Is It Just Me?

Responsibility, Redemption, and Release

Kasim Ali Sidney Jones, Ed. D.

Copyright © 2021 Kasim Ali Sidney Jones, Ed.D.

All rights reserved.

ISBN-13: 978-1-7370905-6-4 (Hardcover)
ISBN-13: 978-1-7370905-7-1 (Paperback)

Niakia Desre' Fontes
June 27, 1995 – February 2, 2019

A perfect angel,

Who's dancing around heaven.

CONTENTS

	Copyright	ii
	Dedication	iii
	Special Note	vii
	Preface	ix
	Introduction	xi
1	Am I Onto Something?	2
2	Did It Start Here?	10
3	Did I Get It Right?	40
4	Where Do I Go Now?	71
5	Seminary Years: Did I Learn?	98
6	From Death to Car Accident to Parenting in the Hood to Chaplain Residency to Doctorate and Beyond	132
7	How Is It Done?	188
8	Can We Heal Together?	259
9	Afterthoughts	305
	Acknowledgments	308
	About the Author	312
	Reference	313

Dr. Kasim Ali Sidney Jones

Special Note

I met Kasim (a. k. a. KJ) when I was about 12 years old, yet it seems longer than the human mind can bear. As I sit back and think of all the years he has contributed to my life, I thank him over and over again. He has helped me heal over each year that has been added onto who I am today. His life lessons and fatherly presence has prepared me for the best moments of my life. Whether it was everyday life, love, the way a man should treat me, or even evaluation within myself, it all has helped me blossom into the woman I am today.

 Reading the portion of this book that was given to me has helped me to open up to not only myself, but those who are around me even more. He has pushed me forward in showing and expressing my love, and accepting it as well, which I lacked for many years of my life. It's like he knows exactly when to push me to do things in life that will help me progress. He randomly comes to me with things that help me in that exact moment. With this book, I have learned things about myself that I had no clue I was hiding under all of these layers of hurt. He hit each layer of past trauma on the head with nothing but the truth. I couldn't be anymore thankful or grateful for the man I am able to call my godfather today. He knows exactly what to do and when to say it. I pray that he continues to be a part of my life because I really wouldn't know what to do without him nor his guidance. It took me years to finally say yes to writing a special note for him. I think it was well worth the wait.

Thank you KJ. I couldn't have done it without you. May our journey together continue to grow as well as grow with new beginnings and closed doors to welcome us into the realm of healed souls; as well as blessing those who get the chance to read this book. May it take you to higher levels of who you are and who you are trying to become in the sense of healing. God knows it is all worth it. I couldn't say thank you enough. So, thank you again and again, Kasim. May your love continue to pour in me as I grow more and more into the woman God has called me to become. I love you much and wish nothing but greatness and success on the journeys ahead of you. Forever and even evermore.

Kionna M. R. "B. B. B." Richards

Preface

It took a long time for me to arrive in this space. Finally, I've acknowledged my need to heal in a way that was inviting and not forced. Nothing earthshattering happened that brought me to this place, even though there were a few transactions that nudged me a little. I know this move was needed because it felt like a natural progression. It was uncomfortable at times, but healing requires some discomfort at various stages. Holding onto toxic, life-depriving issues was detrimental to my overall well-being. With that being the case, I started working not only on this book but myself.

In order to write this book and engage in my own healing processes, continuous introspection had to take place. In other words, I had to distance myself from a number of situations to avoid being distracted and/or overwhelmed by outside influences. By simply being alive and interacting with others, it was inevitably that some things were observed, considered, and examined. However, telling my story as my inner child/young adult mind recalls it was necessary because that is where the root can be pulled up and dealt with. My responsibility was (and is) to exercise discipline in order not to be dissuaded from the mission of this book.

It was my prayer that I was able to not only share honestly, but to have also discovered some things I did not see or understood before. Whether this book achieves an intellectual end or not is the least of my concerns. My goal is to share with the reader by telling my story (within reason). I do not intend to engage in debates, to justify what was or to adjust what is a part of my journey, but to stand in my truth.

*****

I started this book feeling alone in that I didn't see many other Black men speaking out about being sexually abused apart from the limited materials I read and a few celebrities I've heard about. Anger and resentment had to be worked through enough to look beyond my feelings of abandonment and rejection to focus on my healing. When I received the concept and vision for this book, I really didn't consider what was required of me. To be quite honest, I thought I was going to follow "the formula" I had grown accustomed to in my previous works. But that led to frustration as I experienced "writer's blocks" and such. There were many starts and restarts to this project, as well as some exasperation because I didn't know what to do or why the stalls were going on. I had to get to a place of surrender and simply allow what was to be manifested through me to shine through. Therefore, the words you are reading is the result of my obedience. I did not use "the formula." I relied on the knowledge that God had a hand in this process.

    I pray continuously for growth, inspiration, change and the courage, not only for myself, but also for someone who's voice had been silent for so long.

K. A. S. J.

Atlanta, Georgia

2/22/2020

Dr. Kasim Ali Sidney Jones

Introduction

"Perception is everything," someone said. I don't recall the first time I heard this, but it certainly has its place in my life and in this book. The context in which this saying applies is based on my memories, what I felt within and around me, and the impressions that were left upon me. I gave myself permission to tell my story without expectations and/or judgment. I gave myself permission to express myself in a way that was comfortable for me, whether it was "churchy," spiritual, or "alley." And finally, I gave myself permission to fully participate in this process—accepting the good, bad, painful, joyful, difficult, expressive, or enlightening. I embraced it all.

It's amazing how I tend to make things harder for myself because disobedience is a booger. This is the third time I sat down to write this section. I knew I had to continue writing along the direction that my first three books has taken me so far. I knew it would come to this (writing, which is) because it grounds me. You see, reading and writing are therapeutic means for me to relate, learn and rejuvenate, which leads to healing, wisdom and understanding. However, in this case, this project had to be a little different from the others—more straightforward and transparent. I found this to be true because as I prepared for this book, I tried follow the same "formula" or format as I did with *No Shame in the Game* (2013), *Tamar's Healing* (2014), and *Perpetual Victim* (2018). I kept running into blocks where I could not put words and ideas together, as if I did not know the concept, or my interest had waned and I was no longer interested in authoring this book.

I did the best thing I knew would help me to focus on what was before me: I started reading leisurely. I had two books on my peripheral: *Strength of a Woman: The Phyllis Hyman Story*, by Jason A. Michael (2007), and *A Song for You: My Life with Whitney Houston*, by Robyn Crawford (2019). I wanted to read about Phyllis Hyman because she is an artist who would definitely be on the soundtrack of my life. Yet, I was drawn to read Crawford's story first because I really wanted her tell her story as it happened for quite some time. You see, Whitney Houston, Robyn Crawford and I are from the same hometown—East Orange, New Jersey—and I was exposed to different people who were related to them and knew of their story better than I did. But before I could start reading, *I* allowed something to knock me off my square: I got sucked into an anxiety-ridden, alcohol driven situation, which led me to an emotional melt down.

As I climbed out of that dreadful hole, I picked up Crawford's book and began reading. Her words and phrases were so simple and clear that I found myself quickly turning the pages. I had to be patient because I might have missed something because I believed I knew this or that. One night I was reading at work and it dawned on me: You're overthinking this project. My first and third books were written within a matter of months because I allowed the words to come forth. Being aware of this I had to humble myself, pace myself, be patient with myself, and most of all, I had to be kind to myself in this process. These were the things I had been telling others to do. So, I took my own advice.

Having that emotional melt down was useful in its timing because I had to face some old demons I thought I dealt with, and not give into the redundant pattern of ignoring negative behaviors, including my own, in order to get along with others. According to my vent buddy, we processed what happened for hours after it occurred. I was so drunk that I did not remember a lot of what was said and done that night. A key theme that emerged as we talked about it: *triggered*. To be triggered is a person's reaction to a situation, whether it be a discussion (heated or not), a surrounding, a person and/or people. The reaction is so disruptive that it manifests in ways that are not the person's usual way of functioning.

Typically, I would sober up, think about what happened, and then apologize for my behavior, as if I were to blame for what took place. But things were different this time. I decided to change *my* behavior because I was in control of that. I had to remove myself from the vicious cycle I had been locked in for years. I had to change my role in several relationships from that moment on. I needed to get back on the path that God had prepared me for. I had to stop allowing myself to be preoccupied with things and people that were no longer a priority to me. There are standards and boundaries I must adhere to in order to preserve my sanity and restore my peace. No matter how painful it was, I had to stop dealing with some folk until I faced some of my own issues because **I NEEDED TO BE HEALED!!!**

As I continued reading Crawford's words, there was a passage that pierced me to my core. I tried to locate it but couldn't find it, which was rare because I usually remember where I read something that moves me. I knew I had to concentrate and listen as God spoke to me. I needed to be healed in a lot of areas of my life but didn't realize just how much. I kept reading, not expecting anything in particular. I received confirmation in that Crawford mentioned a Teddy Pendergrass song I'd heard two days straight as I rode in my car— "You Can't Hide from Yourself" (1977). It goes to show that things come together when you are open, connected, and obedient.

* * * * *

Is It Just Me?: Responsibility, Release and Redemption will be my way of being honest with myself, and you're coming along for the ride. Yes, I will include supportive information because I embraced my "geeky" side, and this book will be more expressive and sincere. I believe in order to overcome something, you have to face it head-on, called it what it is, deal with it, and then, move forward. I'll be the first to admit that my life was grossly affected by the sexual trauma I experienced. Although I talked about it in *Tamar's Healing*, I was emotionally detached from that process. But it's time to take *responsibility* for myself so I can *release* and obtain *redemption* for this portion of my life. My prayerful intent for openly writing about my life was to help somebody along my journey, and I ask that you pray my strength in the Lord—I learned that in church.

February 7, 2020

Hiram, Georgia

Dr. Kasim Ali Sidney Jones

Part One:

Responsibility

"Every self-limiting thought that you employ to explain why you're not living life to the absolute fullest—so you're feeling purposeful, content, and fully alive—is something you can challenge and reverse, regardless of how long you've held that belief and no matter how rooted in tradition, science, or life experience it may be...."

Wayne W. Dyer

Excuses Begone! (2009)

Chapter One

Am I Onto Something?

When it comes to males who had been sexually abused/assaulted, there's still not enough being said or done, in my opinion. It's still a taboo subject because there are negative stigmas attached to it; yet a lot of suffering in silence occurs along the way. My experience thus far has been a mixture of talking and writing about my trauma, seeking help, and then, not fully processing anything. It's been a rough road for several reasons. Even though it has been years since I was sexually assaulted, I've never truly dealt with it. Before I begin, let me clarify that my assailant was a woman. It's hard for many people to believe females can be that aggressive, but the last time I checked, demons and spirits also appear in the female form as well! The old chauvinistic point of view has blinded so many for far too long, and it has to be eliminated.

As I reflected upon the past 12 months (2019 - 2020), I realized I had never addressed several problems appropriately, which led to damaging behavioral patterns over the years. Although I did talk about some of my experiences in *Tamar's Healing* and the other books, which was a step in the right direction, it was not enough. I had not tackled the emotional fallout that stemmed from being violated in such a way. I agree with the school of thought that says (and I paraphrase), the more you talk about it, the more you can come to grips with your experience. So, here we go.

* * * * *

And so, it happened. It didn't sink in right away because I was in deep denial: "A woman can't rape a man. That's ridiculous." I learned the hard way that this was a myth. There are two camps in this debate: arousal and intrusion. Some say because there was arousal, one was willing; while others say, arousal does not signify compliance. Arousal is the result of a physiological response to stimulation. I agree! That's my story.

Like the average person whom had been defiled, I blamed myself for what happened. I tried to tell myself I should not have been drinking that night. I should not have been in a place where people were smoking marijuana. I even told myself I should have been able to defend myself against a woman. I wanted to explain it away to make it okay. Hell, I even put on a macho mask and tried to convince myself that I *enjoyed* it, "and probably knocked it out the box," when I don't recall what it was like. This sham worked for a while, but then, I had to persuade myself all over again in order to keep this charade going. But there's nothing like the truth!

The Holy Spirit shows us what we need to see, when we need to use it: "But when he, the Spirit of truth comes, he will guide you into all the truth" (John 16: 13, *NIV*). Little by little, I slowly saw what happened that night. And the more I saw, the angrier I became. So, I did the next best thing: I occupied my mind by keeping busy. I went to school full-time, worked two part-time jobs; and if I wasn't doing either, I was drinking and partying (my ass off, mind you), so much so that I functioned off three to four hours of sleep a day. I did not do a lot of serious dating for reasons unknown to me back then my infamous rationalization was: "I ain't got time for that shit! I'm about my business." I developed an unhealthy love/hate relationship with females and did not know it.

It took a long time for me to say anything, let alone accept what happened to me. I'm not sure of the timeframe but my drinking had increased substantially in the process. When I did say something, it was not under the best of circumstances. I was extremely inebriated one night, and it came out in an explosive way. I was so overcome with rage, tears, and helplessness that I shook all over. The other parties managed to calm me, but then, this disclosure was conveniently swept under the rug as if it never happened. To add insult to injury, all of it was treated like a *dirty secret*, a hidden taboo, not discussed again. So, I continued on with business as usual. Grind, grind, grind became my way of life. I didn't know just how much that buried monster was tearing my life apart, so I kept avoiding it.

Looking back, I know the content of my eruption was difficult for the other parties, and it had the potential to be divisively damaging to a lot of people.

Meanwhile, I completed my undergraduate program and started applying to several Master of Social Work programs in the tri-state area (New York, New Jersey, and Connecticut), but decided to attend the Interdenominational Theological Center in Atlanta, Georgia. I planned to major in Pastoral Counseling and Psychology of Religion because I wanted to help others, while serving God at the same time. I tucked those experiences and feelings in a place where no one could see my wounds—so I thought. But, then again, God gave charge over God's angels to help me before I was born.

When the time came for me to leave East Orange, I excitedly packed my things, and stuffed them in a rented minivan, and headed to Atlanta. I made a vow to create a new life and not look back: "I don't have to deal with that shit no mo." I was in for the shock of my life! My issues not only spilled out, but they intensified to the point where they affected some of my relationships, romantic as well as platonic. I found that I could run but I couldn't hide from myself (that Teddy P. song). All of this was in hindsight, of course.

The damage caused by being violated had lasting affects in that I felt exploited and demoralized, subconsciously. I couldn't remember why I had a boulder, instead of a chip, on my shoulder whenever I heard of someone being mistreated, especially if they were close to me. At times, I felt their pain, too much and did not understand why. But, at the same time, a lot of my anger came from not being helped or heard sufficiently. I don't take comfort in saying this, but there are so many men who remain voiceless because of the mortifying stigmas attached to being sexually abused/assaulted and a male.

I've asked myself at least a million times: Are you sure you want to do this (write this book)? You know there are a lot of people out there who will judge you? I may not fully comprehend the potential ramifications for speaking out nor can I see the outcome for doing so. What I do know is I was made for such a moment as this. Someone must speak out because far too many brothers, fathers, uncles, friends, etc. take their trauma to their graves, and for some, an early one, because of what people might say or think of them.

* * * * *

I realized the need for me to do something to help myself. So I worked with a therapist a few years ago. During a session, this therapist sensed something that needed to be explored. He dug around, poking here and there, and then, he asked a question that enabled me to recall something that was very significant. My assailant said something that tarnished my spirit: "I heard this meat was good. Lay yo ass down so I can get some." I was shocked and embarrassed by these words. I couldn't believe I shared them with another person because shame had its ugly claws in me for so long. I said to the therapist, "That's a part of the reason why *I* fucked up so many relationships! *I* messed them up! *I* pushed them away! *I* gave them permission to use and abuse me!" My therapist sat back listening intently. "I run when *I* think I'm going to be mistreated or used, materialistically or...." I said, trailing off at the end. My therapist patiently encouraged me to finish my statement: "You need to say it so you can release it. Let it go!" I fought against it because "men don't supposed to do all this mushy crap," I thought. I dropped my chin to my chest and finally conceded and said it, "Or sexually." I felt small in that moment because of the views I held onto for so long. I was ashamed to admit it happened, and I said this to another man.

    A lot of things changed for me that day. I've encouraged people to be patient and kind to themselves. I had to take my own advice because self-criticism was a trap. I felt that I was not good enough, and my view of myself had been significantly damaged. In other words, I looked at myself differently after that intrusive ordeal. Some of the relationships I had could have been something special had I not sabotaged them. I ended a relationship shortly before I started working on this book. Insecurities, betrayals and other inadequacies did not help our relationship any. It was not until the end of this relationship that I realized how deeply affected I was by a number of things, which were not adequately addressed. Until then, I did not see the connection between that disturbing ordeal and how it left me feeling like a "thing" and/or a service. I did not want to be rejected or denied. So, I started buying friendships and paying for attention to other things as well, which was to my own detriment. What I did receive was not enough because many friendships/relationships were not true, and the attention I received wasn't always good. They became toxic, cruel, and harmful to my psyche and wellbeing. But then, I began to understand myself more because those experiences taught me things about myself that I would not have known without undergoing them.

Being treated like, feeling like, and acting like a contraption or a gadget had a devastating impact on me. This condition is called objectification. It is real and is not to be taken lightly. To be objectified is to "the act of treating people as if they are objects, without rights or feelings of their own" (*Oxford Advanced Learner's Dictionary*, 2025). Many times, it is hard to see or distinguish because it's not understood or is recognized as a normal pattern of behavior for many people. But objectification is a phenomenon that can leave a person in shambles—spiritually, mentally, and even physically. His or her very soul can be distorted in that their self-image, self-worth, self-esteem, and ultimately, their self-respect are deleteriously compromised. Remembering I was referred to as "this meat" so long ago, rocked my world and subconsciously messed with me since then. I had buried that detail for so long that I did not remember it right away, but it still had its grips on me in the way that I related to others. I did not see the person I was before the assault again.

This corrupt view of myself was so engrained that it warped my confidence and my sense of self, even though no one else treated me like that since then. I eventually learned that objectification does not always occur under traumatic circumstances. It can be a slow, arduous process that develops over time, e. from childhood to adulthood. Either way, objectification *is* one of the most soul-destroying stations one could find themselves. When a person sees themselves as a "thing," "good for only," or "damaged/broken," they can also fall prey to additional infringements, and even develop self-destructive patterns of behaviors and views of themselves.

* * * * *

The violation of your body was one of the worse moments of your life. You'd never imagined something so repulsive would have ever happen to you, but there you were and now you're trying to pick up the pieces. Going through the motions, you tried to make sense of it all: Why no one helped you in your time of need, and you've asked yourself how did you wind up in a predicament like that to begin with? You tried to pull yourself together because it didn't look good. A million questions swirled around in your head: Was it my fault? What did I do to deserve this? What was my role in this unspeakable act of violence and intrusion? Is this what I was made for? Am I nothing more than a piece of meat for others to use and enjoy? Am I just damaged goods? Or am I just no good? Some or more of these questions you may have asked yourself a thousand times. You may have felt dirty, soiled, and debased to the point where all you wanted was to get clean. Suddenly, you started coming to your senses: "What am I going to do now?"

There were so many things to consider the moment you realize something had gone wrong: What do I do next? Who do I tell? Where do I go for help? Should I say something to my family and friends? How would people react if I told them what happened to me? What's gonna happen to me if I told someone? Out of all the people around here, why did it have to happen to me? Why didn't someone help me?

The truth is sexual abuse and trauma are real and prevalent to the chagrin of those who wish it never existed at all. Until something changes, we who live with the brutal truth that these things *do* occur and are all too rampant, and is oftentimes ignored, swept under the carpet, minimized, and dismissed. We have to find ways to move pass the tendency of doing nothing to help in the healing process.

* * * * *

I know I've said a lot so far, but I wanted to wet your pallet and set the tone for the rest of this book. This is an audacious endeavor in that it seeks to challenge you to be more compassionate, empathetic/*sympathetic*, and nonjudgmental toward those who have experienced horrendous incidents in their lives, especially males. I specify males because the majority of identified victims of sexual trauma are females. This is due to male representation being highly under-reported (Charak, Eshelman, and Messman-Moore, 2019; Easton, Saltzman, and Willis, 2014; Murphy, Elklit, Hyland, and Shevlin, 2016; Ulman, 2011). It's time to bring this subject matter to light! Although there are other sources that make up this body of work, it is my desire to add to it by telling my story.

Chapter Two:

Did It Start Here?

Knowing the story of how you were born can serve many purposes. I was relieved when my parents finally told me the story surrounding my birth when I was in my early twenties. Until then, I was an angry and confused *little boy* without a clear sense of direction. I was (and still am) pretty much a straightforward person but also passive-aggressive, depending on the circumstance. I had many questions for my parents but did not know how to ask them. This state of mind not only complicated things for an impressionable young man/child, and it also caused me to act out in diverse ways at different times. This state of bewilderment fed an ongoing desire to question my existence and purpose. My parents certainly helped me to see my potential as a child of God, their child, and a citizen of the world.

I am a firm believer in parents and/or elders imparting or blessing young people with empowering words before he or she launches into the world as an emerging adult. It can be problematic if a person, who is unsure of themselves, or is pushed or forced out, so to speak, without receiving this beneficial, instructive encouragement as their anchor. However, the emerging adult must be open to receiving such blessings/encouragement.

I read a Facebook post that said: "Young people, don't let your 'I'm grown' boundaries cut off the wisdom of your elders. If you're not teachable, you can't grow" (Unknown). Let that sink in for a moment. Although I'm not very old, I am considered an elder to some. However, I still reach out to my elders for guidance because no one knows everything there is to know. Every person is responsible for their own journey and has to make decisions for themselves; yet I also understand this priceless pearl of wisdom:

> ...for gaining wisdom and instruction; for understanding words of insight; for receiving instruction in prudent behavior, doing what is right and just and fair; for giving prudence to those who are simple, knowledge and discretion to the *young*—let the wise listen and add to their learning, and let the discerning get guidance—for understanding proverbs and parables, the sayings, and riddles of the wise. The fear of the LORD is the beginning of knowledge, but *fools* despise wisdom and instruction... (Proverbs 1: 2 – 7, *NIV*; emphasis mine).

I've observed a number of behaviors/attitudes that grieves my spirit among a large number of the Millennials, those who were born between 1980 to 1994, and Generation Z, those who were born between 1995 to 2015. These groups are disturbingly different from my generation—Generation X, those who were born between 1965 to 1979—in that the amount of arrogance, lack of respect, and level of disregard is appalling, in my opinion. Some might say I'm out of touch, and I would agree; but some things that are considered the basics in life (again, in my opinion). The most egregious of these is the *I know everything so leave me alone* attitude. Some would argue that most of us older folks were like that when we were young. That may be true to a certain degree. However, there was a line that was not to be crossed, no matter how "grown" you *thought* you were.

When I was coming up, my elders did not interfere with my life very often. But if they saw me traveling down a dangerous road, they pulled me aside to drop some wisdom before moving out of my way— "Do what cha wanna do but I'm just warning you…." I gave some thought to what they had to say, and if I chose not to take heed to their warning, *I* had to deal with the consequences. To tell them to mind their own business, or to even hint at it, was like begging for an ass kicking because, either my folks or their folks would have handled me properly. That was an unwritten law that was not to be tested nor broken. But *some* (not all) of these Millennials and Gen Zs…. I don't know what to say! It's almost as if they were raised by a pack of wolves, rather than respectful human beings. But, then again, that's awfully judgmental of me. Therefore, I chose to stay out of their way. And that's unfortunate! However, I was convicted for these negligent thoughts and actions, and I must figure out a way to reach those I can reach. I cannot imagine where I would be if my elders didn't speak up when they did.

Diane Reeves sang a powerful song, entitled "Better Days" (1987). It was playing in the background as I worked on this chapter. This song is exactly what I mean by "blessing before launching." Reeves offered a soulful rendition of some of the lessons she learned from her grandma and how they helped her. This song is still one that's very inspirational to me. I closed my eyes and pictured myself in my 15-year-old scrawny little body, listening to this song when it first came out. I love this song because there were (and are) a lot of people who poured into my life and helped me to become who I am and will become.

* * * * *

My childhood was not all that bad. Sure, there were some challenging times, but we got by. I was born in Clara Maas Medical Center in Belleville, New Jersey. I was the youngest of four boys before my younger siblings came along. Being the youngest had its advantages and disadvantages. Through my mind's eye, a lot of things appeared to be unfair and/or hard for me. I thought my parents and older siblings treated me as if I were a burden or a nuisance at times. However, I have come to understand that it was not their intent. Younger siblings, especially the youngest, can be seen as pests to their older siblings. They sometimes do mean things to their kid brother/sister, but nothing malicious in nature. I was that curious, mischievous kid, who asked too many questions sometimes, and not enough at other times. Yes, that can be annoying, but they loved me still.

My mother was tough, protective, strict, loving, and strong. She had to be! She had four boys to rear in a community where crime and other behaviors had a strong presence. Yes, my mom had significant men in her life—the late Curtis M. Bey (dad #1) and the late Charles L. Anderson (dad #2)—but as circumstances would have it, she had to do it mostly by herself.

It wasn't until later on in my life that I learned the truth as to why my mom's and father's relationship came to an end, even though they remained friends until his death in January of 2004. My dad died when I was a young teen in May 1986. My dads had a mutual respect for one another: my dad, who was married to my mom, respected the fact that my dad had two sons in his household. My mother, father, and dad believed in the power of education, its value and advocated for it to be an attainment in our lives. "Get as much education as you can," was one of the many aphorisms I heard throughout my childhood.

I asked my mom why she was so hard on me. "I know I was a hard-headed kid," I said, "but why did you ride me like that?" My mom paused and said, "Well, I felt I had to be harder on you because I wanted to make sure you would be alright." Baffled by her response, I asked for clarification. "When you were coming up, I was concerned that the world would take who you were as a weakness," she patiently explained. "You were a sensitive child and needed to be prepared for the world. It was my job to protect you and prepare you for the world out there. There were times when I had to step up and do what I had to do, even when you didn't know I was doing it." That made a lot of sense to me.

I took some time to reflect on what was said as I worked on this section to see if I could recall one of those times when my mom (Momma Bear) stepped up on my behalf. My mom reminded me of an instance when her claws had to come out, and I did not ask for details because some things are better left alone. I knew my mom was cable of not only shield me from dreadful things, but she also did an awesome job of preserving my innocence (thanks, Mom Dukes).

I remembered one situation when "Momma Bear" showed her fangs when I was young—I cannot recall my age. Our minds are so intricately designed that it allows us to suppress certain details of our life's story in order to protect us. Anyway, there was this guy who used to hang out with my mom and her two friends. He was one of the very few adult males my parents allowed into our home.

This guy kept inviting me to sit on his lap. I wouldn't because I knew my parents did not allow me to do that— "No child should sit in no grown man's lap or get between his legs." One day,

I slipped up and jumped on his lap. I don't remember how long I sat there or what happened, but my mother came into the room and saw me sitting there. She calmly told me to go outside to play, which I immediately did because there was a certain reverberation in her voice that said she wasn't going to repeat herself. The look on her face was intense, and I almost felt sorry for ole boy, even though I was clueless as to what ticked momma off. I saw him getting the hell on moments later—running or walking fast away from our house. My mom called me over to our porch and sat down with me. "I'm not mad at you, Sidney," she cautioned. I knew my Mom meant business because she called me Sidney. "You have to listen when you are told not to do something. You are a child," she said, sternly. "There's a lot you don't know, and I will not put up with a disobedient child," she said firmly, which told me something was wrong about what I did—I sat on old boy's lap and it never happened again, with him or any other man.

I can only image what went down in my house while I was outside *playing*. In a way, I worried about ole boy when I saw him scooting from our house. I knew my mom didn't take no shit when it came to her children, and I wondered if she pieced him up a little (kicked his ass). I never knew for sure and I didn't ask. In fact, I never talked to my Mom about it. But I doubt she beat him up because she wouldn't have messed up her house, and by all accounts, it would have been a brawl if she did. One thing's for certain, whatever was said/done made an exclamation point that day. My mom brought me inside, which was as I last saw it, to give me an important directive: "Don't tell Charles [my dad] about this, neither." I was terrified for ole boy and trusted that it was handled by my mom—my dad would have killed him. I never saw that guy in our home again, and the relationship between him, my mom and her friends ran cold.

The takeaway from this illustration is my mother took care of my siblings and me to the best of her ability. It did not matter if I thought I was a pain in the ass, mischievous, or whatever; my mom protected me as best as she could, and she provided for and prepared all seven of us very well. I've said this at least a hundred times: parents, parent-figures and elders can only pour what they have into younger folks. It's up to the younger individuals to do the rest. My mother brims with pride whenever she talks about my siblings and I. I talked to her about the concept of this book and she damned near shouted (or danced). She told me, "Work it out, (a nickname that only my mom calls me)."

* * * * *

Losing several significant people early on in my life certainly caused me to feel as if people were leaving me, and fast. From 1986 through 1988, starting with my dad, a number of people died. As a matter of fact, someone passed away on May 18th all three years. It was tough and I went from sadness to fear quite often. Although these departures were hard to deal with, nearly losing my mother was the toughest. This was when I started engaging in destructive behaviors—namely drinking excessively, which came easy for me. These things brought on my struggles with abandonment and anxieties in the years to come.

My mother was involved in a terrible car accident during the second half of my sophomore year in high school. My family was responding to yet another death—one of my mother's younger sisters, the late Tracy Bryant. My mom's flight to Georgia was scheduled for the following day, a Saturday. She had a preaching engagement the night before and I remember her rushing around trying to get a few things to done. My family kept busy with school, work, and other activities, so there was always something going on in separate places, at the same times. I recall getting dressed to meet one of my friends when my phone rang. Answering that call changed my life in many ways.

I call to mind hearing an unfamiliar voice on the other end of the line. I thought Kris (Kristel, a middle school friend) was playing a trick on me, but I was absolutely wrong. The woman insistently wanted to know: "Are you a child of Shirley Jones?" Just as I was thinking of some choice words to say the voice asserted: "Sir, I need to know who is her next of kin." I froze when I heard "the next of kin" when my dad died. I don't remember what else was said. I had get on the move to find my brothers. That was my thought process.

The next thing I recall was me running down the street with my clothes half on going to find Roy, Sr. at his girlfriend's place. I ran up the stairs to Shannon's apartment and was told they weren't there. I was so frantic that I ran down the stairs with the intent of going to the hospital on foot. Roy and Shannon pulled up just as I made it to the bottom of the stairs. In my mind, all this was happening in slow motion until Roy said, "Get in!" We headed to the hospital in a hurry.

Roy and I arrived at University Hospital in Newark, N. J. moments later, and my nerves were in tatters. Roy, my mom's boyfriend (I think his name was Charles), and I were sitting in a waiting room for what felt like an eternity. They didn't tell us much, and no one allowed us to see my mom for a long time. All I could think of was the phrase: *"her next of kin."* I didn't know if my mother was dead or alive! I went ballistic and they finally led Roy and I into this cold ass room where my mom was lying on a flimsy gurney with the throw (a type of blanket) that she draped across the backseat of her car. At first, I didn't get too close to her because no one told us if she was dead or alive. I was in shock and my memory is a blur as to what I did or thought. I remember our Pastor, the late Elder John D. Coleman, joining us. Roy had to catch me before I hit the floor. I thought our Pastor knew something we did not. As it turned out, my mom was alive but in critical condition, which turned into a coma sometime later.

When I did get closer to my mom, she had blood on her face, glass in her hair and face, and one eye was swollen nearly shut. A tear rolled down her cheek when she heard our voices—I'm not sure if she saw us. I wanted to wipe it but was afraid I would hurt her. I kept trying to cover her with the throw, which was not made for warmth. Momma looked so fragile with her swollen and battered body. Roy and I were trying to wrap our heads around what happened. Elder Coleman prayed for my mom, and then, convinced us to go home to rest. I was worried because we had to tell Duane what happened because he was the last one to see mom before the accident. I burst into tears in the parking lot because I was so overwhelmed as I thought about what happened over the course of a few hours.

Duane was home when we arrive and wondered where we were the whole time. Keep in mind, this was before cellular phones were affordable; so, there was no way to catch up with Duane while we were in motion. But telling him about mom was horrible.

My mom's boyfriend stayed with us for a little while to make sure we were okay. He laced each of us with a $20 bill before he left. That was a lot of cash for a teen back then. I was able to afford my "poison"—Bacardi Silver. At first, drinking helped me sleep, and then, it morphed into something much more than a late-night tonic. I quickly learned I was into something I could not handle. One morning, I took a sip to knock the edge off and before I knew it, I was drinking throughout the day and reached at least a pint-and-a-half a day.

Drinking became the norm for me, and I didn't appreciate how dangerous this behavior really was. If I went without a swig (a sip) for too long, I didn't feel right—I now know it was withdrawals or delirium tremens (dt's). Some of my homies thought we were just skipping out to cut up a little. Truth was, I needed to feed my dependency. As I look back now, I see just how ill-prepared I was during my adolescence. Before this, drinking, I used to shut down and withdraw, emotionally. Drinking took me to another place. It really started showing itself because my demeanor changed and I started lashing out at others. So, rum was not making me as numb as I thought it was. A number of attitudes and behaviors began to take root during this time: nothing mattered and resentment.

My mom awakened from her coma but still could not respond appropriately. I could not understand what was going on. She was connected to fewer machines and tubes, but still not talking. Most of the swelling had gone away, leaving scars that would remain for the rest of her life. I'm not sure how I was able to hold together for so long but I started unraveling fast. I was like a ticking time bomb waiting to explode.

Kris and I talked every day. She was incredibly supportive throughout this period. Kris decided to go with me to the hospital for morale support. I really needed it because I was fighting hard to keep it together, and Kris knew I was not doing well.

On the appointed day of this visit, Kris was very quiet as she sat in the car with Roy and I. I'm not sure if she smelled alcohol on my breathe because I drank as I waited for her to arrive at my house. Roy, Kris, and I rode to the hospital in silence. I was growing weary of drinking and pretending everything was okay when it wasn't—it really wasn't. You see, my mother would have picked up on my behaviors, and Shirley Ann would have stepped in with an iron fist, literally.

Roy, Kris, and I were in my mom's room when the doctors told us my mom had a rough day but I cannot remember why. The doctor left the room and Kris held my hand as I tried to digest what was said. Suddenly, lights started flashing and sounds were frantically blaring. It seemed as if the nurses were not moving fast enough to see about my mom. I grew fearful that something bad was happening and I lost it. Kris pulled me out of the room to console me. Roy was outraged and embarrassed. "You've got to get your shit together before they stop you from coming up here!" he admonished. It turned out that my mom was thirsty and things calmed down once she had a few sips of water. I decided to take a break from going to the hospital until my mom was able to speak to recognize me.

Although I thought not seeing my mom for a while was a good thing, I took it hard because people were abandoning me—that's what I was thinking and feeling. My drinking increased copiously, and it was starting to show. I didn't tell any of my schoolmates or teachers what happened to my mom, but I think Shannon did tell a couple of people. Even worse, I didn't know, nor did I want to admit I had a drinking problem. In my 15-year-old mind, I thought, "people my age don't have those types of problems." Yet I needed to drink to make it through the day. This continued until someone noticed me trying to go to sleep during school hours. Truth was I drank too much and could not stay awake. One of my favorite teachers and a "big sister"—Mr. Daryl Robinson (my band director) and LaKeisha Blue (my big sister)— took notice of my weird behavior and pulled me aside to talk to me. I told them everything that was going on and they vowed to help me. They did as promised and I am forever grateful to them.

Once my mom was able to interact with me, I felt much better on many levels. She was so happy to see my brothers and me. I was relieved to see her smile, to hear her laughter and her voice, even when she fussed me out. Her eyes lit up each time we walked into her room and wanted to know what was going on in our daily lives. I did not trust getting too comfortable with that situation because people were leaving, either they moved away or they died.

Did I Try?

My parents encouraged my siblings and I to enjoy our adolescent years, while being productive and careful. My dad, Charles, encouraged me to get ready for high school, while saying good-bye to junior high. He beamed with pride because I was the last of his six children (his two biological and four additional with my mom) to enter high school. "You're gonna do good," he said. This was one of the last words of encouragement I received from my dad before he died in the spring of 1986.

I injured my knee and had to miss most of the 1985 – 86 school year, which was my eighth-grade year. Kris and Jennetta visited regularly, and they made sure I was not lonely or left out of the loop. It proved to be a long winter that year, but Prince's *Purple Rain* (1984) was on heavy rotation on my family's beta VCR. Watching my neighborhood friends play in the snow was truly a downer but I made it to the spring.

I returned to school when the weather was breaking from winter into spring. I was happy to see my schoolmates and my teachers—Ms. Phyllis Bivins (Language Arts), Ms. Shirley Melvin (Mathematics), Mrs. Wright (Social Studies) and Ms. Gloria Baptiste (Science). It felt good being welcomed back into the fold.

I heard that one of my childhood friends, Asha D., had been looking for me. I was told to meet her at a certain location after school. I was still using crutches at the time, so I could not get around too fast. Asha came to me and said she wanted me to meet someone. A week or so went by and I had not seen or heard from Asha.

One day Kris, Jennetta (another childhood friend) and I were walking home (me, hobbling) from school when I heard a familiar voice calling me from behind. It was Asha and this mysterious girl I had not seen before. Asha asked if she could talk to me in private, which I didn't mind because I was intrigued by the girl with her. "Kasim, Shavonne. Shavonne, Kasim," Asha said before stepping away as we stood there staring at one another in awe. Shavonne was (and probably still is) a beautiful dark chocolate-toned girl with these memorizing, big, brown, almond shaped eyes, and exquisitely high cheek bones. I thought about her a lot from that moment on. Shavonne and I got along very well and soon became boyfriend and girlfriend, even though we both were *too young* to officially date.

One of the highlights of my eighth-grade school year was the Eighth Grade Social—it's equivalent to the "Eighth Grade Prom" in some places. I did not have a date for this event until I met Shavonne. Kris had a date and Jeanetta was not going. I knew I was going but really didn't give much thought to asking anyone to go with me. After meeting Shavonne, spending time with her, getting to a place where I felt comfortable being around her, and eventually asking her to be my girlfriend, I absolutely changed my mind. To everyone who knew about us thought we were a cute couple and it was fitting for us to appear at the Social together. But how we became a couple was one of the sweetest childhood memories I have. I remember the whole scene like it was yesterday because it was all you could imagine a puppy love scene could have been.

Shavonne and I were walking home one warm afternoon. Our friends were happy for us and gave us room to get to know one another. We probably would have held hands had it not been for my crutches. Shavonne was very patient with my situation because I had to stop to rest frequently.

Shavonne's house came before mine. I lived a half a block around the corner. Once we arrived in front of her house, we engaged in awkward small talk for a while, when suddenly, "Will you be my girlfriend?" came out of my mouth. We both stood there for a moment as if we heard something strange. "I'll let you know," Shavonne said with a big smile as she batted those big brown eyes. I slowly hobbled away smiling. Before I could reach the end of her fence, I heard Shavonne call out, "Hey, Kasim! Come here." I turned around and shuffled my way back to her. We stared into each other's eye for long moment before she said, "Yes. Yes, I will be your girlfriend." I had no idea what to say or do next. I was going to ask my god sister, the late Cynthia Clark, about asking Shavonne to be my girlfriend. I didn't know what to do if she said yes or no, but there we were. Believe me, it was an uncomfortable moment but in a nice way. I stared down at my feet for a few seconds, nervous and unsure of what to say or do. Shavonne let me off the hook by saying, "Good night to my boyfriend, Kasim." I was floating on cloud eleven like a scene from a cartoon. That feeling was short lived because I couldn't act too strangely around my mom because I was *not* supposed to date until I turned 16 years old.

Shavonne and I realized the Eighth Grade Social was approaching, we didn't have dates, and we were a couple on the low-low. So, we decided we would meet at Scott's Manor, in Orange, New Jersey, in order to keep our parents off our scent. My mom really wanted me to go with Kris, but our timing was always off—when Kris had a boyfriend, I was single, and when I had a girlfriend, Kris was single. But now we both had a boyfriend/girlfriend at this same time. Kris and I rode to the Social together, but I cannot remember which of our parents drove us there.

Kris quickly met up with her date when we arrived—I cannot remember who her date was because she was on the outs with her boyfriend. I went to find a table where the four of us could sit. It felt like forever sitting there without Shavonne. I went to the lobby to see if she arrived a few of times. Kris stood with me to make sure I was okay. I insisted that she returned to her date the last time I went out to check, which she reluctantly did. I waited a little longer, and then, turned to walk back inside. I felt a tap on my shoulder and turned to see who it was. It was Shavonne, glowing as if she had a halo around her.

Shavonne and I decided to wear pink and white. We wanted to stick with a simple look, but the outcome had a *wow effect* anyhow. I wore a white two-piece suit, like Don Johnson wore on the popular primetime show, *Miami Vice*, with a pink shirt and a white tie. Shavonne wore a white dress that came down to her lower calf and flared out from her waist. I bought her a pink and white corsage, but there was a catch that only a hand-full of people knew about—the flower shop ran out of pink carnations, so they sprayer the edges of the white pedals pink.

Shavonne was so beautiful that day and all of the days that followed, as a matter of fact. Asha took pictures of us, which I still have to this very day, as I pinned her corsage on within of our first moments together.

Shavonne and I were truly enamored with each other in the purest way. We spent time talking and hanging out at our table until it was time to dance. I didn't know it at the time, but Shavonne could really dance, which was a plus because I had always been a pretty good dancer ma-self (I'm just saying). We danced together and was tearing it up. We danced with some of our friends and mingled until the music slowed down. "It's time for the lovers to take the floor," the DJ announced. I looked around but did not see Shavonne at first. Suddenly, I felt a tap on my shoulder—she seemed to be good at tapping me on the shoulder. "Looking for me," she asked with a playful smile. I took her by the hand, led her to the dance floor, and we danced together for the rest of that night.

*****

In the midst of those tender moments, tragedy struck again. This time it was the biggest loss I'd ever experienced up until then, the death of my dad, the late Charles Levi Anderson. He and my mother had been separated for several months and things drastically changed within our family's dynamics, but we survived.

My mother received a jolting call sometime in late March to early April of 1986. "Charles is in the hospital," she explained as she prepared to go to the hospital. I recall Duane and I standing there, stunned by what we just heard. Mom and Roy, Sr. walked out the front door, leaving us behind because we were too young to visit people in the hospital. I was terrified because I had no idea what was going on. Duane and I stayed in the house until they returned.

Mom and Roy came home with dinner in hand—Kentucky Fried Chicken, long before it officially became KFC. My mom kept herself together, while telling us he would be all right. I cannot she how she did it, in hindsight, because it was a lot to take in at a short amount of time. But I didn't buy her story. Duane and I pressed for details. "Charles was hit by a car and has an infection," she said. I started crying because this *infection* was bad enough to hospitalize him. Me crying caused Duane to cry, too. My mother comforted us, while appearing to be a pillar of strength for us. I don't recall too many people comforting her because she held it together for a long time. My mother went to work, came home to prepare or bought dinner for us, and off to the hospital. This went on for a few weeks.

I was leery about going outside or venturing too far away from home or my mom in case something happened. I did not know what else to do. One afternoon, my mother saw what was happening to Duane and I. She encouraged us to go outside to be with our friends before she and Roy, Sr. went to the hospital. Duane and I were trying to decide where we were going to go. I decided to pay Kris a visit because I hadn't spent time with her in a while. Duane was going to visit his girlfriend and was in the bathroom. I was getting ready to leave when the phone rang. Duane yelled for me to answer it, which I casually did. Someone asked for mom to which I told them she was not home. "Please have her to call University Hospital when she returns," the voice asked with an sense of urgency. I asked if there was a message to pass on to her: "We need Charles Anderson's next of kin to make an identification." What in the world!

I was confused and stood there wondering what that message meant. Duane came into the room asking who was on the phone. I told him it was the hospital and repeated the message. "What does it mean?" I asked, on the brink of crying. "We have to wait until mom come home," Duane said, trying to sound positive and upbeat.

It felt like forever before my mother and brother returned home—they went to hospital and was on their way back when I received that call. Duane and I tried to convince each other that the message wasn't bad, that maybe they wanted my mom to come back for paperwork or something like that. The last report I received regarding my dad's progress, a week or so before this call, was he recovering well.

There is a major element I need to include: Charles had a first wife, I'll call Wilma, with whom he had two sons with—my stepbrothers. Knowing this will be crucial to this story.

My mother and Roy finally came home shortly after that call and our discussion behind the possible meaning of the message to

Mom. Duane and I went down the stairs to meet them in the kitchen. "I thought I told y'all to go outside," mom snapped without looking up. "Ok, what's the matter? Why y'all looking like that?" she asked once she turned to face us. Duane told her the hospital called and wanted to talk *Charles' next of kin*. Duane and I stared at my mom as she quickly processed what was said. She did not call the hospital. Instead, she told Roy they were going back to the hospital to see what was going on. My mother never let on that she did or did not know what that message could have meant.

 I decided to go see Shavonne because I knew she would comfort me and I wouldn't be too far from home. I told her about my mom being called back to the hospital. Shavonne was sweet and kind to me and provided a positive distraction. I ended up staying out longer than I intended. It was okay because I was with Shavonne, which helped me feel better.

 I went home once Shavonne and her sisters went inside for the night. I lived around the corner from her and could see my house from the end of her block—the corner of 18th Street and Eaton Place. There was a bunch of people on my front porch and on the sidewalk, which wasn't unusual, especially on warm spring nights. I didn't rush as I walked home.

 I felt something was off the closer I got to my house. Laughter or some sort of noise usually accompanied a crowd that size, but silence hovered. No one said much nor did they look directly at me as I approached. I cannot remember who told me what happened, nor who was present. I did not want to leave the house or my family after that. I wanted to tell Shavonne my dad was gone but could not do so. I called Kris and told her what happened. She and her mom came to my house, immediately.

At some point, my mother called her mother-in-law, Grandma Anderson, who was an emotional wreck. My mom told her we were on our way to visit with her for a while. Grandma was so happy to see us and graciously invited us to make ourselves at home. I don't know exactly who else was there, but I do recall people my age were present. Grandma was so engrossed by grief that she had no filter as to what she said. The kids were excused from the room with the adults, but still heard what the adults were saying—some of it I did not want to hear. The adults were either crying or mad as hell. At first, I couldn't understand what the anger was about, even before we arrived at Grandma's house. I started hearing bits and pieces of what happened to my dad and was thrown off balance. My cousin told me it was Wilma's fault that my dad was dead. I had no understanding as to what they were talking about.

The visit came to an emotion peak when I heard the adults' voices rise to yells. We, children, fell silent. Some were crying, me being one of them, while others were livid. I remember one of my cousins becoming so enraged that he had to punch some pillows piled on the bed. A lot was said that night and I'm not sure my mother intended for my brothers and I to hear a lot of the details the way they came out. Grandma tearfully pled, "Please, please don't y'all get ta fighting over my dead son! Please, please!" I cannot remember what else happened or when we left. My mother explained what happened to my dad when we returned home, "because y'all gonna hear much more than what y'all heard tonight."

This is what I remember my mom saying that night: Charles was hit by a car and did not go to the hospital for weeks after the accident. Wilma kept him home and "took care of him." She fed him dope (street drugs), which led him to being rushed to the hospital because his injuries became infected. Once he was in the hospital, Wilma and my mother chose opposite visitation times so they would not be present at the same time. Wilma visited dad after my mother left that day. "Wilma raised so much hell that he (my dad) had a massive heart attack and died." My mother did not appear to be very upset by this because her last visit with my dad was *great*— "Charles accepted God into his heart and that's good enough for me. I'm okay." Receiving this information prepared me for the three-ring-circus to come—the wake, the funeral, and the interment (burial).

My eldest brother, Willie (aka June), who was in the U. S. Army at the time, came home for the funeral. My mother brought us into the dining room area of our home to talk to us. "A lot of people are pissed off and they wanna whoop Wilma's ass. I'm not worried about her and I don't wanna do anything to her. Y'all stay away from her and everything will be all right," she said softly. I got a couple of nudges from my brothers, which meant "this means you."

The wake and funeral were held at Perry's Funeral Home in Newark, N. J. and the burial at Evergreen Cemetery in Hillside, NJ (I think). There were so many people there. I felt the love and respect for my dad because he was a good man.

Several people, whom I had not seen in years, remembered me as a little child and were amazed by how much I'd grown. Several of them said I was "growing to be a handsome young man," but I didn't feel that way. I saw cousins I hadn't seen in years. One cousin, Stacy, caught my eye. Stacy and I were tight when we were younger, even though she had a younger sister my age (Stacy and

Duane were the same age, while Yolanda and I were closer in age). From the moment we saw each other, Stacy and I supported one another throughout this sad occasion.

The wake was very emotional and intense because grief was oftentimes accompanied by anger. There were at least two instances where someone nearly jumped on Wilma. I accompanied Stacy and her sister outside because we needed air. I floated numbly through, behaving myself as my mother told me to. I kept looking around the large room almost wondering why I was there.

The next day, at the funeral (or Homegoing Service should I say) there was even more emotional than the day before. A lot of tears flowed as "It's So to Say Good-bye to Yesterday" played—the original version, sung by G. C. Cannon (Perren and Yarian, 1975). My mother finally showed emotions during dad's final viewing. I was a few feet behind her. June and his longtime friend, Rick, were not positioned behind my mom at first. Once they saw her swaying side-to-side, they were able to catch her before she hit the floor. I don't remember where Roy and Duane were, but I do recall looking for them desperately. I didn't see them until we arrived at the cemetery, I think.

It was a tough time for me and I grew tired of looking the other way and ignoring snide remarks from Wilma. My temper boiled over during the interment portion of the services because she said something that set me off. Stacy and another person pulled me away until it was time for us get back into the cars.

We did not attend to the repass because there was too much drama, which was cool with me. I was happy to go home to spend time with Shavonne. My mom insisted that we resumed our adolescent lives and move forward. This was an important time for

Roy and I because we were achieving milestones that year—Roy graduated from high school and me from middle school.

The end-of-the-year festivities were memorable for me. We were off for the summer following our graduation ceremony, with high school coming that fall. I almost didn't participate because this boy, who didn't like me, tripped me up during free time in gym and I reinjured my knee. I had to wear a leg brace and use crutches until the beginning of that summer.

* * * * *

I really enjoyed the summer of 1986 because of Shavonne's presence. We spent a lot of time together. Taking walks in the park, holding hands, and just being with each other. That was enough for me. Shavonne was my first love and my first heartbreak. Shavonne once told me she felt safe being around me and she brought out the protective side of me—not in an aggressive way.

All these things were done in secret because I was not allowed to openly date until I turned 16 and Shavonne's mother wasn't with it, either. I asked Asha why she brought us together. She said she thought we "made a nice couple and y'all deserved each other." Our innocent puppy love romance came to a screeching holt when someone in the neighborhood discovered we were dating—most likely that guy my mom distanced herself from years earlier, the one she chased away from our house—and told Shavonne's mom. She went ballistic and we quickly felt the backlash.

Shavonne's mother pulled me aside and made me to feel as though I was not worthy of her daughter's attention, like I was a deviant, flawed person. She threatened to tell my mother about what Shavonne and I were doing, which was pretty much pure puppy love. Shavonne's mom forewarned me to "stay away from my daughter or else I will tell your mother what's going on." To make sure I complied, she told Shavonne I threatened her. I wouldn't have done anything like that. Plus, I was terrified of my mom—Shirley Ann did not tolerate us disrespecting adults at all, and had not begun my rebellious phase at that point.

The next time I saw Shavonne, she looked at me with total disgust and contempt. Our favorite song was Billy Ocean's "Suddenly" (1985), but it abruptly changed to Lisa and the Cult Jam's (1985) "All Cried Out." Even though I understood Shavonne's mother's concerns, her approach was not appropriate for a child, in my opinion. Shavonne and I did not get the chance to talk about what happened until 20 or so years later because her family moved away unexpectedly.

Not only was my heart broken, but my feelings of abandonment also deepened. Shavonne and I were cordial toward one another once we returned to school. We started talking beyond the "hello" and "how are you?" Shavonne started dating this guy, who did not like me and delighted in the fact that he was dating my ex-girlfriend. However, just when Shavonne and I agreed to meet somewhere on school grounds to talk to about what happened between us, but she disappeared—this was sometime in the fall of 1986. We did get talk sometime between 200 and 2005.

*****

I have to share how Shavonne and I were able to talk after 20 or so years later without giving too many details (confidentiality is attached). I was working at a state child protection agency and Shavonne's name came up. I didn't think too much of it because this was not the first time I encountered someone I thought I knew. Once a possible person was identified, I contacted them by letter, inviting them to call me to further discuss why I reached out to them. If this person agrees to participate in this process, I notified the principle to inform them of my findings. Once other steps were taken, the identified person would either deny or confirm knowing the other party—blah, blah, blah.

Shavonne reach out to me one afternoon. At this point, it was strictly business for me because I did not think much of this interaction. Shavonne agreed to the terms described in the letter, and agree to submit to have background check. After these things were successfully completed, all I had left to do was paperwork. But something wonderfully strange happened shortly in this process.

I called Shavonne and finished what I needed and was ready to end this call. "Sir," Shavonne said, "I have some questions that might be personal for you, if you don't mind." This was an odd request and it caught me off guard. Shavonne alerted me of her hunch and asked where I attended middle school. I told her Hart Middle School, John L. Costly. And then, she asked if I attended my "Eighth Grade Social." Once I confirmed my school's location, we both fell silent for what seemed to be an eternity. Shavonne said, after a few moments of silence, "I looked at your name and wondered… What is your full last name?" this shocked me because not many people knew Jones would not have been my full last name had my dad lived longer—he wanted to officially adopt us and our names would have been Jones-Anderson. This question stunned me, and then followed by, "Kasim," pronounced the way it was back then. "Yes," I said, fighting back tears. I asked if I could I ask her a question (the one that only a few people could answer) to which she consented: "What color was your corsage and why was it special?" The flower shop where I ordered her corsage ran out of pink carnations, so they sprayed the tips of the white carnations pink. When Shavonne answered correctly, we both fell silent, again, save for a few sniffles. We agreed to talk once I was finished with work.

I was totally floored because I was just doing my job when this happened. I never would have imagined this happening after all those years. It was a beautiful thing. The last time we saw one another was the fall of 1986.

I called Shavonne back after I finished my duties for that day. This happened on a Friday afternoon. We talked for hours and it was amazing. We agreed it's not often that people get the chance to reconnect after so many years. Shavonne shared that she and her sisters endured a lot of chaos back then. We understood we had no control over what was going on because we were kids. We shared a number of things the other was not aware of back then. Shavonne and I were able to forgive one another and received closure.

Needless to say, it took some time for me to get over Shavonne back in the 1980s and this exchange brought some relief. I endured so much loss back then, and she was a huge source of comfort through some of it. Just being in Shavonne's presence made a difference for me, even when she did not know what to say or do. There were times when Shavonne simply held my hand and quietly sat next to me. Shavonne never made demands or caused me to feel threatened or uncomfortable. She provided a sense of peacefulness during a period of calamity. Shavonne taught me the value of being present and feeling genuinely loved. I strongly believe she could have been the love of my life had we been given the chance.

Shavonne was the first person I connected so tightly with wherein words were not necessary—I experienced this level of intimacy maybe once or twice after her, but eventually treasured the lessons that were learned through my encounters with her.

Why Did it Keep Coming?

I shared those stories to demonstrate how some of my challenges presented themselves earlier on in my life. These feelings, behaviors, and actions didn't appear out of nowhere nor did I conjure them up. They were brought on by people and circumstances. Not only did I manage to survive this tumultuous time in my life, I also saw how people behaved when they were in various modes (i.e., fear, anger, desperation, insecurity, jealousy, confusion, etc.). These characteristics helped me to learn how to observe people's words and actions.

All of those events occurred by the end of the first half of my freshmen year at East Orange High School—the home of the mighty, mighty Panthers! I heard so many scary things about high school before I arrived. I needed to get acclimated this new environment. Having people I knew from middle school and my neighborhood made it a little easier. Shannon (my future sister-in-law at that time) was there as well, but I tried not get in her way because she was a senior and she had her own thing going on. I had to tap into the resources I was given before I got there. I had supports on the personal level, namely my god sister, the late Cynthia Marie Christina Renee Clark (she loved saying her full name) but she went by Cyndi.

Cyndi was a warm, caring, giving, loving person who I count myself blessed to have had in my life, even for that brief amount of time. Cyndi had a condition called Systemic Lupus

Erythematosus (or Lupus). By the time we met, her case had advanced and she had several surgeries because, unfortunately, the treatment was not as innovative as it is today. None of us in my neighborhood really understood just how ill Cyndi truly was, but we all loved her deeply.

At first, Cyndi was this mysterious person we only saw getting in-and-out of her grandmother's car, coming in-and-out of their apartment building. I do not remember exactly how we met her. I think someone introduced themselves to Cyndi as we were sitting on the front porch. I loved her because she spent time with me and treated me as her own little brother, even though she had two younger brothers and a younger sister. Cyndi reinforced the need for me to attain a good education and helped me to start believing in myself because "you're a smart, handsome young man." In fact, she encouraged me to ask Shavonne to be my girlfriend. Cyndi told me about her health , but we didn't focus on that. She taught me *so* many other things about life—like the my appreciation of good music, history, and fairness. Cyndi excused my antics as I transitioned into my high school experience and encouraged me to get involved in extracurricular activities.

I was beginning to catch my stride by the end of my freshmen year. I joined the marching band and spent a lot of time at band practice afterschool and hanging out with my newfound friends. Cyndi understood and was busy enjoying her relationship with her boyfriend/fiancée, Marc (I cannot remember his last name). Cyndi and I made time for one another whenever we needed one another. My mom, Cyndi, and my other god sister, who's name happens to be Cynthia J., worked together at Kids R Us—Shannon and I worked there in the afternoons after band practice. I used to see Cyndi before she left for the evening. She always asked how school was going and supported me as I prepared for the HSPT (High School Proficiency Test). I had to pass this test in order to graduate. This was an important task, and Cyndi knew I needed to do well.

One spring morning, Cyndi called while I was getting dressed for school. I had an eerie feeling about this call. She did not sound well at all. Cyndi asked me to let my mom know she was not going to work that day. At first, I thought it was morning sickness because she was in her first trimester of pregnancy, but it just didn't feel right. I offered, rather pleaded, to come sit with her, but Cyndi declined— "You need to go to school and get ready for that test. I'ma be alright." I begged anyhow but she was not having it because my education was a priority. I relented, even though I wanted to be with her, and went to school.

The first part of that day was okay because I was able to focus on the things that were going on around me, but at some point, I was distracted by a sinking feeling that something was wrong. I couldn't shake that feeling off no matter how I tried. I managed to remain in school the entire day and went to work as usual. I simply did not want to accept what was stirring in my spirit.

I arrived at work and that lingering feeling was still on me, only stronger, and I did all I could to move past it. I went to my mom and asked if she felt something stirring in her spirit to which she said yes. My mom told me she had been feeling this stirring all day, "and she explained that it started this morning. We agreed to talk before she went home.

I found my mom and my other god sister, Cynthia J., sitting in mom's car, lollygagging as if they didn't have anything else to do. Usually, they would have been long gone, but there they sat. I knelt on my Cynthia's side of the car and talked with them for a while. While doing so, I was able to see inside the store from where I was situated. I saw the store manager run to a department manager, Diana, first. They conversed and the department manager burst into tears. Then, Cyndi's supervisor, Maria, appeared. The store manager said something to her, and she, too, started to cry. They all looked toward my mom's car for a moment. The three of us wondered what was going on and why were they gawking at us. The store manager came towards the car. I stood up and wanted to run in the opposite direction but froze in place. She said something to my mother, but I don't remember what it was. My mom asked me if I heard what was said to which I didn't. She got out of the car, took me by the arm, and explained, "Cyndi passed away this morning…." I felt as if I was going to pass out but was too shocked by the news. My mom stayed with me a while longer and tried to convince me to go home with her. I declined and remained at work.

I couldn't believe Cyndi was gone. She told me she was going to be alright, but she was gone—my trust and abandonment issues were inflamed even more. I stayed at work but ended up going home early, anyhow. I talked to Cyndi's paternal grandmother, who was present when she died. She was devastated. I could not understand what happened as I numbly floated through this mourning period, which was during the Easter season 1988.

The store closed for the wake and the funeral, which was interesting because the customers did not get angry but sent condolences to Cyndi's families—both her biological and extended families. It took a while for me to forgive Cyndi for leaving when she did. I eventually came to an understand: her body was battered and she was tired. I had a challenging time trusting people for many years after all these things transpired.

* * * * *

Time went on and I resumed my life as a teenager. I focused on school, band activities, and work. It wasn't easy at first, but I kept looking for positive experiences. I loved participating in EOHS' bands (marching, concert, and military). In a lot of ways, it was a positive outlet for me and others. I soon came to realize several of my peers were going through some things that were not obvious to everyone. Situations like ours made us who were to become. As for me, it took some time for me to arrive at a place where I started enjoying the positive things happening around me. I still believed there was good in everybody, while ignoring their agendas and motives.

Chapter Three:
Did I Get It Right?

As I started settling into my teen years, I began to rebel. I was a PK (Preacher's Kid) and grew tired of the rules, double-standards, and expectations other people had for me. I'd heard some horrible things about PKs, while at the same time, I'd seen preachers' families being taken for granted and abused. One of my friends, who was also a PK, was amazed by how Duane and I held it together for so long. They started rebelling long before we were teenagers and "didn't give a shit!" I tried my best to do right by my mom, because I knew she would cut up with me. I believe people knew this and took advantage of it. Moreover, I wasn't feeling these duplicities anymore. One of my favorite responses was: "My mom's the preacher, not me."

Duane and I were expected to "behave" and "act like you know how to act" all the time. Many people thought we should have known the Bible from front-to-back, and when we did not…. I tried to live up to those ideals, but they proved to be too much. I was ready to bust out and be me, whoever that was. I began experimenting with some things I was not allowed to even think about before, mainly partying and drinking.

Sundays were very long. Duane and I would be in church from morning into the evening most Sundays—Sunday school, morning service, afternoon meal, afternoon service, and sometimes, evening prayer service. At one point or another, we sang in at least two to three choirs, served as Junior Ushers, as well as other collateral duties. Making plans on Sundays, other than church, was a waste of time because we had to have our asses in church, period. I loved the Lord and all, and still do, but this was a bit too much for me. My mother believed in the "age of accountability," the coming of age at 13 years old, and would not budge— "If Jesus did it, you will too!" Of course, we tried the "I'm sick" routine, but it didn't work because "they can anointed you with oil and lay hands on you." I couldn't wait until I turned 13.

Duane and I attended one church primarily for a number of years, and accompanied my mom whenever she went to different churches to visit or bring the Word. These churches were in *an association*, but not always in a formal sense. Most of the time, two or more churches had causal connections like the pastors were cousins (and nem) or friends, etc. It was within these so-called associations that I ran into the most trouble. Folk thought they could say crazy things to me and I wasn't *supposed* to say anything back. But I had a slick mouth on me, and I clapped back when I had to. One "deaconess" told me she was going to "slap the shit out" of me. Can you imagine how laughable this was? I felt this incident was not worthy of me telling my mother about because Shirley Ann did not play when you mistreated her kids.

I placed quotes around this person's title because she had a nasty spirit and was just mean as hell. That same deaconess encouraged me to get with this girl who was known for her hook-ups and being loose (promiscuous). She pushed us to do something we had no business doing, only to give her mean ass something to talk about. But I didn't fall for it.

There were instances when I saw preachers and others do some grimy shit without caring who saw and/or knew what they were doing—not even children. People were quick to say,

"Preachers are humans, too," whenever it served them best. I knew it was true, but I also saw people (the congregants) enticing the male preachers by sitting on the front row with no pannies (panties) on and screwing around with them. I've seen this type of behavior too many times but said nothing because I knew some things were not meant for me to see or talk about. There are so many things I will take to my grave, but I tell you, a lot of it was disgraceful. Several of those people actually helped me to figure out who I was and served as excellent examples for what I was not supposed to do.

I started enjoying church when I was away from my mom's influence. I loved going to churches that did not know I was a PK. I know this might sound funny, but I felt like I could blend in with the crowd and enjoy the service. If it had not been for these encounters, I would have stopped going to church at 13 years old. Being exposed to different church environments allowed me to see beyond the churches I attended on a regular basis. I visited one of my friend's church one time and saw someone I knew. I had to damn near beg that critter not to say anything about me being a PK. I simply wanted to enjoy the singing, hear the Word, and then, go home.

One of the worst things about being a PK was the extraordinary amount of restrictions my brother and I had to live under. We were supposed to take on my mom's fiery exhorter personality, admonishing God's people to repent and be saved. There was no room for deviating from this plan because God *showed* them something and didn't give us a clue. I eventually learned that God does not reveal something about me to someone else without giving me a clue. This is why I get so annoyed when people follow behind others (preachers, singers, and the like) in order to "get a word"—lowercase *word* was intentional. I grew tired of people *speaking over me*, because the same tongue that was prophesying was the same one cutting me down— "He ain't gonna be nothing but a tack head (hoodlum) when he grow up...," "Yup, that one is gonna be an addict," or "he gon have kids everywhere." PROPH-A-LYING!!! No, I didn't let these people speak over, pray for, or lay hands on me when it was time for me to go away to seminary—ya kiddin' me (in my Jersey accent).

My mom, my pastor, some of my cousins, and others did their very best to help me understand my spiritual gift(s). The more I comprehended, the more I wanted to run from it because it required me to be more responsible. I wasn't ready to do that at that point of my life. I knew there was a calling on my life from an early age, and I was also aware of my spiritual gift. But *I* wanted to live a little before I tapped into that part of me. Like several other things in my life, I didn't know what to ask of others or what to expect. Those who were close to me used to say things that were obscure and mysterious, thinking I would understand what was being said or not said. All of this started when I was seven or eight years old.

I had to learn how to pray for myself in specific areas of my life. I knew my mom and others had my back, but there were some things I had to learn to do for myself. Me being me, I made this process hard at times. I reverted back to a familiar cop-out several times: I ran. When I see this type of behavior in teens and young adults today, I want to say, "I really understand how you might be feeling." Yet, when I was their age I had to learn on my own because I was surrounded by warriors, who knew who I was because that's how God works—God provides for you along your journey. I had to find out what a crucible was and why it was necessary. In hindsight, some of the pressures of acknowledging the calling upon my life was self-inflected because I wanted to be like other people my age and have "fun." I had to recognize I was set apart and was not supposed be like the typical or ordinary. With that being so, solitude would become a considerable part of my life. I tend to withdraw without knowing it sometimes.

As a PK, I thought it was extra hard because I believed "I should have known better," but what did I know? I've talked to several PKs through the years and many of them had mixed feelings about being a PK because some didn't let others' thoughts, opinions, or perceptions interfere with their lives. I must have missed that class. I had no clue what it meant to be a PK. It was hard at times because if someone knew my mom and I didn't know them, they would tell on me (snitch) when I did my dirt. It was bananas. I wondered how my mom knew so much, especially when I thought I was extra careful in doing my dirt. I know it takes a village but dang. I felt paranoid at times because I didn't know who was watching me—and telling on me. One lady said, "I told your mother because you should know better." The funny thing was she should have been watching her own children, especially her daughter. Say no more.

Did It Stop Me?

My first personal challenge forced me to put what I knew to the test. One of my parents' sayings, especially my mom, was: "Stay a child while you can." This used to get on my nerves, especially in my teen years, because I thought I knew everything there was to know about life. I started taking on adult responsibilities and making grown folks' moves like it was so easy. My mom repeatedly told me to slow down, "You have plenty of time for that." No, I had to act like an adult right then and there.

My mom did something I now know was difficult—she stepped aside but remained close enough to reach me. I thought I won the battle with my mom's *meddling* because it was my life, and no one had the right to tell me anything. Like I said, I swore up and down I knew all that I needed to know about life, and I had a handle on what I was doing. I was clueless and was too arrogant to admit it. My mindset and attitude were obvious signs of my immaturity.

Yet, I plowed through, full steam ahead. Life was good and I was doing my thing—finishing high school, working, and taking care of my *readymade family*. Although things were moving along, the pressure started building and I found myself constantly hustling and not really taking care of myself as I should have been. I was so focused on attaining what I wanted that I ignored the warning signs my body was sending—slow down. I'm tired. This physical and mental fatigue was so obvious to others that they began trying to get me to see what they saw. But "A hard head makes a soft tail all day." I was stubborn as hell because *I knew everything* and wasn't going to let anyone *run my life*. My defiance was to my own detriment and the clock was ticking against my health.

The flu season of 1989 – 90 was alarming because other infections were running rampant as well. I was still doing everything I was committed to and spreading myself too thin at the same time. This was supposed to be my senior year. Instead of focusing on what I was going to do after high school, I was so busy hustling trying to keep my thing going in that moment.

My mom stepped up to tell me I had too much going on, "and if you don't slow down, its gonna catch up with you." I always had a comeback and I thought if I just continued doing what

I thought I had to do, so that my mom would be pleased with the outcome. Little did I know I was walking around with a flu-like virus that would disrupt *my* plans.

Sidebar: It is beneficial to have people who truly love you near, especially those who are not afraid to tell you the truth. If you're smart, you'd put your pride aside and listen to good counsel, because to have people like that in your life is a blessing. To take them for granted or ignore good counsel from loving, wise people in your corner is a big mistake that carries large ramifications in the long haul.

My mom had been saying I looked tired all that week, but I didn't listened to her. She continually told me to rest— "Take a little time to rest. Everything will be there when you get back. Just take one day to sit yo ass down somewhere." Nope! My foolish behind believed I had to do certain things myself because I had a lot to do. In truth, my mom knew what she was talking about but I was so obstinate that I didn't want her to be right. In hindsight, my mom was doing her job and did not want to see me hurt. All of the rippin,' runnin,' and ignoring that my body was telling me it was getting weary, my illness quickly came to a head.

One day, after going to school all day and band practice afterwards, I went to work knowing damn well I wasn't feeling well—the virus had been running its course all the while. Like a trooper, I thought I was going to push through my day, go home and rest overnight; and then, get up the next day and do it all over again. But that virus had another agenda all together. I walked around with a fever that steadily climbed as the day went on. I ignored the symptoms and didn't say anything. I just kept going, *making moves*.

I arrived at work early as usual. I struggled because I was so tired and sore. I thought it was odd because I didn't do anything that would have caused my body to act like that apart from band practice. Again, I ignored the symptoms. I thought if I sat down and took a break before I started my shift, I would've been fine. I tried to convince myself I would be *aight*, but it didn't work. In fact, I felt worse. I tried to stay at work because I had to get my coins to keep things moving. The fever caused me to feel hot and flush to the point where I almost fainted a couple of times. One of my coworker/friends looked at me and said, "You look like shit! Go sit down. You need to go home."

I decided to call my mom. She knew something was wrong immediately, and she knew I was not drunk. My mom went into *Momma Bear mode* and started snapping orders: "Sit down and stay there. I'm going to call the store and let them know you are coming home. I'm calling Roy to pick you up. Get off the phone (click)." Roy arrived within 15 minutes with a look on his face that indicated things were serious. We rode home in silence. Roy glanced over at me from time-to-time. His facial expression grew more and more concerned each time he looked at me. I was oblivious as to what he saw.

We arrived home in what seemed like no time. Roy tapped my arm while saying, "Let's go!" and nodded toward the front door to our house. Roy led me up to my mom's bedroom. She took one look at me and started issuing commands like a five-star general who was warned of an oncoming attack. Because I was a minor, Mom was still responsible for my well-being. She mom gave Roy my health insurance card and said, "Take to him to Saint Barnabas cause that's where our doctor works. Tell 'em Kasim is a patient of Dr. R. and they'll take care of him." Roy whisked me out the front door and into the car again. He whipped that Grand Am like he was a seasoned ambulance driver without sirens blaring. I was confused because I thought I was going to stay home, take some medicine, go to sleep, and then, be back on my grind the next day. The last command I heard my mom snap was, "Call me after the doctors see him."

I'm not sure what happened but Roy got me to the hospital quickly and sprang into action once we arrived. He got some nurses' attention, making sure they checked me in, and then, they whisked me into a room before I had the chance to sit in the waiting room. I looked around wondering, "What the hell's going on?" One of the nurses took my temperature at a registration station. She jumped up, grabbed a wheelchair, and pushed me to be triaged to a treatment room. She told me to take off my clothes and put on a hospital robe—"I'm going to get a doctor right now!" I was really baffled by then. I froze and asked Roy what was going on. I had no idea of the condition I was in. Roy told me he would be back, but I grabbed his arm before he could walk away and begged him not to go. He helped me off the bed for a moment and led me to a mirror on the wall. What I saw scared me! My face had a slight droop and I sounded like my mouth was swollen. Roy and I quietly removed my clothes, put on the robe, and waited in silence.

Suddenly a doctor and a nurse rushed into my room and started probing, prodding, poking, and asking a lot of questions. I was still stunned by what I saw in the mirror. Roy answered some questions as best as he could and stepped back to let them do what was needed.

One of the last things I can remember was the doctor taking my temperature, saying to one of the nurses, "We've got to get his temperature to come down." They put an IV in my arm, told Roy they were going to take care of me, and advised him to call my mom. Roy's face was wrought with concern, as if he messed up. That wasn't it! He had to call **<u>Momma Bear</u>** to tell her what was going on. I fell asleep at some point.

I woke up the next day feeling groggy and disoriented. My mom's face was the first one I saw since I went to sleep the night before. Mom's grimace quickly turned into a smile when she saw my eyes opened. "You're probably going home today," she said, attempting to sound blasé. I wanted to know where I was and what happened. Mom said I didn't need to worry about that, "I got you. You gonna be alright." She alerted the nurse of my awakening and the doctor was called in to talk to us. The doctor said I could go home but had to be on bed rest for a few days "until the infection passes through your body." My silly ass was more concerned with having to sit down for a while rather than focusing on my recovery. The doctor continued on to say, "We kept you to monitor you because of your high temperature and blood pressure, because it almost triggered paralysis. In other words, he nearly suffered a full-on stroke because of the clotting and infection in his body. It was a light stroke, if you will, which was a BIG warning sign." My mother looked at me with an expression that said, "DAMN-IT!" But me, I looked as if it was nothing, but then, the doctor said, "Son, you're a blessed young man."

I was under my doctor's care and missed more than 18 days from school in addition to the other days for appointments. I learned that if I had not gone to the hospital when I did, my condition would have been much worse. So, my recovery was longer than originally anticipated. In accordance with New Jersey state law, I had to repeat the twelfth grade. I had already turned 18 years old that year, and my grades were subpar, which meant they didn't have to allow me to return the following school year. I didn't know this at the time, so I focused on catching up on what I missed. I started going to all of my classes and doing the work, which gave me an edge for the next year.

My mom and I received a letter from the school towards the end of the year. This letter informed us of my being ineligible to graduate that year, and the date for a meeting to discuss my future and what would be required of me. Basically, this meeting was to determine whether I would be able to return or not. This situation became real because I didn't know what was going to happen.

Things were tense at home in the days leading up to that meeting, because I was the only one there with my mom and Tihira—my brothers moved out and were on their own. There was no one there to mediate during our discussions. My mother told me to think about my future and make a sound decision. There were no more threats or strong-arming because, after all, I had been making *grown folk moves* before then; so, it was all on me. I had a lot to contend with in my mind. I had plans to move on into adulthood for starters, and this situation would set me back another year. I talked it out (processed) with my mom and others. I received mixed responses about what I should do. Some of the input reminded me of all the crappy predictions I'd heard when I was younger, which flamed my rebellious streak even more—"I'll show their asses!" But for the time being, I decided to wait until the meeting to see what would happen.

Before this letter arrived, I realized I had the ability to succeed academically. I had no idea this would be the road I would travel later in life. I was accustomed to the *get over mentality*, where

I looked for shortcuts and *work arounds*. I thought I was city slick in a couple of classes, and tried to do the least amount of work, looking for the best grades. But then, I started applying myself more after being called out. The class that forced me to move differently was Senior English. The teacher of this class, Mr. D., didn't play when it came to his assignments—whether you did the work, or failed. I had to read a book and do book report as a part of my final grade—the other parts were a final exam and a recitation of a silique from Shakespeare's *McBeth*.

There was a booklist you had to choose a book and then sign-off on. It was "a first come, first served basis." All of the books on the list had a meaning to life theme to them and not hard reading at all. I chose "Brian's Song," by William Blinn (1971/1983). Well, I decided to half-ass it by reading a few of chapters of the book, and then, wrote the book report. Mr. D. gave me an *A* for creativity but an *F* for not following the real story line. He gave me another chance to read the book, *the whole book*, and resubmit it. I had two weeks to do all of this. Receiving A+ as a final grade sparked my love of books, reading, and learning. I still have the book I read back then, and I still remember some of the words from that Shakespeare silique.

* * * * * *

The day of reckoning arrived. My mom and I climbed into her car and quietly drove to the school for the meeting. My mother was about the business, while I quaked in my boots. The secretary, Ms. Mc., asked for our names, looked at her appointment book, and then, looked at me with a screw face before instructing us to take a seat. I discovered the meeting was with the meanest, the toughest, took-zero-shit-from-no one Vice Principal, Mrs. P. My mom looked at me and said, "Ain't no time for panicking now. You better pray."

Mrs. P. called us into her office and invited us to make ourselves comfortable, but how could I when my future was so uncertain. Mrs. P. laid down the law. She told my mother everything, from my shitty attendance to my "half-ass'd grades," and my lackadaisical attitude toward school, in general. She then turned her sights onto me. "It looks like you're no longer a minor, Mr. Jones," she growled, while looking down at my records. Mrs. P. stated the obvious, that I would not graduate in the ensuing days because I missed too many days, "even though they were for medical reasons." She demanded that I give her a reason why she should readmit me for the next school year— "Why should I let you back in here next year?" I told her I wanted my high school diploma because I wanted to make something of myself.

My words hung in the air for a few moments. The tension was so thick you could've cut it with a butter knife. I glanced over at my mom. She grunted and turned her head. I felt like everything was falling down on me for real and no one was able to help me.

Mrs. P. broke the awkward silence by saying, "Against my better judgement, I'm gonna let you come back. But if you mess up once, just once, you're outta here!" She glared at me for a moment before reaching for a legal pad. "Here are the conditions," twisting her mouth into a tight curl, "if you make anything less than a B, you're out! If you miss one day without a legitimate reason, you're out! If you mess up any other way, YOU ARE OUT!" Mrs. P. paused for a few moments to let that sink in. "Do you know of anything that will get in your way? Speak now or forever hold ya peace," she snapped. I thought for a moment and informed her of my job. I was bound by a legal contract until October of 1990. "Is that right?" she asked my mother, who validated its authenticity. Mrs. P. rubbed her chin, glared at me, and told my mother she expected big things from me— "Because I know he can do the work." She smiled and shook my mother's hand; and then, took my hand and barked, "Don't mess this up."

My mom and I left that meeting silently because we hadn't had the chance to process what happened. "Don't mess this up," she warmly. "You have a chance to do something good and make something of yourself." I knew it was true because I knew a few people Mrs. P. didn't allow to come back. I felt this was my opportunity to do the work and shine at the same time.

My purpose became clear: Put in the work to get that high school diploma. I developed a *Nothing will stop me* frame of mind. I not only worked my "grown folks' gig" all summer and fall but I got serious because Mrs. P. wasn't playing when she said, "You are out," if I didn't do what I had to do. I knew I had to get my high school diploma because it had been instilled in me since I was a child. It was almost a no brainer but I had to sweat it out until the opportunity was presented at that meeting, because it was not a guaranteed option. I was relieved to know I was invited back. I also knew I could not afford to botch this second-chance.

Some of the decisions I made during the next three or four years were touch and go. Yet most of my positive moves were not as hard as the not-so-positive decisions (and outcomes) were. Deciding to return to school while working that *grown-up* job was hard as hell but it reinforced the work ethic I'd acquired from my parents. Once that contract was finished, I had enough money to pay all of my senior dues and most of the expenses. I applied that same mentality with my schoolwork. I had two or three mathematic classes, biology, as well as other subjects that I either missed or failed, but needed. My schedule was no joke all year long. However, I managed to earn all A's and B's except for one C, which was in the first quarter. I made Honor Roll three out of four marking periods. In doing so, I annoyed my mom because she knew I could do this all along. I was overjoyed during the graduation ceremony and Senior activities.

* * * * *

Once high school was over, I had to get on with my life. My two closest friends were preparing for college, and I had no clue as to what I was going to do with my life. My mom gave me a little time to celebrate before dropping the *adult responsibilities* speech on me. I understood where she was coming from because it was time for me to start taking caring for myself. I had a lot to consider as an emerging adult and knew my mom would call me to task if I started to slip. It was time for me to start charting my own path.

My folks did an excellent job up to that point, and this could only be seen in the way I proceeded. There are so many opportunities presented to you when you're young —some good, while others may not be favorable. Navigating this field is akin to trial by fire because you can only receive advisement on the decisions you have to make and deal with the consequences of those choices. The rest of my life was before me and the decisions I made would affect my future—scary shit!

My parents' warnings about the call of the streets echoed in my mind. After graduating from high school there were many opportunities to party to which I did my share. By the time I'd reached the "legal age" to do certain things, they were no longer exciting because I had been doing them for years. Once I was outside the safe walls of high school, there were countless things showing themselves. It was very important for me to tap into the resources instilled in me since I was a child. I thank God for those lessons.

The drug and flashy lifestyle was very much visible in the early 1990s. It was a glamourized lifestyle of decadence on many levels of society. Yes, there were messages out there discouraging drug usage, but the pull of the drug life was strong and many fell prey to it. My folks admonished my brothers and I to do the "right thing," which translated into the "legal thing"—earning money in such a way that you were not fearful of the law due to illegal activities. My older siblings were living on their own and did not have problems with the drug life. It was my turn to find my way. As tempting as the drug life was, I got a job after my talk with my mom.

My mom was clear about me getting on with my life. She encouraged me to find my place in the world because "Everything ain't for everybody." This was a great piece of advice because there were so many options out there. Coming from a military family, my first choice was to join the U. S. Navy like Duane—Willie and Roy, Sr. joined the U. S. Army, and so did my father and my dad. I went through all the steps but was unable to serve due to a pre-existing medical condition. I was devastated at first but I had to move on to find something else to do.

I was interested in so many things, which only made things more complicated. I considered attending the DeVry Institute to study Computer Programming, which was a big to do at that time. I checked the program out and discovered it cost just as much as a bachelor's degree and it was not guaranteed that you got a job. I felt stuck. I could not figure out what my next move was going to be. Once again, my mom stepped up to encourage me to do something I thought I would not do again: I enrolled to take classes at Essex County Community College (also known as Essex County College and ECC) in January of 1992.

Making the decision to enroll in college, per my mom's suggestion, wasn't hard. In fact, it seemed natural being that my curiosity had been ignited during my last year in high school. My mom pointed to the fact that I seemed to enjoy learning new things. I agreed but had another motive: I wanted to prove all those people who said I wouldn't amount to shit wrong. The experience I had in high school helped me to see myself differently because several people helped me to believe I could do whatever I wanted to do. Coupled with this knowledge and the opportunity, I had a defiant streak that fed my sense of determination. This made the next step in my life's story much sweeter.

Was I on the Right Track?

Transitioning into adulthood was interesting because I quickly learned it required a certain level of humility. The next two to three years of my life were impactful. Many of the lessons learned influenced who I was becoming, even to this day. My mother taught me not to be ashamed to ask questions or for help when it was needed. So, I kept my eyes open to see how things worked. Of course, there were times when I wasn't paying full attention to what was going on, but I did my best to be aware of my surroundings. My dad told me several times, "When you set out to do something, try to learn as much as you can [about it]." I had to draw from that wisdom to keep learning, and not just from books.

My first job after high school was at Pathmark Supermarket on Bergan Street in Newark, N. J.—across the street from University Hospital. This was my second supermarket gig, only this time I was working legally. I was hired to work in the non-foods/pharmacy department, which was something different for me. The crew I worked with was very helpful and competitive because they did not like being scrutinized by upper management. My Department Manager, Joey, and his Assistant Manager, Rob, were great guys who looked out for their people. The Assistant Manager, an older gentleman, took me under his wing because he had a fatherly touch and patience to boot. Not only did Rob show me the ropes, but he also dropped gems of wisdom here and there. Rob was intrigued by the fact that I was starting classes at the local community college and talked about school a lot. Most of all, Rob was impressed by the way I carried myself, even though I looked like your average *knuckle head*—it was the clothes. I credited to my parents, which caused Rob to nod his head slowly and rub his chin— "I like that." Me being curious, I asked why he said that. "I've heard that so many times before, but it was the way you said it. You really meant it," he explained. Rob was a quiet, soft-spoken man, who said what meant, and didn't mind explaining things. We had many good laughs together, while getting our work done, of course.

Several other people helped me to figure things out. I had to lean on what my mom told me when I was in high school— "You're the one in control of your life. Nobody can take care of you better than you." I kept that in mind and made it habit, especially in those days, when I was so impressionable. I really looked up to Rob, and figured I needed more individuals like him in my life who would support and guide me onto higher heights; people who were able to recognize my potential and could help bring it out.

January 1992 rolled around quickly, and I was ready for a new challenge: college. I reported to where I was instructed in my welcome letter and was assigned a Student Ambassador, who would show me around the school's many areas, sections, and services. Essex County College brimmed with activity. People were always moving about, especially in the afternoons and evenings. Not only was it a place of higher learning for adults, but these students were serious about what they were doing. It was intimidating at first, but I eventually found my rhythm.

I was in the right place at the right time. I was assigned an ambassador as soon as I walked into the Students Life office. He introduced himself as Raheem. He was an older man, in his early thirties, soft-spoken, and intelligent. Raheem was like a younger version of my dad. He described himself as an "old soul" and made no qualms about it. Raheem made himself available to me, especially when we had time between classes. This guy had a quick, strong mind, and was constantly reading and thinking about some relevant topic. Raheem had this saying, "Challenge your mind not to be lazy." I thought he was a *deep brutha* and wanted to learn more. My mom always told me to listen to the Spirit, "and you won't go wrong." I knew there were wolves in sheep's clothing, but Raheem seemed safe to be around.

One day, Raheem and I were hanging out in an outside area on the campus. The season was changing and the weather was just right. He look at me and said, "I know who you are. Kindred spirits draw one another." I was absolutely lost! Sensing I didn't know where he was going, Raheem asked, "What is your gift?" The confusion cleared up because I caught on to what he was asking—he was referring to my spiritual gift. In his usual fashion, Raheem began to teach: "Some people can take you only so far along your journey. God assigned others to do the rest." We agreed upon a mentor/mentee relationship that day. Raheem knew I did not like being treated like a PK; so, he rarely quoted the Bible, and did not ask me to do so unless it was fitting.

Raheem did not like the fact that I was still in the partying phase of my life. He was cool and was not too harsh (judgmental) about it. He could tell when I partied hard—among other things. One of the downsides of being around kindred spirits is you became sensitive to one another's moods and energy, even when you do not want to be.

Raheem continued feeding my inquisitive spirit by giving me this powerful reading list and a copy of James Allen's (1903) *As A Man Thinketh*, which I still have. I have read this wonderful little book several times through the years and gained inspiration each time—I also gave my mentees and younger siblings a copy.

The first time we discussed *As a Man Thinketh*, Raheem was impressed by my comprehension but questioned my application as evidenced by this question: "And you do what?" After hearing this question several times, I asked what he meant, "because you keep asking me the same thing over-and-over again." Raheem paused for a moment and stared at me. In my naiveté, I thought he could be pensive at times, especially when I wanted to do what I wanted to do without question. "You're still trying to impress people," he said without flinching. Dumb-struck, I had no idea what he was talking about. "You're not ready," he asserted in the most condescending tone I'd heard from him at that point. Raheem encouraged me to think about that discussion and we would talk about it later. So, I went on my way, concentrating on the tasks of the day.

I thought about what Raheem said and realized I ignored things when I did not want to face or deal with them. Raheem was not trying to hurt me or keep me from living. He was doing what he had been charged to do—speak the words that stirred in his spirit. Raheem was able to *SEE* the lost little boy in me but didn't want to push too hard, too fast. He understood, in my opinion, how damaging it could have been if I were *not ready* to wrestle with certain issues in my life and he pulled them out too soon. It took a couple weeks but we talked about what he was hinting at in depth.

I told Raheem how a number of people used to speak negatively over me and how I did things "just to show their asses." Raheem posed a question that served as the catalyst to deep consideration that day: "You know everybody has a job to do or a role in this life," he began, and I paraphrase. "Well, it's the same on the spiritual plain. Everybody has assignments, whether they know it or not. So many people don't know we are mere vessels created to serve an ultimate purpose. Distractions are intended to take us away from our paths. What convinced you to believe the hype (someone else's story, opinion, or perspective)?" I had to give it some thought because I had never asked this question before.

If you'd asked me to give one word to describe myself back then, and even now, I would say tenacious. Tenacious would be a suitable adjective because I didn't like being blocked as I tried to function on my own, although it wasn't always in a healthy way. I would push people away who seemed to be against me, even if I could not articulate what I was feeling. I wanted and needed someone to push me in a way that gave me room to figure some things out without being told or given all of the information easily.

Meanwhile, I discovered a link to why I tried to *impress* others in some ways, while not giving a damn in others. Although it was significant in the grand scheme of things, I suppressed it's meaning for many years. I tried to avoid thinking about dark times in my life when I was emotionally and physically abuse by an unlikely source.

The situation I shared with Raheem involved my seventh-grade Science Teacher. This person was not fit to work with African American children because of his deep-seated biases. They did not seem to be sensitive to my age group or culture they served. The average age of a seventh grader is 12 or 13-year-old—early adolescence. Not only is one in search of their identity, he or she is highly impressionable. So many things occur during this stage that it may be considered "the toughest years" in life.

I'll be the first to admit I was clown back then, with an explosive temper to boot. The crew I ran with was very good at cracking jokes or hiking on others. We all had some crazy shit going on in our personal and/or home lives. My tomfoolery was a cry for help and I didn't know it. My science teacher enhanced my struggles by humiliating me in front of others (my peers and teachers alike), and eventually, physically striking me.

I attended a middle school where my primary classes (English, math, science, and social studies) were taught by a team of teachers. These teams had leaders who served as the spokesperson, advocate, etc. for the teachers and the students. My name came up several times during some of their meetings because I acted out in their classes; but I did my work in all my class except one: science. Little did I know my Science Teacher had made several recommendations for me to be placed in an emotionally disturbed self-contained class (Special Education). It could not happen because there was a criterion that I didn't meet. I did not know what happened behind the scenes until I was in high school.

My school had a swimming pool and most of us learned how swim as a part of our physical education (Phys. Ed.) curriculum. One of the safety rules was no glass was allowed in the locker rooms or the pool areas, but I had a mason jar with my lotion in it—hold that point.

My science teacher, who was working his agenda to get me out of the general population, stepped up his game with provocation and other things that agitated me without being seen or heard. This teacher used to set me off by whispering things like: "you little monkey," "stankin' piece of shit," "ya black ass buffoon," to name a few. Each time he said or did those things, I erupted in the worst way. To make matters worse, it appeared as if I didn't have a reason to act out that way. I would tell my mother, she would call the school, and nothing could be done "because we can't prove it." The other teachers on my team and school officials could see was my behavior, but unbeknownst to my mother and I, they had their doubts about what was going on in my science class. The other teachers wondered "why it wasn't happening in my class as well."

Back to the story. Phys. Ed. came the period after my science class, and the whole team went to those classes at the same time. Our class had swimming and we were escorted to the pool area by that science teacher. For some reason, I did not walk to the pool area with my class. I rushed down the stairs quickly because I had to be dressed and ready within certain amount of time, or I couldn't participate and received a zero for the day. In my haste I did not see that teacher coming toward me. I looked up and there he stood with a menacing look on his face. I knew I was in trouble instantly because I was cornered. "Oh, there you are, ya dumbass muthaf**ka," before backhanding me across my face with his leather grade book. I swung my bag as hard as I could, striking them in the face, busting their bottom lip with my mason jar.

By the time I arrived home that afternoon, the imprint of his gradebook was clearly visible. My mother rushed me to my eye doctor, and my injuries were documented. My mother went to my school the next day and calmly stated her issue with this teacher, which was probably scarier than other parents who had a problem. As for that science teacher, they were fired and stripped of their license to teach in the state of New Jersey.

Raheem sat quietly without interrupting or drifting off. That was the first time I'd talked to anyone about that situation in years. I had not dealt with what this ordeal had done to me, emotionally and intellectually. I did what I knew best at that time: I suppressed it. Pushing my feelings down was what I thought I needed to do because I didn't want to add another burden on my mom, who was going through a lot back then.

When Raheem finally spoke, it was almost as if he was cold and indifferent toward what I'd shared with him. "Yeah, I get that. When you gonna shake that shit off and keep it moving?" I was stunned and felt my anger rising. So, I challenged: "What the hell is that suppose ta mean? Didn't you hear what I said?" With the patience of a true teacher, Raheem looked me straight in my face and said, "I get that but when are you going to work it out, put it in its place, and then, move forward." Just like that, my anger dissolved into clear, solution-based thoughts.

This was a revealing moment for me. I already knew I was not limited intellectually, because I was earning A's and B's in my classes, so learning was not an issue. Raheem had a good point because not dealing with certain aspects of my past was holding me back.

I dreamed of moving onto a four-year college someday. Raheem and my "unofficial academic advisor" kept saying, "This place is getting too small for you." I was comfortable at ECC and did not want to leave. I wanted to graduate the following year, and then, make my next move. Raheem's verbiage changed from "You're not ready" to "Whenever you're ready." My unofficial adviser encouraged me to really think about the benefits of transferring to a four-year college. I asked why they felt this was a good move at that time, and they said: "You need to be somewhere that challenges you. This place was a good starting point for you, but now it's time for you to move on." I offered my pathetic excuse about wanting to graduate before attending a four-year institution—I had this thing about finishing what and where I started. My advisor gave me this look and said, "I tell you what. You do your homework in finding the school of your choice, and I'll pay all the fees." I thought for second and said, "It's a deal," while shaking their hand. My advisor assured me this was a good thing to do "because they're gonna accept all of your credits."

I discussed my thoughts with my mother because she was (and still is) my chief advisor. My mother listened as I made my case. We were riding in her car, heading home. I was still blabbing on about my plans when we arrived. My mother asked questions here and there and listened as I went on talking. I finally finished and asked her what she thought. "Well, son," Mom said with a dramatic pause, "whatever you choose to do, I support you." I was ready to go.

I contacted the three schools: Fairleigh Dickerson University in Teaneck, N. J., Jersey City State College (now known as New Jersey City University) in Jersey City, N. J., and Kean College (now known as Kean University) in Union, New Jersey. My best friends attended the latter two—Minnettia was at JCSC and Anjamilah was at Kean. Fairleigh Dickerson University was ruled out quickly because it was too far away, and I did not want to live on campus. I visited the other campuses several times before, as you can imagine, and they both had their own appeal. I wanted to look into their psychology departments to see what they had to offer. In the end, I chose Kean because it felt like home—you know, Anjamilah was ecstatic.

I had a lot of positive things going on by this time in my life. I stayed in touch with both my mentor and my "unofficial advisor," who was true to their word. Not only did she pay all the corresponding fees for admission, but they also purchased half of my books for my first semester at Kean.

My mentor and I met in the middle of the day on Saturdays because I had to work in the evenings, and Raheem went to class in the mornings. Although I was making positive moves in working and studying, I was still partying and engaging in "empty relationships" and destructive behaviors. To me, it was all a part of being young. Raheem was still saying, "Whenever you're ready," even though I was in a good head space. This went on for a few months before Raheem and I parted ways because we moved on with our lives.

Raheem and I met at a well-known eatery spot downtown Newark, N. J., off Broad and Market (Streets)—you rarely heard or said Streets. This place served the best pizza in the area and was always packed with people either sitting down to eat or grabbing a slice to go. Prior to this meeting, Raheem said he wanted to talk about *As a Man Thinketh* some more. I agreed and didn't think about it until a day or so before we met.

I went to work and "clubbing" the night before and was gearing up for round two later that night. My life consisted of a routine—I worked, studied, and partied, repeat. I had been in a toxic relationship for a few years and wanted to spread my wings a little. I was mindful to pay my bills, work hard for what I wanted, and not be a burden on anyone, especially my mom. In my mind, I was doing pretty good. However, I was still suppressing and ignoring my need to heal in order to move forward emotionally, mentally, and spiritually.

Two vices kept me from participating in the healing process: women and parting, which was fueled with alcohol—so you can say there were three vices. I had always been a "one-woman's man." I didn't engage in more than one relationship at a time, not because I was a goody-two-shoe, but because I didn't know (and still don't) how lie well enough to cover my tracks. So, it was easier for me to be monogamous in my romantic relationships. As for partying, I've always been a good dancer and drinker. Going out to clubs with my friends and girlfriends became a distraction from doing what I needed to do for myself.

Back to my meeting with Raheem. He was talkative and animated while we were at the pizza spot. Raheem talked about some his projects, his new relationship, and his decision to move onto a four-year college. I had never seen him smile so much since we met. Raheem asked me for an update on what was happening in my life. Raheem, as always, listened intently. We decided to walk to our stomping ground, the Essex County College campus, which was a few blocks away. I didn't pay attention in that moment, but I talked the entire time we were walking.

Once we arrived at a shady spot on campus, it was game on for Raheem. He commended me for "keeping yourself busy," and skillfully brought *As a Man Thinketh* to the forefront. Raheem asked for my perspective because "It's been a while since we discussed it." Little did he know I brushed up a little before we met. Of course, I went on a tear about what I *thought* I knew. Raheem politely interrupted with a simple question: "So, why do you party every week and sleep (have sex) with those girls?" I was caught totally off guard because I was not prepared for him to go there. I offered every excuse I could produce in that moment, and Raheem just listened. I don't think he blinked. Out of sheer frustration, I said, "Shit, man. I don't know! That's what young people do: We eat, sleep, drink, and [y'all know the other one]!" We sat in awkward silence for a while until Raheem looked at his watch and said, "Look brother, it's getting late and you gotta go to work. I'm not trying to tell you how you should live, but you should KNOW why you're doing what you're doing. I suggest you stop until you figure it out." We agreed to meet the following week, exchanged salutations and hugs before parting.

My defiant ass went out that night, partied extra hard, and went home with my girl. "F**k his uptight ass," I thought. I went about my regular routine, and then, something happened that brought everything to a screeching holt: I became gravely ill on Friday, April 22, 1994. I remember the exact date because it was the night Richard M. Nixon died.

I had plans to go clubbing with my girlfriend and friends that night after work—my crew and I started partying on Thursday night and didn't end until Sunday morning. We had a good time the night before and was bucking for a repeat. I started feeling funny during my shift. First, I had this strange tingling in my lower right chest, close to my abdomen. I didn't pay much attention to it because I drank and I chain-smoked the night before—I smoked a lot whenever I drank. Suddenly, the tingling turned into a burning sensation, and full blown pain. But, oh no, I was still trying go out that night.

I went home to get dressed, thinking it would pass. The pain increased to feeling like someone hit me in my ribs with a ball-point hammer. It was horrible and I think I blacked out for a moment. I asked (begged) my mom to take me to the hospital. Of course, she took me to St. Barnabas Hospital, where Dr. R. worked. I learned of Nixon's death while waiting to be seen. I was diagnosed with Sarcoidosis ("an inflammatory disease that affects multiple organs in the body, but mostly the lungs and lymph glands. In people with sarcoidosis, abnormal masses, or nodules (called granulomas) consisting of inflamed tissues form in certain organs of the body"— mayoclinic.org, 2019) in my lower right lung and was told to follow up with my primary care physician as soon as possible.

I didn't get the chance to meet with Raheem that weekend. When I called to tell him what happened, he came to my house to make sure I was okay. I insisted that we talked because "I really gave some thought to your question." Raheem didn't want to disturb my convalescence, but I insisted, "I'm fine. I need the mental stimulation." He laughed and relented. I assertively explained the roles that partying and having premarital sex served at that time— "They help to keep my mind off the dark thoughts and memories." Raheem listened carefully, as usual. He told me no one could rush the healing process— "You're ready when you get ready." I asked about his journey because many times wisdom comes from experience. It was both interesting and comforting to know where he was coming from. I decided to embark on a journey of "dealing with my own shit," rather than running from, suppressing, and ignoring it. One of the most important things I'd learned from all this was you can never "get over" bad or traumatic experiences. You must work through them and learn how to live, in spite of them—the issues from your past. This was something I needed to know because there were some things coming in the next few months that would have an influence on my life for a long time to come.

Part Two:

Redemption

"Turn Your Pain into Power."

Annie T. Shaw-Spellman said to me many times (not sure if this was her saying).

Chapter Four:

Where Do I Go Now?

Life as a college student, a worker, and an emerging adult was interesting because I started growing as a person, while coming to grips with my past and how some events were shaping who I was to become (and still becoming). There were times when I stayed in the moment when addressing a traumatizing situation; and then, there were other times when I chose to be distracted, both constructively and destructively. I did these things because I believed they preserved my sanity. I maintained a full schedule that gave me a chance to learn and earn money. I was a full-time student and a part-time worker my first year at Kean College. This worked out well because I was still partying but not as much as before because the demands of school and work had increased. I was living a "balanced life," so I thought.

    I seriously thought about making some changes in my life. I had been doing several things for quite some time, such as clubbing, engaging in empty relationships, and drinking excessively; but not focusing on what I really needed: my healing. Not only were they becoming unhealthy, but "played out" (boring). Considering some of the advice I had been given over the years, I started looking at my life and where I could go. I was not as jaded as I'd come to be, but I was getting tired of being an "ole mean ass." I did certain things to protect myself from allowing many people get too close to me. It was time to move onto new experiences in life.

I started taking life a little more seriously because it wasn't (and isn't) all about partying and playing around. I had to grow up and be accountable for my actions. I had to allow maturity to take its natural course in order to become the man I was made to be. No more blaming others for what I did or did not receive up to that point. I couldn't depend on others to provide for me anymore. I had to take control of my own life and destiny, in partnership with God, of course. No longer a little boy, I was a young man and had to carry myself accordingly.

My folks repeatedly warned me, "Be careful of who you spend your time with," "Everybody's not happy for you," and "If you wait on someone to feed you, you'll starve to death." In other words, some people don't want to see you happy or successful in life, and I was responsible for the decisions I made. To a certain extent, some people will do what they can to knock you down or block your path. I was starting to see that more and more.

You might experience a few more obstacles along your journey if you continuously get in your own way. However, you must be patient with and kind to yourself if and when you go off course because it's a part of your journey. You must not remain distracted because the devil's loose and will do all he can to keep you away from who you were designed to be. I also learned that the enemy would try to mock God by presenting bad intentions with sound arguments. But I was seeing a better way to live and had to be disciplined in order to reach my goals but then, on that frigid winter night, my life was changed—see Chapter One.

Can I Dance?

Ever since I could remember, I had been a pretty good dancer. I've heard stories about me dancing before I was two years old. Since music was a big part of my home life, it only made sense that I was in tune with different beats and rhythms. It turned out that Willie (a. k. a. June Bug or Jr.) and I were my mom's dancers until my younger siblings came along. I copied a lot of what I saw my big brother do until I was able to pick up from other places, such as TV and other people. I was blessed to have seen Soul Train and the Legendary Soul Train Dancers as a child. Some of those dancers moved so well together that they almost seemed as one, equivalent to "tictocing" today. There were a lot of dance shows on television in the late 1970s and 1980s, and I became accustomed to picking up, copying or "biting" dance moves I'd seen. But then, I learned to develop my own style, which helped me by the time I reached high school.

I shared this piece of information as a way to demonstrate how I learned to cope, why I engaged in certain types of relationships (both platonic and romantic), and why I carried myself the way I did after being sexually assaulted years later. There were many aspects of my life I had to take a long, hard look at so I could understand myself better because I so desired to become a better version of me. Reaching this stage in my life didn't happen overnight. It took a lot of pain, therapy/counseling, mentoring, love, and acceptance to arrive where I am today—an imperfect vessel being mended. Therefore, I decided to identify some of behaviors, thoughts, and actions to find out how they developed, and then, make plans as to what had to be done to address them—this will go far beyond the writing of this book.

The first behavior I distinguished was my alcohol use/abuse. I used alcohol for several reasons to achieve different outcomes: to escape memories, to calm my anxieties, and to numb the pain. In an abnormal way, intoxication steered me away from dark places in my mind and provided an interference so I didn't have to deal with a lot of heavy shit right then and there. This would my second bout alcohol abuse. "The more I drank to relieve my shame-based loneliness and hurt, the more I felt ashamed. Shame begets shame," Bradshaw (2005, p. 36) shared. Intoxication caused more problems because sometimes my thoughts and feelings intensified, which caused me to be even more emotional in the form of sadness or explosive anger. I could be what is called a "mean drunk," where I lashed out at others, oftentimes for no specific reason. The impact of my self-medication was described in the following manner:

> The cycle begins with the false belief system shared by all addicts: that no one could want them or love them as they are. In fact, addicts can't love themselves. They are an object of scorn to themselves. This deep internalized shame gives rise to distorted thinking. The distorted thinking can be reduced to the belief, "I'll be okay if I drink, eat, have sex, get more money, work harder, etc." The shame turns what Kellogg has termed a "human doing," rather than a human being (Bradshaw, 2005 p. 36).

Addictions are oftentimes indicative of emotional trauma and/or pain, and the behavior(s) sets out to ease or mask the pain. Rum was considered my best friend back then. She helped me to evade pain, fear of stigmas and shame. She took my cares away, gave me an escape from my responsibilities for the moment, and made me fearless at times ("liquid courage"). However, Lewis (1995) asserted:

> ...Denial and forgetting require a refocusing, removing attention from the events that caused the shame or from the

shaming experience itself... ...*people attempt to rid themselves of the unpleasant shame feeling*. The critical feature of all forms of dealing with acknowledged shame is that the sufferer must first "own it" before giving it away. *In situations of unacknowledged shame, the individual works to avoid "owning" shame* (pp. 139 – 140, emphasis mine).

Don't get me wrong, acknowledging your shame is not an easy task; and it is not a quick, "microwave" procedure. Owning one's shame may require plenty of support and time. I'm a living witness! Although I made efforts in the past, shame prevented me from fully accepting what happened to me.

I truly believe God is a God of healing and can remove the stain of shame in an instant. I also believe, as Paul declared, God allows us to remember and feel it (the thorn, 2 Corinthians 12: 7) so we can minister to others. Therefore, I had to (and still have to) put in the work and *endure* the discomfort that comes with this process. In fact, Kaufman and Raphael (1996) wrote:

> Coming out of shame is a journey toward wholeness and self-respect. These are the fundamental building blocks of what we somewhat ambiguously refer to as *self-acceptance*. In order to become whole, we must embrace all of the facets of our being—including those parts we have disavowed or cast away. *We can never become whole by disavowing essential aspect of our nature. Wholeness is never attained by splintering the self further, only by uniting and integrating it more completely. We transform shame, and in so doing become whole, by actively reowning all of those rejected orphans within us*. That is the path of healing, the

path that ultimately leads toward realizing inner worth and securing self-esteem. If shame is the source of low self-esteem, dignity and pride in self are the source of high self-esteem. Not only must we develop an inner source of valuing and pride in self, but we must also acknowledge shame and thereby redeem it. (p. 110, emphasis mine).

In *Tamar's Healing* (Jones, 2014), I discussed a phenomenon where people felt comfortable with randomly sharing their sexual abuse/trauma with me. Sometimes this happened when I didn't feel like hearing it. I would ask the person, "Why are you telling me this?" before I understood what was happening. There were times when people said they were "talking about this for the first time," "I don't like to think about it, but...." Even if we were total strangers, they shared the most dreadful experience(s) of their lives. In those instances, it never became a "my experience was worse than yours" type of pity party. I would disclose it depending on the situation, because by doing so could have made things worse for the other party. Only a few people could tell I was praying as they were speaking. People genuinely did not know why they were sharing nor did I. Something beyond both parties orchestrated those encounters and I know it was God. It was as if they were telling Jesus what they were struggling with, and I just happened to be there with them in the flesh. I don't know where they were on their journey or what they were going through, but their sharing served a purpose for them.

This sharing may have been as Lewis (1995) described, a person's "owning their shame." As for me, it took many years for me to acknowledge that a depraved spirit within that woman (my assailant) led her encroaching upon my person and my dignity straddling me like an animal or thing to meet her aberrant needs.

Until then, I did not want to feel the emotions that were associated with the fact that I had no control over that situation; that I was not given the choice to be a willing participant. The truth was: A woman *did* take advantage of me. She was cunning enough to lie in wait for an opportune time when she did not have to use force to attain her wretched desires. So, alcohol consumption numbed and diverted my feelings and thoughts from my immediate purview. I simply chose to shut them out. Lewis (1995) explained, with profound clarity, the effects of prolonged avoidance, denial, and/or covering your true emotions in the following way:

> In the case of emotional substitution, especially for sadness and anger, we have the opportunity to look at patterns of substitution over time and in interactions. ***Single instances of shame can lead to sadness or anger as substitute emotions.*** However, during prolonged instances and interactions, in which sadness or anger are consistently substituted for shame, sadness turns to depression and anger to rage (p. 141, emphasis mine).

This statement encapsulates what replacing and/or masking shame can lead to. For me, because my perpetrator was a woman, and no one knew what happened, I had to do something to keep it out of view, to suppress it.

There were times when I was around this person in various settings, for assorted reasons/occasions. I had to act like all was well in the world in order to avoid conflict. And to add insult to injury, this "woman" acted like nothing happened or she did not carry out an act so reprehensible. What's more agonizing was she made a point to interact with me. Relocating to Atlanta was not the solution because my heart, mind, and body never forgot or recovered.

It took some time for me to realize I had been trapped in a ferocious sequence of patterns in order to keep this information hidden. Sexual and physical happens in too many families and communities, especially when individuals feel that they need to protect the perpetrators to "preserve the peace." "The dark secrets that are so carefully guarded," Bradshaw explained, "get revealed and uncovered because the children act them out—if not in this generation, then in the next, or the next" (1995, p. xiii). This became my greatest concern—that my holding onto this secret will come out in a damaging way. Bradshaw continued on to say:

> When such traumatic events are denied and made into dark secrets, a family's loyalty to the secret may appear in subsequent generations as reclusiveness, morbid ear, obsession with death, bizarre and unexplainable death-defying crazy behavior, and suicide attempts on an anniversary or the same age as the first death (p. 29).

Although the context of this quote pertains to suicide, it can be seen in other destructive behaviors. In the case of sexual abuse/trauma, it can appear as sexualized behaviors, inappropriate relationships, and, unfortunately, multiple victimizations.

My concerns involving my withholding information is the long-term effects it may have on my psyche. However, I rest assured in knowing that I am moving forward because I am cognizant of these concerns and I must do what is necessary to protect my well-being.

Behaviors and patterns can develop that holds the survivor captive in that he or she suffers long after the initial event(s) occurred. This anguish might be a direct result of keeping the secret and/or protecting others, while agonizing in silence. "…[W]hen shame has been completely internalized," one writer said, "nothing about you is okay" (Bradshaw, 2005; p. 33). Because the survivor takes on much of the blame, responsibility, or may be safeguarding others, they create and sustain their own private hell and other forms of "self-deprivation,"—I heard someone use this phrase a few years and it stuck. Bradshaw continued on to say the following:

> …You have the sense of being a failure. There is no way you can share your inner self because you are an object of contempt to yourself. When you are contemptable to yourself, you no longer in you. To feel shame exposed in a diminished way. When you're an object to yourself, you turn your eyes inward, watching and scrutinizing every minute detail of behavior (p. 33).

I think this might be a suitable place to briefly discuss some of my past relationships, both platonic and romantic. I engaged in what some might call self-deprivation due to my diminished ability to trust people, my lack of faith in relationships, and my tarnished self-image, self-worth, and self-esteem, which I grasped in hindsight. Immediately after "the incident," I stopped dating, and did not screw around very much. I kept busy with "constructive" activities to avoid intimacy on many levels. However, before I continue, I would like to share one writer's description of intimacy, and what's needed to achieve such a connection:

> Intimacy requires the ability to be vulnerable. To be intimate is to risk exposing our inner selves to each other, to bare out deepest feelings, desires, and thoughts. To be intimate is to be the very ones we are and to love and accept

> each other unconditionally. This requires self-confidence and courage. Such courage creates a new space in our relationship. That space is not your or mine; it is mine (Bradshaw, 2005, p. 235).

I didn't trust most people let alone myself and didn't make efforts to continue many relationships nor developed new ones. I'm not sure if anyone noticed what was happening—hell, I didn't until recently—if so, no one said anything. There were inquiries into why I did not have a girlfriend or why I wasn't dating much, but I do not recall many instances where I was encouraged to do so—snide remakes do not count as encouragement. Kaufman and Raphael (1996) said this about some of the barriers that keeps us from achieving intimacy:

> Our inner relationship includes the characteristic ways we treat ourselves in every major circumstance, from triumphs to defeats, and in every minor one as well. It's ongoing and constant, whether we're tuned in to it or not. It's the ways we speak to ourselves the thoughts and feelings we have about ourselves, but it's also actions—the way we behave toward ourselves... By shaping this emergent inner relationship that we come to have with ourselves, shame places a distinctive stamp on identity, thereby exercising a powerful role in directing, distorting, and even crippling identity.... (p. 111).

Even as I write these words today, some 20 plus year later, I fought back tears and I didn't know if it was because of the sexual assault, the withdrawal, other issues, or all. I thought about a statement I made earlier about not being treated like a "piece of meat before or since then." The truth is I did engage in some "relationships" that were exploitive but not blatantly as with my perpetrator. I went about in those relationships passive-aggressively as evidenced by a lack of commitment, longevity, and sustenance. They were simply "hook-ups" and "side-piecing" that went on too long. Worse part of this was, I allowed it and went along with these types of "relationships." However, it's important to note that I did have a few meaningful relationships as well.

The bonds of loyalty within my family were also tested. It was difficult to trust many of my family members because I felt that they failed to look out for me. Whether this was true or not, that's how my mind perceived the situation at that time. In hindsight, they probably did not know what happened. The dynamics of several bonds had been compromised since then. I'm well aware that one source of this quandary is based on my withholding information for the sake of keeping the peace and to avoid shame. But, then again, "Silence breeds shame every bit as much as shame breeds further silence," Kaufman and Raphael (1996) wrote. "The two are locked an endless cycle of mutual reactivation" (p. 111). Hmmm....

*****

There was an extended period of time I found myself so screwed up emotionally wherein my self-esteem was shot to hell, and my self-confidence plummeted. I second guessed myself often, and my moods were out of whack. I was in state of regression and didn't know it. Although I continued interacting with others, oftentimes not by choice but by circumstances, I stayed to myself most of the time or with a select few. I was in denial on many levels, and I could not accept there was something amiss in my life. I immersed myself in my "priorities" (distractions) and did not try to further complicate my life.

When I did participate in other activities, it was with the few people I felt safe being around. Periodically, I wanted to do more but didn't because of my trust issues, which affected my ability to engage in close relationships, for the most part. There were quite a few women I would have liked to get to know or even date. I never gave myself permission to do so because I didn't feel confident in this possibility, which attributed to my "self-deprivation." However, Kaufman and Rapheal (1996) offered hope in situations like this:

> Self-esteem rises and falls along with the vicissitudes of shame. For self-esteem to reman securely anchored within us, we must learn to tolerate recurrences of shame, know how to release shame without internalizing it further, and develop tools for effectively counteracting the sources of shame throughout the life cycle... [Because] Our capacity for intimacy can be damaged by the ravages of shame. In order to experience intimacy, we must be able to approach others and also be willing to be approached my them. We must convey out interest openly... We must allow ourselves to communicate the excitement we feel in discovering new friends. We must also enjoy communality with others. In that process, we open ourselves to each other and become deliberately vulnerable (pp. 110, 111 – 112).

*****

Attending Kean College was a place where I began to grow. The campus was big enough for me to mix in with the crowd, yet small enough to not be easily overlooked. I transferred in as a Psychology major but switched to Social Work soon after arriving. I found that

Social Work was more diverse than psychology. I continued taking psychology classes because I wanted to become a counselor/therapist.

Anjamilah introduced me to a wonderful woman, named Paula, before I transferred to Kean. Paula worked in the admissions department and was a professional dancer. She was also a student in the Counseling Education graduate program. We quickly befriended one another. I would visit and talk with her frequently. We engaged in deep, heart-to-heart chats between my classes. Paula was so intuitive and was able to sense that I was wounded and guarded. One day, she showed me where the Student Wellness Center (I think that's what it was called) was located and encouraged me to check it out. I decided to give it a try.

After visiting the Wellness Center, I decided to sit down with one of the counselors to address my lack of emotional connectiveness and indifference. Being that I was cautious about what I would and would not talk about, progress was slow, and I eventually stopped going. I continued struggling to the point that I show very little emotion apart from coldness and/or meanness.

Academically, I kept working hard; in fact, too hard. I would soon discover. I started taking classes within my major and two of my Social Work professors took a shine to me. Although I did well in their classes, they noticed something unusual about my efforts. They didn't jump to conclusions but they observed before approaching me.

One day in the fall of 1997, the beginning of my senior year, the two of Social Work professors called me in for an informal meeting. I was a little skeptical because I could not think of a reason why I was being summoned to this meeting.

We met in a conference room where we were able to sit comfortably. The female professor took the lead and reassured me that this ad hoc meeting was a good thing. She told me to relax while they asked a few simple questions. Their questions related to my study habits, preparation for tests and writing papers, and my learning style in general. They knew I was working hard as evidenced by my grades—A's and B's—but their concerns related to how I was getting it done. The male professor said (and I paraphrase), "We noticed how tired you look whenever an assignment is due." He also inferred to the amount of time and energy I put into my assignments, which was accurate because I put in a lot of both. The female professor chimed in and suggested that I visit the Learning Center (I think that's what it was called) to figure out a better way to study and learn. I was relieved because I knew I was doing my best to learn what was presented in my classes and worked extra to keep up. They gave me a few time slots I could go to the Learning Center and a contact person.

I walked away from this meeting feeling good but apprehensive about what transpired. A part of me was happy someone wanted to help me, and then, somewhere inside I did not want to trust others or their processes. I thought and prayed about it for a couple of weeks before I decided to do anything. I did not consult anyone because it was a personal issue and I needed to figure it out for myself.

I called the Learning Center to inquire first, and then decided to give it a shot. I was administered a battery of tests and, I believe, one was an Intelligence Quotient (IQ) test. I was assigned an assessor/teacher, who explained my test results. The test determined I had "learning differences." Meaning the way information was taught was not conducive to how I learned.

Therefore, I worked harder to make it work. The assessor gave me a learning plan, which included ways to help me learn and retain new information. They recommended that I considered what was said and call them back once I decided if I wanted to move forward.

It didn't take long for me to choose to go along with the learning plan because I believed the Learning Center was willing to help me acquire new and helpful learning tools. Besides, I had nothing to lose but much more to gain. If the tools did not work, we could figure out ways that suited me better.

I met with my teacher/coach, developed a schedule, and started working on understanding my learning differences and how I can improve the way I learned. It was a little challenging at first because I was used to learning the other way, which was not effective for me, and was being introduced to new methods. But I hung in there knowing there was something to gain from this experience. The skills I obtained helped me to learn in a more efficient manner.

*****

As it was with my senior year in high school, I had an interesting schedule for my senior year at Kean. I had a 7:30 a. m. class and a late one too—I cannot recall what time the late one started and ended. Biology was the early morning class and Social Statistics was my late class. I kicked myself for waiting until my senior year to take them, knowing these subjects were the ones I struggled with most. These classes really tested my resolve because I knew they were the obstacles to finishing this program.

I had to muster up the discipline, the focus and the determination needed to reach my goal of attaining a college degree. However, it appeared that my course load required more time than I had. I had to decide quickly: run the risk of failing everything or withdraw from Biology and Social Statistics and take them another time. I chose the latter because my first semester was loaded with major classes apart from the two highlighted subjects. It turned out to be a wise choice.

I had the opportunity to meet some phenomenal people while studying at Kean College—the status and name was changed to Kean University that spring. I was really inspired by a wonderful professor and a Distinguished Visiting Professor—Drs. Melodie Toby and the late Reverend Samuel Dewitt Proctor. Dr. Toby taught Black Liberation and Black Theology and introduced me to the concepts of the late Reverend Dr. James H. Cone, the father of Black Theology—I was blessed to have met Dr. Cone later, while in seminary. Dr. Toby was passionate about Black Liberation and Black Theology. She would light up as she explained various parts of Dr. Cone's theories and applications. Because I showed a real interest in Black Theology, Dr. Toby encouraged me meet our Distinguished Visiting Professor, Dr. Samuel Dewitt Proctor. I had no idea who Dr. Proctor was because I was being exposed to Black Theology for the first time in Dr. Toby's class.

Dr. Proctor released his last book prior to coming to Kean that semester. I was intrigued and planned to stop by his office the next day he was scheduled to be on campus.

I received shocking news from the financial aid office concerning my Pell Grant: it was ending that semester and I had no idea of how I was going to pay for the rest of my education. I left the financial aid office and headed to Dr. Proctor's office in a daze. I tried to shake it off before I arrived because I wanted to make sure

I was able to engage him appropriately.

Dr. Proctor's door was opened slightly when I arrived, which made me hesitate for a moment. Dr. Proctor heard movement and called out, "Come on in." I pushed the door a little and apologized for interrupting. Dr. Proctor graciously insisted I was not bothering him. He was a kind, grandfatherly man of distinction. "Son is there something wrong?" he patiently asked after a few moments of my visit. I denied anything bothering me at first because I didn't know Dr. Proctor and didn't go there to dump my problems on him. Dr. Proctor gently insisted, and I told him about my financial aid situation. He patted my hand softly and warmly said, "The solution is quite simple. Get a loan." I sat quietly for a moment. "That's what they're there for," Dr. Proctor explained. He shared some of his educational experiences and how student loans helped him. "Learn how they [student loans] work so you can go on and earn that doctorate degree," he said with certainty.

I walked away feeling honored to have been in Dr. Proctor's presence that afternoon. I later learned he was considered a giant in academia and in the fight for civil rights. Dr. Proctor was so patient and benevolent in the way he spoke to me. I couldn't wait to tell Dr. Toby about how Dr. Proctor helped me, a total stranger, to find a solution to my problem. She replied, "See there, wisdom." I shared what Dr. Proctor said: "He told me I was going to earn a doctorate degree." Dr. Toby paused for moment before asking: "Why not?" I didn't have an answer because I barely entered college in the first place. "And study what?" I inquired. She told me I would figure it out in due time. Drs. Proctor and Toby were the first of several people to tell me I would pursue a doctoral degree, even though I'd never considered it to be in my future. It just wasn't in my preview, but the seed was sown.

I managed to make it through the school year and took Biology and Social Statics over the summer at Essex County College, and then, had the credits transferred to Kean. It was much more manageable for me. The class sizes were smaller, and the professors were able to help the students more in the classroom versus assigning office hours or telling us to "get a tutor." They even encouraged us to form study groups inside and outside the classroom. Both professors said they would do whatever it took for us to learn the material needed to pass these classes. I had a wonderful experience in both classes and wanted to learn the information. They taught me to be steadfast in my pursuit of higher education.

Where Did This Come From?

The next phase of my education came with a twist. I started applying to Master of Social Work programs in the tri-state area (New York, New Jersey, and Connecticut). Graduating from Kean University's Bachelor of Social Work (BSW) program afforded me a higher status in that I had completed one year of graduate studies before graduating with my bachelor's degree. Because I had been immersed in the Social Work environment and mindset for so long, I thought I was supposed to complete the Master of Social Work (MSW) program as well.

I started applying to several MSW programs, hoping for the best. I did not have the best G. P. A. (grade point average), but I had a desire to further my education. I didn't stop to consider other options beyond the MSW programs. In the end, none of my top choices accepted me into their programs. I was deflated. I had never felt so rejected in my life, but I was not willing to give up hope. I had no idea I would travel in an amazingly different direction—SEMINARY.

Not long after I acknowledged my calling into the counseling ministry and was denied admission into the last MSW program I applied to; I began to pray for guidance. I could not believe I was at another place where I felt lost, again. In some ways, I needed to rest. I had been working in an adult psychiatric day center for some time before I graduated from Kean University and enjoyed working in that capacity. But furthering my education burned in my spirit like a five-alarm fire. I kept my eyes and ears open for other opportunities, and in doing so, my need to follow God's lead was confirmed.

One of my god sisters, Keesha, and I were catching up on the phone one day. We laughed and joked as we always did. Keesha inquired about my graduate school search. Apart from my mom and my pastor, she was the first person I shared my calling with: to become a Pastoral Counselor. Keesha immediately suggested that I spoke to her father-in-law, who was a Vice President at Interdenominational Theological Center (ITC) in Atlanta, Georgia, at that time. She told me he was a reliable source of information regarding what ITC was about and its function. I took her father-in-law's contact information and told Keesha I would give it some thought and call him.

Meanwhile, I received a call from my mentor, Raheem. We caught up on what was happening in our lives. I was about to graduate at the end of the year. I wanted to invite him to the ceremony. He agreed to come and told me he wanted me to meet someone and serve as their mentor. I was a little unsure at first, but Raheem explained some of this person's demographics, challenges, and age. Intrigued by what I heard, I agreed to meet them. We planned to meet at a neutral location for this introduction. Raheem left out one vital piece of information about this young person and kept it that way until the meeting.

I arrived at the designated place and noticed Raheem chatting with an older woman, and a teenaged boy was standing next to her. Walking slowly toward them, I tried to observe as much as I could before I was in their presence. Raheem saw me and beamed with pride as he introduced me to the woman: "This is one of my mentees..." (blah, blah, blah). We exchanged salutations. Raheem told the woman I would be mentoring her child. I extended hand to the teenaged boy, "Nice to meet you." Raheem and the woman stared at me for a moment before he said, "No, no, no. He will not be your mentee." I apologized and waited, thinking another boy was somewhere around. Raheem announced, "Oh yes, here they come." I was unaccustomed to the use of gender-neutral language back then and didn't think anything of it. I turned in the direction they were looking and saw a girl walking in our direction. I looked past her and wondered where the boy was but did not see him because "Surely Raheem is _not_ talking about this girl," I thought. Lo and behold, Raheem started his introduction— "KJ, this is Annette...." I politely shook her hand while glaring at Raheem.

Raheem picked up on my facial expression and excused us for a moment. I positioned myself with my back to the woman and teens. "**SHE'S A GIRL!**" I said through clenched teeth, "I don't wanna mentor a girl." Raheem assured me we were a good match and promised to talk about that later. "I'm not promising nothing," I snapped with a menacing scowl. We returned to the group. The woman broke the ice by saying I looked familiar and asked, "Who's ya folk?" I told her my mother's name and she replied, "Uh huh." We all sat down to talk for a while with Raheem facilitating the discussion. He asked if I knew Annette or seen her around to which I denied.

We continued talking with Annette chiming in here and there. There was an uncomfortable moment of silence, before the woman asserted, "You know, I think you ought to know, I know your mother." I maintained my poker face and glanced at Raheem. She continued on to say, "I think you can do something with my daughter. Will you be her mentor?" I thought for a few moments, weighing the pros and cons with the greatest two being: Raheem chose me to be in this girl's life, even though he could have asked a woman to do it; and she was a girl! I wanted to explode because they were looking at me and waiting for a respond. I thought, "Oh shit! What the hell is going on?" Annette spoke up, "Is something wrong? You don't like me or sum'n'?" We locked eyes for a moment before I asked, "Do you always look adults in the face?" Raheem, the woman, and the other teen looked on in silence. "I was taught to look a person in the face when I'm speaking to them. No disrespect," Annette explained. (Side note: My people (peeps) from the East Orange/Newark are frequently described as gruff and harsh. It's not true. It's our way of cutting to the chase, chop it up (have a discussion) quickly, and moving on).

Raheem knew I was going to speak my mind and probably knew Anette would too; so, he leaned back in his chair and listened. I started by thanking everyone for inviting me, and then, told them: "Usually, I don't deal with girls, but I like Annette. She got spunk." Both Raheem and Annette's mom appeared to be relieved. "I'll do it under one condition," I said and paused for a few seconds, "if everyone agrees to hold off on telling me what her talent is."

Raheem sighed, agreed and so did everyone else. Annette's mother thanked me and said, "I think you're going to be a good fit for Annette." Me being inquisitive, I asked her why she thought so. She nodded in Annette's direction and said Annette should respond to that question. "I'm usually shy, unless I'm doing what I loved, *but I'm talking to you for some reason*," Annette revealed before looking down at the table.

Annette, her mother, and I talked about meeting times and days, exchanged contact information, and began building rapport. We all joined hands and prayed together before going our separate ways. Raheem and I walked together and talked for a moment. He wanted to know how I felt about this arrangement— "You know your heart and spirit can be at odds sometimes." I was more than intrigued at that point because I wasn't interested in her talent at that time, which shocked them when I asked them not to tell me about it.

Something Annette said reverberated in my head the rest of that day: "… *but I'm talking to you for some reason*." I tried to put it aside while I was at work and school, but in quiet moments her words echoed in my mind. My coworkers noticed my somber mood and left me alone for the most part. I apologized and told them I had something on my mind, and I was okay.

I prayed that God would show me God's will in this situation because I didn't work with girls for several reasons, especially teenage girls. I wouldn't see Annette for another week or so, and I wanted to be sure of what I was getting myself into; after all, the Spirit guides us in all truth. I continued on with my regular routine and tried not to think too much about the "Annette situation." However, I repeatedly heard the phrase, "there's a reason," or something like that, all that week. Eventually, I decided not to back out on being Annette's mentor.

Raheem and I talked about my thoughts, feelings, and plans as to how this mentor/mentee relationship should be established in order to make all parties comfortable. One of the things I asked about was the advanced age of Annette's mother. Raheem smiled and said, "I'll let that work itself out between y'all." I thought that was an odd response, even though I had my own thoughts. We agreed I should talk to Annette and her mother about establishing this relationship in and around the home first, "That way we can get to know one another, build trust, and vibe off one another." Raheem was visibly excited and added: "Don't forget your gift. It is the reason why I felt this would be a good match. I'm not telling you a lot because that would take away from the bonding [process], and Annette is old enough to share when she's ready." I thanked him for saying that because that's what I wanted to know and it is something I still practice to this very day—get to know the person first, when it is appropriate, before getting secondhand information. I also informed Raheem of the rationale behind all my questions and hesitations. Raheem said, with the wisdom of an old sage: "Sometimes we find our redemption in unlikely places." He let that hang in the air for a moment. I took a deep breath before saying, "Okay."

Annette and her mother agreed to us visiting in the home before venturing out— "It's for our own good [protection]," I advised. To my surprise Annette and I bonded quickly. Yes, she was very reserved—I would not say shy—but became lively once we grew accustomed to one another. I quickly noticed there was a lot Annette was not saying and I did not press too much, or too fast.

I arrived at Annette's house one afternoon, expecting to chill on the front porch because it was a nice spring afternoon. Annette met me on the sidewalk and was excited for some reason. "What's with all this bubbly stuff?" I asked. Annette explained she had something to tell me, "Can we go to the park?" I told her to pump her brakes, "I'm going to say hello to Mom Dukes first."

I found Annette's mother was in the kitchen cooking dinner, which was smelling good. She turned and greeted me with a warm smile and said, "Annette seems to like you, which is rare. She asked if y'all could walk down to the park to hang out for a while. You okay with that?" she asked while sizing me up for a reaction. I agreed because I felt we were at a good place by then. I headed toward the front porch and heard someone singing. I stopped to listen for a moment. The voice was rich and mature. It was Annette! I made noise to let her know I was coming out. She stopped in the middle of a riff. There was something very familiar about her singing voice (hmm, put a pin that).

Annette popped up from the porch swing, asking if we were good to which I said, "Let's roll, kiddo." We talked and laughed as we walked toward the park, which was a few blocks away from her home. Annette grew quiet for a few moments before asking if she could tell me something about her— "After all, I feel like I can trust you," she said. I told her it was okay. "Remember when I told you I was talking to you *for some reason*?" Annette asked and I said yes (Of course, I did! It rang in my head for about a week). She shared that her mom was her biological maternal grandaunt. Annette lived with her aunt for a few years before they made it official and her aunt became her adoptive mother. I thought that was cool because I had a sister around her age. "Wait there's more," Annette announced. She teased me and became melodramatic: "Now don't fall out when I tell you this. You ready? I'm a singer." I teased her back by asking, "Like a real (professional) singer?" It made sense based on what I heard moments before, but there was a piece missing that would not come together for couple of years after we stopped working together (I will not reveal too many details in order to protect all parties' privacy).

Annette seemed shocked when I didn't get excited. "What, you didn't hear me?" she asked with a little spice on it. "Yeah, I heard you. I was wondering when you were going to tell me," I said with a straight face. "That's what's up," Annette said. She went on to explain how people tried to use her because of her affiliations, which I asked not to reveal at the first meeting— "I'm not impressed by celebrities because I know a few, myself." We pounded it out (fist bumps) and continued on with our discussion. Annette seemed more relaxed because she saw that I was genuinely not interested in other people or their status. I explained that our time was for us, "Unless these people affect you and how you're doing. I'm not impressed or interested in hearing about them." Hearing that helped Annette tremendously.

Annette and I worked together for almost two years. She was my first official mentee, and we learned so much from one another. Now that I think about it, she was also the first person to say, "I don't know why I'm telling you all of this." We mirrored each other in many ways in that we endured experiences that should have broken us. Annette inspired me by the amount of confidence she gained since then. I asked Annette how she was able to perform without hesitation. She boldly declared, "It's a gift from God. And when you know this, you let the Lord use you." I was like, "Come on with it. So, what's your other gift?" Like I was with Raheem, she was puzzled. "Singing is your talent, what's your spiritual gift?" Annette laughed and said without hesitating, "Discernment, no doubt." It took a moment for it to sink in before she realized what happened: "Wait! Why did you ask me that?" I remained quiet in order to give her space to process on her own. Before long, Annette said, "Oh! I *SEE* you."

I really enjoyed working with Annette and was able to follow what she was doing, professionally, over the years. She was able to accomplish several feats, while blossoming into a respectable, beautiful young lady. Once I was aware of her talent, she let me in on one of the songs she sang on. Annette tried some of ad libs and riffs out on me as she was developing the concept for her part on that song. She asked for my opinion one time and I tried wiggle my way out of giving it—"I'm not letting you off the hook that easy. I know who ya momma is," said with a smile. Annette played the demo of her stacked voice (one person singing all of the background parts). Before I could ask, "All that is me," she said beaming with pride. Annette's question was about a riff she did while harmonizing on the bridge. "My only advise as a lover of music is don't record something you cannot repeat live," I encouraged her.

What I heard that afternoon appeared on that artist's song just as she practiced in my presence. I was blown away by her natural, vocal aptitude and her humility. Annette went on to work with other artists and producers. My heart melted when she was called on stage to sing with one of my favorite artists. As a matter of fact, she did a part of our handshake during an appearance on national television a couple of years later. We were heart-broken and proud when I told her I was relocating to Atlanta to attend graduate school.

Let me fast forward to tell you what happened down the road before I forget to share. They say it's a small world and that may be true, but I believe in God's divine providence in that God ordered our steps and supplies our needs, even before we are yet in our mothers' womb. It turned out that Annette and her family crossed paths with some of my family members and others. It turned out that I *did* hear some of her early projects—that's how I knew her voice. I laughed when I discovered her famous affiliation and beamed with pride when I saw or heard her appear on that artist's project. Annette's story makes me feel honored to have been present in her life.

I moved on, taking experiences that helped me in some ways and stifled others with me. As I mentioned before, I went to Atlanta to move forward with my life. I met people from various places, at a variety of stages in their lives. I was in Atlanta to not only go to school but to figure out where I was going in life. There were several parts I figured out quickly, such as my need to be connected to a local church, while others took years. Overall, my seminary, chaplain residency, and doctoral studies were life-changing times for me.

Not only did I find a new church, but I also found new mentors. Having people in your life to assist in your development is absolutely necessary. I definitely needed guidance because I didn't know anyone who went to seminary. I discovered seminary definitely was not Sunday School shortly after my arrival. The Interdenominational Theological Center (ITC) was a place that strengthened my faith because it was where I was stretched and tested. The work in the church and the community was where my real learning took place, but seminary was the gleaning ground. I quickly joined the church I visited several times, served in its Youth

Ministries, and eventually, became Youth Pastor (twice).

Chapter Five:

Seminary Years: Did I Learn?

I began my studies at the Interdenominational Theological Center (ITC) in early August 1999. The weather was hot and very humid. I'd just left a 30-day heatwave in New Jersey only to endure another one in Georgia. John F. Kennedy, Jr., his wife, and her sister had recently died in a plane crash, which sent many Americans in a state of grief. As they said, "His death marked the end of Camelot." Kennedy seemed to have been showing signs of possibly entering the political arena at the time of his death, but those hopes were gone. I scratched my head because his sister, Caroline, was still around, but she did not want to dabble in politics.

I arrived in Atlanta a couple of days before orientation and moved into my dormitory. I was warmly welcomed into Bennett Hall (Morehouse School of Religion) by the Resident Assistant, Daniel. He was a Baptist preacher and proud to have come from a long line of preachers before him. Daniel showed interest in who I was and where I came from. He laughed when I told him I was a *PK* and was majoring in Pastoral Counseling. I also noted preaching was not my first calling, "but to minister to those who are suffering is where I'm supposed to be." Daniel advised me to be mindful of my calling because "you're going to be around a lot of preachers, and they will automatically think you do, too." I wish I would have remembered that advice. Daniel took me around to meet some of my peers and showed me where the main parts of our campus was so I wouldn't be late for orientation the next day.

Orientation was quite interesting, to say the least. It began with breakfast in the dining hall. I was at ease in the first few hours because I really hadn't wrapped my head around the fact that I left everything I knew in New Jersey to come to Atlanta, GA to prepare for my calling. Once it did sink in, I remember thinking to myself, "What did I do?" I heard several presenters say things like: "This is not Sunday School," "You'll learn the history and meaning of your beloved Bible," and "This place can either be a seminary for your higher learner or a cemetery for your faith." I sat there listening intently, wondering: "Are these people outta their damned minds?" In a strange way, those statements caught my attention and I took them as a form of intimidation, a sifting process. I decided, right then and there, I was going to hang in there no matter what, unless they threw me out.

I was somewhat naïve but hopeful about this endeavor because it signaled a new beginning for me, and I was very excited to be in my family's home state. I received a jolt when it came to some of the behaviors I observed of some seminaries within my first few months, namely the academic integrity of some of my peers. Don't get me wrong, I was not blind to the fact that some students cheated, bought, and sold papers, passed tests on; but in seminary…!

The work was grueling, demanding, and downright overwhelming at times (most of the time), I'll admit. A lot of the information was new to me as well as many others. We had to ask questions in order to gain some traction with those profound concepts. If you did not have efficient study habits and methods, you'd found yourself lagging behind. Unfortunately, a number of seminarians had a sense of entitlement, where they were supposed to get these perks. They either cheated or relied on their denominational connections to carry them through this strenuous journey. This disturbed me because I had to work my ass off just to have a clue. I didn't know who I could talk to about this, so I sucked it up for a while.

I found myself connected to in a local church. The pastor of that church inquired about my progress in school. He attended ITC and was familiar with the coursework. I told him about some of my concerns and how they were affecting me. With the patience of an old sage, Pastor listened. Once I finished, he said, "I understand your struggles because there were cheaters when I was there. Do what you feel is right and keep working hard." I joined that church soon after this discussion. Pastor and I forged a connection, which mirrored my relationship with my dad—loving and tumultuous at times.

There were other relationships formed during this period that were impactful. I dated some and was engaged to be married (again) for a brief time. I figured the second time around might have been it. I also met people with whom I consider friends for life. These individuals kept me grounded and reeled me in when I needed it most. The pressures of being a seminarian, and later, an ordained minister, were suffocating and restrictive at times. You see, you have to be very careful about who you associate with, not only as a minister but as a child of God—this too, I had to be relearned over the years. Who you are is very important in the sight of God, and if or when you drift away from your authentic self, you will be "out of order." But God is so loving that God will forgive you and lead you back on track if you are willing.

I found my rhythm at ITC and was proud to be a member of Morehouse School of Religion. I was aware of the purpose for my being there. My major was Pastoral Care and Counseling/Psychology of Religion. I was not aware of the support I had behind the scenes, Dr. Al When I met him, Dr. Al was kind toward me. Dr. Al was the Jarena Lee Professor of Pastoral Care and Counseling Department and a prolific figure in his field. He was my advisor and genuinely showed interest in my learning experience, which I needed because I felt like a fish out of water at times. Dr. Al checked in on me from time to time to make sure I was okay.

Meanwhile, my unresolved emotional issues started to rear their ugly heads as I started to adjust to my new life in Atlanta, GA. Weird dreams and flashback came into the picture, which never happened before. I went to the Campus Chaplain, Dr. Helen, who was also an awesome therapist, to see if she could help. She told me she would help me to figure out what was needed before referring me out for long-term therapy if that was necessary. Initially, I attributed the dreams to me being homesick because I had never been away from my family for an extended time before then. That might have been possible, but the flashbacks were related directly to my trauma.

It took some time for me to openly share with Dr. Helen and I wasn't sure why because I went to her for help. In hindsight, I believe I was hesitant because of my trust issues, even as I recognized my need for assistance. Once I did tell her what was going on, Dr. Helen thanked me for confirming what she suspected and said she had the perfect therapist for me.

The therapist Dr. Helen referred me to was a Sexual Trauma Specialist and was highly regarded as one of the best in Metro-Atlanta area. I pushed myself to go because I didn't want to be put on a long waiting list. It was reassuring to know that Dr. Helen cared enough to point me in this therapist's direction. I trusted her judgment and figured I had nothing to lose and everything to gain.

Dr. B.'s office was easy to find and not too far from campus. I felt somewhat at ease as soon as I reach the front door. A woman was in the waiting room and appeared to be with someone. I took a seat and quietly waited. A door opened and a teenager walked out—it turned out that the woman was waiting for her.

Moments later, Dr. B. came to the door , greeted me, and motioned for me to follow him. I wondered if he knew who I was. "I see a set number of people a day to keep the foot traffic low," he explained. Dr. B. invited me to sit in a number of places— "wherever you feel comfortable." I stood at a window for a few moments, while Dr. B. patiently waited. Many thoughts ran through my mind: "Should I leave?" "Should I stay and give this a shot?" and "Why am I here?" I chose to stay and took a seat near a window, while staring at some random object. It was eerily silent for a few moments with only the sound of water running in a fish tank. A few minutes later the strangest thing happened: I started to cry. Dr. B. slowly offered me facial tissue without saying a word.

The tears stopped moments later. I had no idea where they came from nor did I feel them coming. Dr. B. patiently waited until I collected myself before slowly engaging. He started by saying he booked a longer session because he wanted start building rapport. He did not want me to feel rushed or pressured. Dr. B. thanked me for coming and commended me for choosing to do something to help myself. I nodded slowly because I didn't know what to say.

Dr. B. is the therapist I mentioned in Chapter One. I was inspired by the work he was doing. I continued seeing Dr. B. for several months and cannot recall why I stopped. With his help, I started dating again (or tried to), even though dating was not something we spent a lot of time talking about.

People tried to link me to someone they knew. There were two persistent, loving people in particular, who introduced me to several women. Some were bizarre, on the rebound, or just not a good match for me. One of the women I was introduced to thought she was my mother (controlling) one moment, possessive and insecure the next. She confirmed why I believed (and still do) there were far too many people sitting in churches, week after week, with undiagnosed mental health conditions, and not receiving the help they needed. Anyhow, we were getting along well at first, then suddenly, she started flipping out one day. I saw signs before this particular day, but they were not really bad. It was early enough in this "relationship" that I did not have a lot vested to walk away with, as they say, "nothing ventured, nothing gained." One morning after I got off work, I called her as usual. She started making demands, telling me how I'd *better* do this and that, and would not let me get a word in for about 10 to 15 minutes. This irritated me because I didn't see it coming nor why it was happening. It was creepy because it was like I was speaking to someone else. I said a few choice words before hanging up as she went on to tell me what I could not, should not, and the like.

My plan was to just leave her alone because, honestly, she scared the shit out of me. She called at least ten times that day, she talked to the person who introduced us, who, in turn, started calling me too. Soon both of them started asking other people if they saw me around and/or if I was okay. I felt that this behavior was a form of stalking. I finally had enough and called the "matchmaker" to ask them to stop calling me for this woman, because "She's a weirdo and I don't want see or talk to her anymore." With great concern, they asked what happened and was shocked by what was reported— "Oh no. I'm *so* sorry. If I knew she was like that I wouldn't have introduced you to her." In short, I revoked their *matchmaking card* and asked them not to introduce me to anyone else.

The other person tried to "hook me up" with so many women that it felt like they were introducing me to people they randomly met on the street although there were quite a few, three of them stands out in my memory—Carrie was on the rebound, Roshelle was on the rebound, and Susan wanted to jump my bones the first night we met face-to-face.

Susan was the most shocking of them all. I liked her, and we talked on the phone for a couple of weeks before we met face-to-face. We agreed to go on a double date with Frankie and Beth (Frankie and I held similar views regarding first dates, which is why it was a double date). Don't get me wrong, I'm not a prude because I did my share of dirt, but I wanted to do things differently this time.

We all decided to go to a public venue where it wasn't too intimate yet not too crowded. We chose an outdoor festival downtown Atlanta and had a great time. It was everything we'd heard from others who attended this festival in the past. Frankie, Beth, Susan, and I went to a popular restaurant afterwards. We laughed and talked about some of the things we saw that afternoon.

This date took place on a Saturday and everyone planned to go to church the next day. The four of us hung out at the restaurant a little longer than we intended but it was okay because we were having a good time. Susan seemed to be as nice in person as she was on the phone. We talked about family values, friendships, and faith a lot. So, I felt we had a basic understanding of one another and where we might have gone in this budding relationship.

Things took a scandalous turn as we were getting ready to leave the restaurant. We rode together for many reasons, one being to relieve the awkwardness of the occasion. I felt this date should have been a group effort because Susan and I really didn't know one another very well, and I was still a little shaky about the whole dating thing.

Beth went to the restroom before we got on the road. Frankie, Susan, and I waited in the bar area. Frankie gave us space and was happy to see us getting along so well. Then suddenly, in what appeared to be an accident, I saw the top of her undergarment—her thong was exposed. I turned my head quickly because I thought it was a mishap. I looked at Frankie but he had no clue as to why it happen. So, I chalked it up as a mistake and moved on.

Beth appeared and was ready to leave but stopped short and glanced at me without saying anything. As we walked toward the car, Frankie and Beth were ahead of Susan and I, giggling as if they were a new couple. Susan and I were quieter than we had been the entire day—I believe Frankie and Beth sensed something was wrong but didn't say anything. Frankie opened both the front and back passenger doors to allow Beth and Susan to enter first.

Just when I was ready to let the first thong incident go, Susan showed not only her underwear, but Frankie and I saw just about all her ass followed by a mischievous grin. We froze for a moment, wondering if we saw what we *knew* we just saw. It was a long, quiet ride to Susan's house. I stared out the window most of the time. When we arrived at Susan's place, I walked her to her front door, extended my hand once it was opened and was out with the quickness. Beth was like, "Dang! No kiss, no hugs?" Absolutely not!

I got back in the car and the three of us did not say a word for a few moments. Beth asked if I was okay, and of course I said yes. Frankie said he was sorry I had to go through that— "She seemed like a nice young lady." Frankie and I explained what happened to Beth. Her voice sunk into disappointment as she said, "I'm so sorry." We actually laughed about what happened.

Frank, Beth, and I laughed about how Rochelle and I met, dated, and ended just as fast as we started—I dated Rochelle before Susan. It turned out Rochelle was on a "mini-separation," and her heart and mind was on her fiancée, whom she married and divorced. I was simply making time with her, which wasn't so bad because I knew she was absent even as we were together. It was the same with Carrie. I became annoyed with the dating process because I had been trying to meet and date people, but they turned out to be "no go's." I started feeling like a pitstop in women's lives. I'd had enough and told everyone to stop trying to link me up with who they wanted or thought I should meet. I wanted to start meeting people on my own, at my own pace. I no longer wanted to be bothered with romance at the moment. I simply wanted to focus on why I was in Atlanta: school!

I returned to my school grind and was working the graveyard shift as a security guard, which worked out perfectly because I was able to read, write and study without being disturbed very often. My classes became more demanding as I progressed onto the next level. I knew how much I could handle and decided to slow the pace down a bit. Instead of graduating May of 2002, I opted to graduate the following year. There was a lot of pressure to excel and the coursework was just too much for me to pile on as recommended.

Meanwhile, having a good paying job afforded me the ability to move off campus, which was the best move for me. I was grateful for the campus experience, being that I had never lived in an environment like that before, but there were far too many distractions for me. After having such a disappointing time with dating, the last thing I wanted to see was barely clad, beautiful Black young women prancing around in every direction. Even though this happened just about all year round, have mercy when it really got hot…! The more I tried to concentrate my schoolwork and other priorities; the more complicated things became. Walking to the library, for example, was like a game of chutes and ladders. I had to constantly cross the street in order to avoid the Clark/Atlanta women—there was a women's dormitory on the same street as mine. Keep in mind, I was a little older and I knew why I came to Atlanta. I couldn't afford to fall off track. Believe me, the struggle was real because there were beautiful women everywhere. It was like being in a sea of tantalizing chocolate covered strawberries, while on a diet.

One night I decided to go out with some of my peers because it was Spring Break and we did not go home for different reasons. The purpose was "to blow off some steam" after our midterm exams. Again, I was naïve to think anything of it because we were a bunch of preachers and seminarians. I was shocked to find we were heading to a popular strip club in Atlanta. In hindsight, I wasn't all that shocked because I saw this type of behavior as a PK. I was appalled because some of my peers made it seem as if we were going somewhere quiet and uneventful. I *never* wanted to do dirt with preachers and seminarians. I know that sounds hypocritical, but that was not my thing at that time. My partying days were slowing down to few and far between. I had no plans to return to those behaviors IN SEMINARY, because I was ready to move on and establish meaningful relationships. Once again, I felt like the odd man out. Many of peers were dating and having good ole time (read between the lines), while I was focused my "priorities." Therefore, I knew it was time to make some moves to get off campus.

    I talked to my Pastor and mentors about what I was experiencing. It was embarrassing at first, but when I explained my position, they all agreed it was time for me to find my own place. My academic mentor, Dr. Al, encouraged me to focus on other productive things, such as writing. He suggested that I participate in an independent study so I could research, read, and write freely. I agreed and registered the next semester. I worked on this project a whole semester and then some after that semester ended. I later asked Dr. Al why he wanted me to complete this study, and why he had me to submit so many drafts. Dr. Al quietly elucidated, "You need to get used to writing and submitting multiple drafts for your future studies." I accepted his explanation for what it was and did not inquire again until years later. Dr. Al also told me to avail myself to many of the actives that were to come on campus. I didn't know Dr. Al would be promoted to another post soon after this exchange.

    I had several opportunities to either meet or be in the presence of several influential figures in the Black Church and academia while attending ITC. One of the first was none other than the late Dr. James Hale Cone. Dr. Cone was one of the figures ITC's student body revered because he was the father of Black Theology. The campus was abuzz as he was coming to our campus after a recent book release.

You should have seen how people, who had never heard of Cone prior to arriving at ITC, behaved. I promise you I had never seen so many militant folks in my life. They were, as someone said in a private discussion, "A bunch of half-cocked idiots, running around with half-truths." I took this to mean people who really did not grasp Cone's concepts but were on the bandwagon anyhow. "It's like the old saying: There's nothing more dangerous than a person with partial truths," the other party explained. I made it my business not to go gong ho over something I did not have an adequate comprehension of from that point on.

I had to wait several years later, despite the explanations I had heard, to find out what was the motivation behind Cone's theology. I wanted to know how he came to develop such a critical body of work. Dr. Cone answered all of those questions in his last book, released posthumously, *Said I Wasn't Gonna Tell Nobody* (2018). Reading this book was like looking into Cone's mind as he told his story. It was as if he arrived at a point in his life where he was ready to answer a lot of questions people asked through the years. I really found inspiration in reading this work. I also took courage from reading one of his other books entitled, *The Cross and the Lynching Tree* (2011). Both works presented a bold perspective on two of the most controversial topics in American history: racism and lynching. In the end, Cone's words not only showed me how to present my point of view, but also the need to take a look at myself within a given context before opening my mouth (or using my pen) to say things I don't have a decent level of comprehension, period. In this case, introspection, as Van Der Kolk (2014) explained, is the ability to "notice what is going on inside us and thus allow us to feel what we're feeling" was a vital piece for me to move forward in my quest to find peace. There's always work to be done but one must start with themselves.

Some of the other people I was exposed to while at ITC were Bishop Vashti Murphy McKenzie, the first woman to be elected Bishop in the African Methodist Episcopal Church in 2000. If I recall correctly, she preached in ITC's chapel shortly before her election. Other figures were Reverend Doctor Jeremiah A. Wright, Jr., Dr. Jaqueline Grant, one of the founders of Womanist Theology, Dr. Noel L. Erskine, the late Dr. June Dobbs Butts, and a host of others. I can say ITC presented a plethora of perspectives that challenged my mind. Other memorable scholars were the late Dr. Jonathan Jackson, Dr. Carolyn Ann Knight, Drs. Wallace S. and Helen Hartsfield, Dr. Riggins Earl, Dr. Mark Ellingson, Dr. Willie Goodman, Dr. Mark Lomax, Dr. Temba Mafico, Dr. Carolyn A. L. McCrary, Reverend Doctor Sherman Pelt (Baptist Polity), Dr. Anne Streaty Wimberly, Dr. Stephan Rasor, Dr. Elizabeth Walker, Dr. Michael I. N. Dash, Dr. Tumani Mutasa Nyajeka, the late Dr. Edward L. Smith, Dr. Melva Wilson Costen, Dr. Kenneth E. Henry, Monifa A. Jumanne, Dr. Randall C. Bailey, Dr. Robert Michael Franklin (President, 1997 - 2002), Bishop Oliver Haney Jr. (Interim President from 2001 to 2003), Michael A. Battle, Sr. (2003 to 2009), and it's current President and my former classmate, Reverend Matthew W. Williams.

Encountering so many scholars, who looked like me, inspired me to study harder and do my best, especially in the areas that were new to me. Well, that was just about all the subjects because this setting was not, as they said from the beginning, Sunday School. Many concepts caused me to wrestle with my understanding of different Bible stories and characters. Respectfully, I told some of my professors about my lack exposure to a lot of the content they presented and greatly appreciated their enthusiasm. But that was not always the case because there were some professors who pulled outlandish stunts to prove their points—let's leave it at that.

*****

I had the awesome opportunity to serve as Youth Pastor at the Chapel of Christian Love Missionary Baptist Church in Atlanta, GA, from 1999 – 2008, 2010 – 2016. I found that serving as Youth Pastor was more than *babysitting* or keeping youths *entertained* during service. It was a lot of work, prayer, and patience. Establishing connections with youths is not always easy because you have to show them you are committed to and really care about them. I learned so much in this capacity because I had to work with the entire family at some point, which taught me diplomacy and fortitude. I developed some bounds I consider lifelong and maintained a connection with many individuals and families I served. I really enjoyed the fruit of good works in my time there. However, there was a downside to serving in that capacity as well. Working with and encountering different, and sometimes difficult, personalities was my greatest challenge. This oftentimes required a lot of behind the scenes work and *politicking* to get many things done.

I stuck to my guns about not allowing people to set me up with women who they consider *a good match* for me. I started to think people saw me as desperate and lonely, but that was far from the truth. I was (and still am, with my jaded self) convinced people truly believed you are not happy unless there's someone in your life, romantically. I never accepted that because I knew I could be miserable by myself; while at the same time, I could be happy by myself as well. However, it wasn't about unhappiness, companionship, or loneliness at that time in my life. It was about accomplishing a goal and preparing for the next phase of my life. I didn't need additional since relationships require time, energy, and work. I'm a true believer in God's timing, and not rushing it. There were a number of people who tried to use Scriptures to persuade me to hit the dating scene, but it didn't work because I knew what was best for me. So, I waited.

They say, "Good things come to those who wait." My good thing came when I least expected it. I was working on a project for a class (cannot recall the name), where I had to identify an area or program to enhance based on a targeted observation. I had been going to the Chapel on a weekly basis for quite some time. Again, I was about my business and not what others deemed priorities in my life.

One day I took notice of a woman, named Cheri, who had been at the Chapel all the while. I believe we both took notice of one another around the same time. My project supervisor and Pastor called ahead to let me know he was running late, so I had to sit in the same space with Cheri. We engaged in small talk, and then, our eyes met. My supervisor came in and led me into their office to discuss the progress of my project. They provided great feedback and offered suggestions for future direction. When we finished this discussion, my Pastor said something that caught me off guard: "I was late on purpose," with a mischievous grin as he nodded in Cheri's direction. We talked a few moments longer before I left his office still wondering about his comment. I stop to say good-bye to Cheri, which turned into a full-blown discussion. We exchanged phone numbers and I headed home for the weekend.

Neither of us called that weekend, and I didn't make a big deal out of it. In fact, I didn't tell anyone about Cheri and I exchanging numbers. I played it cool because I didn't know if we were going to talk outside of the office nor if we should. I cannot recall who called whom first, but we started talking on a regular basis (this was the fall semester of my last year at ITC, 2002).

Cheri and I decided to go out on a date, which included her son, Samuel. We went to a family friendly place and had a good time. Cheri later told me, "If my son didn't like you, there wouldn't have been another one. But he thinks you're cool." This was the beginning of our relationship.

I went back to the Chapel that week and my supervisor was grinning ear-to-ear. He immediately said, "She's has been smiling for a couple of days. You put a move on her." He laughed out loud, which was unusual, and with a swift shift he said, "Alright now. Pay attention. You're getting what you prayed for." I made a mental note of that statement.

Cheri and I connected very fast. She introduced me to her family, and I did the same with my extended family and friends. My birthday was approaching, and my friends decided not to plan anything too big because they felt it was best that I spent that special day with Cheri.

I was so busy with school and work and didn't realize Cheri, my supervisor and others had concocted a scheme to surprise me for my birthday. On the day of my surprise outing, Cheri had me to come to the Chapel to pick her up because she had a lot of stuff to tote home. I arrived on time and noticed the blinds move as I walked past her window. I didn't pay it much mind because there was an air condition unit below that window. I walked in and there were several balloons, cards (a giant one and regular sized ones), and cute beer cake. Cheri softly sang happy birthday and excitedly said, "I hope you don't mind, I made plans for us this evening." How could I say no after seeing her big smile. Cheri informed me that her parents wanted us to stop by because they had something for me as well. Cheri thought it would be a clever idea to drop off my gifts at her house, which was cool with me because the balloons were blocking my view anyhow.

We arrived at her place and it was quiet, which caused me to wonder where Samuel was. She quickly disappeared while saying, "I'll be back in about 10 minutes." It gave me a chance to think about what was happening: Cheri had planned an entire evening for us. I felt special and decided to enjoy the moment and let my guard down a little. "Oh yeah, there's beer in the fridge," Cheri called out. Again, I was impressed by how much thought she'd put into this day. Cheri quietly appeared wearing a pair of jeans and a red blouse because it's my favorite color. Cheri said, "I've planned a special night, and all you have to do is drive and enjoy." I was game because I had not had a woman to take great care in planning anything for me in a long time.

Cheri and I headed to her parents' house. For the first time, Cheri took my hand and placed hers it in. She smiled from ear-to-ear. This was the first physical contact we had up to that moment. Cheri pointed at the radio and said, "That's our song," referring to Ashanti's (2002) "Baby." She told me she thought of me whenever she heard that song. I blushed as she pinched my cheek—"Awe! You like that, don't you?"

Cheri became more animated as we approached the exit ramp to her parents' house. She called ahead to tell them we were about five minutes away. "Oh, I think you're going to like my folks." That was odd because I had already met her parents, then it dawned on me, she may have been referring to her siblings.

We arrived in front of her parents' house and I notice a red balloon tied to the handrail of the front porch. No one was outside and the house seemed quiet. Cheri and I took our time getting out of the car, walking up the driveway, giggling and holding hands. We were so into one another that we didn't realize we were being watched by her mother and sister. They were all smiles, and I was a little embarrassed when I saw them. I also noticed them nudging one another and nodding their heads. Her mother met us at the bottom of the steps and told me to enter the house through the side door, while leading Cheri up to the front door. I didn't know what to expect. I didn't know that her two brothers were in the house, too. I did expect to be *looked over* by the men in Cheri's life at some point, and this was the day! I tapped on the screen door. I heard Cheri's dad call out for me to come in. Once I was inside, two young men, who resemble Cheri, appeared. At first, they bore menacing expressions on their faces but softened shortly after entering the room.

If there was one thing I didn't forget about meeting the family and friends of a woman I dated was the *sizing up* portion, because I've done it several times as well. Cheri's father had already invited me to take a seat, in a specific seat, mind you. He introduced Cheri's younger brothers to me. I shook their hands and exchanged salutations. One of the brothers offered me something to drink, something smoke, something toot—test #1. I accepted a beer. The other brother chimed in, "You sure you don't need anything else?

You look nervous." I stated I was good, "Beer is fine." The first brother handed me a bottle of beer and I opened with my hands and drank out of the bottle, which seemed to please them. These men were important to Cheri, and I knew it. I also knew they would have smelled a phony a mile away, so I didn't try to be anyone other than myself.

Cheri's father and brothers had a number of questions for me, and I answered them within reason. The father took the seat facing me as the sons began their Q & A session from both sides of the table and remained standing. One brother asked what I did for a living and where my "folk" were from. I gave my answer, which seemed to satisfy them. The other brother asked, "You mean to tell me, my sister snagged a preacher. How did that happen?" The sons looked to their father as he continued to glare at me. The older son asked, "So tell me this, what you doing with my sister? Y'all doing it?" That caught me a little off guard because Cheri and I were adults. If we were "doing it," which we weren't, it was none of their business (in my head). I responded, "No, it's not like that. Cheri and I are not on that level. That's not what we're about." The father called his grandson, Samuel, into the room and asked, "Have you met Kasim?" Samuel said he did and added, "He's cool." Samuel came toward me, gave me a pound, looked at his grandfather, who nodded for him to take a seat.

There I was in the presence of the most significant men (and a child) in Cheri's life. Once Samuel was seated, the brothers sat down, too. Everyone was quiet for a few moments before the father spoke. With a serious countenance and a lower tone, he said, "Now son, if I can call you son," to which I nodded yes. "Cheri is ours and we don't want to see her hurt anymore. We wanted to talk to you, so we can see why she's…" the father stopped to look around at the sons and told Samuel to go get the mother and daughters. Once everyone was in the kitchen, the father continued, "Cheri has been smiling for the past couple of weeks and talks about you a lot." Cheri's mom was standing behind her, and grabbed Cheri's shoulders before saying, "I think you bring out the best in our daughter. Her father and I talked about this the first time we met you." I looked everyone in their eyes without saying a word. I heard my mom's assuring me, "Remember, the Spirit will guide you in all truths."

Cheri's mom announced, "I know y'all have plans but hold on a sec." She left the room for a moment and reappeared holding a gift bag, a card, and Cheri's sister came from behind her brothers holding a cake. They sang happy birthday and Cheri's sister said, "I hope you enjoy the rest of your evening, bruh." Cheri blushed a little as she came to stand next to me.

Cheri and I stayed a little while longer. Her parents insisted that we leave because, "Y'all don't wanna be late." Now, I was really intrigued by what Cheri was up to. She had been giggling and smiling the whole time we were with her family. I finished my beer, said good night to everyone, and we were back in the car again.

I was overwhelmed by everything that happened up to then and didn't know what to do with those feelings. Cheri asked what I was thinking. "I don't know. Why did you go through so much trouble for me?" I replied without expecting such a straightforward answer: "Because I think you're special and you should be treated that way," she said. And then, Cheri leaned over and kissed me on the cheek. SOLD!! She had me.

We drove from her parents' house as Cheri was giving the directions, turn-by-turn. She was elated, and her eyes sparkled in the cool October air. I decided to turn off my suspicious mind for a little while. I recall the afternoon sun was behind the trees as we rode with the windows half down to enjoy the autumn breeze. I held Cheri's hand as we rode to some unknown destination. I drove for about 15 to 20 minutes as Cheri told me to make a few turns before we arrived in front of this nice restaurant.

I parked where Cheri pointed. I got out, opened her door, and helped her out. We walked in and was met by a greeter, who immediately led us to a table by the wall to the right. I was captivated because the greeter didn't say anything but knew where we were to be seated. We sat there for a moment before I said, "You are good." Cheri smiled and said she had help and everything was going as planned. The restaurant was a new steak house and recommended by her parents and my supervisor, who was the one responsible for linking us together. My supervision brought Cheri to the restaurant the day before to make the arrangements. I was thrilled to know she and others went to such lengths to plan all this for me.

Cheri and I started moving *too* fast. Certainly, we were getting to know one another, building trust, and bonding well; but we started making moves that should have waited (in hindsight, of course). I was so caught up in everything that I ignored the heeding of a few important people around me— "Pay attention." We enjoyed being with one another, that's no lie. However, some things were out of order. "You're getting what you prayed for," came to mind a few times. I ignored it because Cheri and I had developed strong feelings for one another by this time.

Others noticed how our relationship was forging ahead as well. I remember we were visiting her parents and was sitting in the basement with Cheri's father. We were chilling when he said, almost randomly, "You're a good guy and you seem to have a positive influence on Cheri. What's your intention for her?" It startled me for a moment because I wasn't expecting this talk at that moment. He apologized and said he did not want to put me on the spot, but "I know happiness when I see it." I did not know what to say in the moment, so I remained quiet. Cheri and her mother entered the room, and she noticed the confused expression on my face.

Cheri and I hung out and ate dinner with her parents. We laughed and joked most of the time, which was good for me. As we prepared to leave, I gave Cheri's mother a hug and shook her father's hand. He gave me a nod and a wink without saying anything. I nodded in return.

Cheri and I walked to the car in silence. "So… why are you so quiet? What did my daddy do? I hope you're not mad or anything?" I assured her nothing was wrong but had something I wanted to talk to her about to which she slowly nodded her head in conformity. We knew we had deep feelings for one another, but we had not talked about them at that point. Cheri expressed her desire to talk to me about something important as well.

Riding home that night was somewhat awkward at first because there were a lot of quiet movements—I purposely left the radio off to give us an opportunity to be in the moment without distractions. Cheri took my hand in both of hers and asked, "Can we talk later?" I agreed and flashed a warm smile. She reached over and turned the radio on, which softly played the "Quit Storm." Our song came on and we sang along as we rode home.

This entire situation was bizarre to me because, after all, I spent much of my time focusing on my grind and not being out there looking for anyone at that time. Quite honestly, I did not see this one coming. Once again, I heard my supervisor's voice: "This is what you've prayed for." I was prepared for this but didn't want to ruin it. So, I gave myself permission to live in the moment.

Cheri and I arrived at her place and sat in the car for a while. We both waited for the other to speak first, but after some time, she insisted that we went inside, "I don't want these nosy folks in our business." Before I could take the key out of the ignition, you'll never believe what came on the radio? Silk's (1995) "What Kind of Love Is This?" We listened to it before we went inside. "Does that answer your question?" she asked as I opened her door.

The song broke the ice for us. Cheri told me: "I saw you before you noticed me. I knew you were a good man, even then." I'd already known Cheri had a discerning spirit, as well as her family members, including Samuel. She went on to share how she waited for me to speak because "I didn't want to get in your way." I shared where my mind was and admitted that I, too, took notice of her. "Why didn't you say something? I was right there." She giggled and patted my hand, "My shy guy."

We laughed and talked until the wee hours of the morning. There were times when Cheri and I didn't talk at all. I quickly realized our bond was as such that we didn't need to talk a lot, especially in the company of others. Something amazing happened that morning: Although there was no sexual contact that day, our bond grew stronger! We maintained an appropriate yet intimate spacing the entire time.

One of the most important rules of thumb when comes to relationships is to _not_ let others into it—not even mentally. Cheri and I agreed to spend more time together, that way the three of us could form a tighter bond. That was not unreasonable because we had good times together and needed to learn how to be a strong unit. People started showing a lot of interest, or should I say too much interest, in our relationship. I honestly do not believe everyone was against our being together. We were genuinely happy. But there were those who were not happy with themselves let alone for someone else. We withstood attacks by praying and communicating.

Our first and only Christmas together was wonderful. We spent time with her family and my extended family but chose to spend Christmas day in church and with one another—just the three of us. Somewhere between Christmas and New Year, Cheri and I were having a serious discussion regarding our relationship. I do not remember most of the content, but what stands out is one critical exchange. "I could marry you," she blurted out. "So why don't you," I replied. Stunned, we stared at one another in silence. I asked her not to answer until the time was right. Cheri nodded her head as she quietly shed a few tears. "Joy?" I pointed. She nodded yes. We called Samuel into the room and we prayed together.

I took this moment very seriously because I was experiencing something that was beyond my understanding. My first step was to call my mom to seek counsel, and most importantly, to get her blessing. I talked to my mom about Cheri and the direction I believed our relationship was heading. I knew how much my mom wanted me to be happy and supported me in most of my decisions after I stated my case. You see, this was not the first time I talked to my mother about relationships and marriage. My mom was delighted because I was showing signs of happiness, which she had not seen in quite some time. She also knew this had to be something special because I was mostly about my grind. (Side note: I believe my mother understood the real reason why I avoided relationships.) I asked her not to share her thoughts completely until it was the right time. My mom said she would be praying for us and hoped for the best.

I waited until January to start communicating with our parents. I really wanted to talk to my dad, but I had no way to catch up with him without Cheri knowing about it. I wanted honor her dad by showing him respect.

I finally had a moment talk to Cheri's father alone. I remember feeling so nervous that I started sentences, and then, stopping before I finished them. I took a deep breath and asked Cheri's father for her hand in marriage. Cheri's father stared at me for what felt like hours before asking: "What took you so long?" He busted out laughing while extending his hand. He called out to his wife, daughter, and Samuel, "Y'all come here." All of them came running into the room, wondering what the urgency was about—I didn't tell Cheri I was going to have this discussion with her father. "Cheri, you be quiet," he said sternly. "Bae, he wants to marry our baby. What you think?" Cheri's mom remained silent for a long time to which made me feel uneasy.

Cheri's father then turned to Samuel and told him to sit on his knee as he explained what was going on. I asked Samuel directly if I could have his mother's hand in marriage. He paused, looked around the room, clearly thinking about what was being asked of him. "Yes," like a little old man, "because you treat us nice and you love us." Her mom, who was already in tears, said, "I told you he was going to ask. Yes, oh, yes you can marry my daughter!" Cheri's dad agreed with his wife. Once the hugs were over, we sat down in the "pit" (a lounging area) with the elder couple facing us. I knew something serious was about to happen.

Cheri reminded me to call my mother to receive her blessing as well. Cheri's mom asked that we prayed first, which was the best thing. I called my mother and told her where we were and what just happened. She laughed and asked, "Did you pray about it? Did you and Cheri pray about it? And did y'all pray with her son and her parents?" Cheri's mom announced, "We just finished praying a minute ago." My mom indicated she prepared me well— "That's my son." The parents said it was time that they truly blessed us by "speaking life" into our relationship— "because tests are about to come." Yup! But did we take heed to this warning?

Our parents talked to one another most of the time and Cheri's dad said something that stuck with me to this day: "He knows what's coming their way, and so does she." The mothers also said something about kindred spirits, which only meant we all knew what our spiritual gifts were. Long story short, we were told to beware of the people around us and to do what we felt was right for the three of us.

I decided to wait until Valentine's Day to pop the question, only if I was moved by the Spirit. I may act a fool on many things, but I knew what to do in important times of my life. Cheri asked her parents to let Samuel spend the night if they didn't have plans for themselves. Their Valentine's activities were postponed because Cheri' mother didn't feel well. We arranged a time to take Samuel to her parents' house. We visited for a while and prayed with her mother before we left. She felt feverish when I touched her forehead, and she assured us it was getting better. Cheri's parents rushed us out the door and wished us a great night.

Cheri and I agreed not to go too far out of the way in what we did for one another because we wanted to spend a quiet night at home. I cooked Cheri a pot roast dinner garnished with mashed potatoes, fresh green beans (or string beans), candied yams, and rolls. Cheri baked a cake because I cannot bake well. We also had Champaign and ate by candlelight, which I cannot stand but did it for her. Once we finished our dinner, we watched a couple of movies, or at least that's what were supposed to do, because we dosed off to sleep here and there.

The night went perfectly. In fact, we slept most of the night—it was the food. I woke up just as the sun peeked over the trees, grabbed the ring out of my coat pocket, awakened Cheri gently, and got down on one knee. She started crying instantly. I asked, "Do you still feel like you can marry me?" She giggled and said, "Of course I can." "Let's do it," I said. And you know how the rest of the morning went.

We didn't tell everyone about our engagement and decided to wait until we talked to key people first—our family and friends, our Pastor and his wife, my mentor and his wife, as well as some people in the Chapel's Youth Ministry department. People speculated anyhow. Pastor was told about Cheri's ring by several (messy) people, and he cautioned them not to jump to conclusions. When we did tell Pastor about our engagement, he was delighted and congratulated us profusely. We asked Pastor to arrange a meeting to bring key people together under the impression that he wanted discuss Youth Ministry matters. "Let's make it interesting,"

Pastor mused. "Let's act as if I don't approve of you two working as a couple around the children and teens of this church." The three of us laughed and decided to have the meeting the following Sunday. Keesha, my god sister, was not involved in this meeting because she already knew about it. We got a good laugh out of how this meeting was probably going to go down.

On the appointed day of this meeting Cheri, Samuel and I sat together during service for the first time in weeks. We got a few funny looks but paid them no mind because we weren't doing anything to anyone, save for being happy. Pastor finished his sermon and asked that the listed people meet with him in his study after the service was done.

All of the people who were invited to this meeting gathered in Pastor's study wondering what the purpose of this meeting was. Cheri and I played along by acting as if we had no clue. Pastor entered moments later, took off his robe, and sat at the front of the room with an uneasy look on his face. He thanked everyone for coming in at the last minute. Pastor explained he invited key people in the Youth Ministry Department, as well two church advisors, because he wanted to address *some developing concerns*. Pastor was a great actor and remained in character the entire time. "Several families have expressed some concerns," he announced with a dramatic flair, "and I wanted Reverend Jones and Sister Cheri to be present as we discussed them."

Pastor acted as if his heart was broken. He went on to pose this question to the group: "Do you think Reverend Jones and Sister Cheri working together with our children is improper?" No one answered at first. "Some of our parents said their children, especially the younger ones, are asking questions about them," he continued. The group members looked at one another, sort of confused, and then at us. Pastor's wife spoke first and asked: "I'm not understanding what's going on. What is the question? Are you overly affectionate while you're here or in the presence of the children?" he asked us. We denied, while maintaining straight faces. "Do y'all talk about your relationship in their presence?" Again, we said no. "Then, I don't see what the issue is," she said appearing to be agitated and annoyed, "So, what are we really talking about?" My mentor's wife, who was known to have no filter, spoke up and requested to be accused in advance, "Pastor, may I speak frankly to this young couple?" which he nodded yes. She asked, "Are you happy together?" to which we nodded yes. "Then live your lives!" Everyone else concurred. Another member declared, "I don't see why we're discussing this. They make a nice couple and they ain't hurting nobody. Pastor, tell them folk to leave them alone."

Pastor asked Cheri and I to come to the front of the room and face everyone. He assured everyone it was his responsibility address such issues. "Do you have something to say?" he asked. Cheri said something about not wanting to offend anyone, which caught me off guard because I didn't know she was going to say that. So, I had to show her up. "Y'all wanna know what I think about all of this?" in louder but controlled voice. Everyone froze for a moment. I paused for moment before saying: "We're engaged!" It was quiet until it registered, and then, the woman who worked with me for years slipped up and shouted: "Aww shit!" before bursting into a huge belly laugh. They all laughed because they thought people were really complaining about us.

Pastor assured them there were no real complaints and asked them to vote on whether we should announce our engagement to the congregation to which they unanimously agree. "Okay. Let me know whenever you are ready," Pastor told us. Everyone agreed to keep this news to themselves by not confirming or denying any knowledge of the truth.

The next couple of weeks were filled with prayer, midterms, and work. Cheri, Samuel, and I had many discussions about how to carry ourselves, handling "church folk," and how we could support one another. Talking about these things caused me to reflect upon my experience as a PK (Preacher's Kid), and how I could help Samuel navigate this unknown territory. I did not want to taint his experience with my jaded view.

Cheri and I had to figure out how to be a couple, while ministering to others. In other words, we had to set boundaries because I had been the Chapel's Youth Pastor a few years before Cheri and I met. I wanted them to know my love for them had not waned, and I was not going to abandon them. Cheri was wonderful because she wanted me to do more and be present when needed. I emphasized wanting to be respectful of her and Samuel, while not being neglectful of their needs as well. Being a ministering family can be stressful if mindfulness of our needs are not recognized and appreciated. However, the members had to also be mindful of our sacrifices because they were so used to me showing up for just about every event the youths were involved in. Cheri and I intentionally incorporated weekly "Quality Time," where we spend couple time or family time together.

We decided to make the announcement the week after spring break in order to give most of the congregation a chance to return from their trips. We asked Pastor to make the announcement for us because Cheri was not comfortable in front of large crowds.

I know this may sound funny, but I was a little nervous because I didn't know what to expect from the congregation—we were a motley crew who loved one another, even when we were at each other's throats. Pastor asked us (all three) to stand as he announced our engagement, and the congregation clapped, cheered, and wished us well. We were met with the same positive enthusiasm as Pastor asked us to join him on the receiving line at the end of the service.

My life was moving along well. I took a trip back to New Jersey to attend my mother's Ordination Ceremony. We thought my ceremony was going to come first and I would have been able to lay hands on my mom, but it didn't work out that way. It was still special because I was able to participate in the service by delivering the opening prayer. My mom was so happy and so was I.

Unfortunately, this trip was the first real sign of cracks in my relationship with Cheri. Cheri and Samuel did not join me on this trip because of "schedule conflicts." That's the story I'll have to live with, but in hindsight, she just didn't want to go. I started noticing that Cheri declined a few invitations from my extended family, namely traveling to Columbus, GA to meet my eldest brother. My brother and his fiancé, at the time, were planning to get married that same year as us and wanted to discuss ways to avoid scheduling them too close to one another. It never happened and, as it turned out, our weddings would have been one week apart.

I realized my relationship with Cheri had changed and the red flags really started to show. Her attitude shifted and her behavior became more controlling, possessive, combative and she really didn't want me to spend a lot of time with my people. It was not all on her because I condoned most of her attics by not addressing with them.

There was one incident that pretty much sealed the deal for us. My best friend came to Atlanta and we made plans to spend time together, and Cheri knew it. My roommates and I invited several of our friends over for a little cookout. Cheri was also invited, and once again, she declined.

I really wanted to Cheri to meet my best friend because she wouldn't see her again until our wedding. Cheri still refused. Regrettably, that day turned into a huge fiasco because Cheri called and left a threatening message with my roommate, which sent everybody into ready mode. It was so embarrassing. Everyone looked at me crazy and was angry (pissed off) because some had their children with them, and Cheri was acting like a mad woman for no reason. My best friend pulled aside and pointed out the obvious—"This shit is not cool!" She introduced me to Blu Cantrell's *Bittersweet* (2003), which eventually served as my "breakup" cd.

Things went from bad to worse. Cheri and I clashed over many critical elements, such as child rearing, finances, educational attainment, substance use, work, to name a few. One of the few times we did attend an outing with my people, Cheri and I quarreled. She'd already had an attitude, which didn't help. So, I ended up taking her home. My friends were leery about inviting her to other events from that point on. Two of my closest friends sat me down for a heart-to-heart (intervention) because things were reaching dangerous levels, which was out of character for me since I was not about that life. I had been in a toxic long-term relationship before and they knew it. Major points addressed were the controlling behaviors, possessiveness, and isolation. This sit-down made perfect sense to me. Having people who truly love you and care about your well-belling really makes a difference in life. I really started paying attention to not only Cheri's actions but also my own.

God has a way of protecting us from ourselves, even when we're unaware of our need for it. I was preparing for graduation from ITC, which included a number of programs and ceremonies. Each time a school or church event was coming up, Cheri and I were at odds. In fact, we fought more often than we got along. I kept praying for those things to get better, while knowing they would not.

Once she missed the voting for me to become an Ordination Candidate and the actual ceremony, I knew it was pretty much over. The good thing was had Cheri and Samuel been present for the Ordination Ceremony, they would have been prayed over and linked to me for a long time to come, even after we broke up. All that was left of this relationship was going through process of ending it, which was not easy because we participated in a lot of manipulation, mind games, and emotional abuse. This is what we call "soul ties." It's one of those situations where you must do as Jesus admonished his disciples in Matthew 7: 21: "But this kind does not go out except by prayer and fasting." (*NIV*).

With all other things considered, I had great end-of the-year experience. Like other commencement periods of my life, I had a lot to think about. I knew my relationship with Cheri was pretty much over. I had a lot of decisions make because a great deal of time, money and work went into preparing for my future. I needed to determine what my next educational move was going to be if there was going to be one. There was no time to allow distractions and other issues to creep in and disrupt my life. I had to move forward.

Chapter Six:

From Death to Car Accident to Parenting in the Hood to Chaplain Residency to Doctorate and Beyond

Once I graduated from ITC and all of the church ceremonies were behind me, I had some important choices to make about my future. In some ways, I felt that my educational journey was not over, and I needed to figure out what that meant. Yet at that moment, I needed to rest and make some money. I had been working with children and teens for a while and felt good about what I was doing with them because it was productive. But I needed to find my way because things were hazy. I appreciated God's providential care, which included God's timing, and I was mindful of doing things the way they had to be done. So, once again, I focused on my grind and kept my eyes, ears, and nose open for new opportunities.

Positive things started happening for me as I worked hard to make a difference in the lives of young people. I continued serving as Youth Pastor, and the agency I worked for afforded me several opportunities during my tenure. These things served as confirmation for all my hard work with this population.

After hearing: "You won't really learn your craft until after graduation" so many times while in the classroom setting, I quickly found it to be true. I worked with a number of *troubled* youths, and adults, for that matter, and was able to connect with the population I was most passionate about. I had my eyes on the state's child protection agency for years but could not contribute and complete my studies at the same time. You see, they came under fire a couple of times and had several high-profile cases, and there were a number of significant changes happening. I had to bid my time, be patient, and keep my opinions to myself until the time was right. I had a few critiques and felt that they were useless if I was not able to contribute to making a difference within the system. So, I shut my mouth and prayed for the children/teens in the state's custody.

I was making a difference in the lives of those I worked with and ministered to. I later discovered I was working with several children who were in the state's custody. They were doing well and thriving. But it almost felt as if I was pitching in without a clear purpose and/or direction. I continued praying and watching for where I needed to go. Meanwhile, something strange started happening, people started disclosing their sexual trauma without provocation. I was a little confused at first but when it occurred repeatedly, I knew God was moving. All I could do was hold their stories in confidence. I continue working and ministering for several months without disruptive events.

Do Things Change Swiftly?

After the 2003 – 2004 holiday season I still hadn't given much thought to my next move, career wise or educationally. I had been in school for most of my life and wanted to rest and enjoy life a little. But when you have a calling on your life, and you've acknowledged/accepted it, your life is not your own. I dealt with a comparable situation before, where I wanted to do my own thing and it didn't work out. It was a distressing time and I did not want to grapple with that again. I hung out with a select few people and had fun, but nothing too crazy. I was still mending from my failed relationship with Cheri and wasn't thinking about jumping into another one at that moment. I focused on how I could move forward instead. Besides, I had not had the chance to weigh or explore any my options and did not want to be tied down with complications.

My world changed after receiving a call from my mom one afternoon. Although it was unusual for her to call me in the middle of the day, I answered her call without thinking anything of it. I was told to go sit down. "Now you have my attention," I thought. My mother informed me of my father's death, and I that needed to come home as soon as possible. This was the Wednesday after Martin Luther King Day 2004, and he passed the day before. She also told me the service would be held that Friday morning. I believe this was by design, but Duane and I still made it home on time.

I was stunned by what was said and went looking for my supervisor to inform him of my need to go to New Jersey. The first thing that came out of his mouth was, "When are you coming back?" I wasn't sure of anything at that moment. This person (replaced "person" for the word I had in mind) had the nerve to inquire: "Were you close?" I couldn't believe what I heard. I was disturbed because he was dead-ass-serious. "Are serious? We're talking about my father. Why would you ask me that right now?" was my response. I was through and cannot recall the rest of this exchange.

Preparing for unplanned trips are not only stressful and tricky because there are many things to be done in short periods of time. There's no time for frivolous activities that would have to wait until your return. My mom, my brother, Duane, and I communicated and supported one another throughout this process. I had a great network here in Atlanta and did not have to worry about too many things, save for getting home. I did just about everything in shock and could not process much because I had to get home to New Jersey. I grabbed one of the suits my father bought me. I remember him saying, "Get something sharp. I want my son to look good on Sundays." And that's what I did. His passing happened abruptly for me. I did not have a lot of information, which was okay because I could focus on those details once I arrived home.

I packed my things, threw them in my car, and hit the road, heading north. I left Atlanta that Thursday afternoon and arrived in East Orange, N. J. early Friday morning. To this very day, I cannot remember if I drove straight through the 11- to 13-hour trip. I do recall my thoughts racing at times causing me to have to refocus and concentrate on the road.

Things happened so fast and I wasn't prepared to keep my emotions in check. I walked into the room where my father was lying and was conscious enough to pay attention to what was going on around me. My mom, brother and his family had taken their seats—my mom sat near some people I didn't know but they favored my father. One of the women said, "Look, he does exist." My mom proudly said, "Yes, that's my baby." I thought it was in poor taste and bad timing. That statement did something to me that I still cannot explain. It was as if I was the subject of some family folklore. Not only did those words sting but her facial expression was that of contempt—as if I'd done something wrong. Yet I stayed in pocket (behaved myself) out of respect for my father.

I went to view my father's body and then sat next to Duane. Stunned, I started asking questions because I was incensed by what I saw. My father had this grayish-silver paste on his mouth because his lips dried from dehydration. I didn't know exactly what happened to him at that time because I did not have the chance to speak anyone. But I knew what that paste meant—some foul shit happened to my father. So, I sat there brewing. Duane gently grabbed my arm and looked at me, and instantly knew I would be okay.

My uncle, Reverend Jerome Calloway, officiated the service. A lot was said but most of it is a blur, but then "Dance with Father," by Luther Vandross (2003), started playing. I put my hand on Duane's and before he could move, I was outta there with my mother in tow. She caught me in the hall before I could locate the exit. My mom hugged me as I cried like a big baby.

A plethora of thoughts raced through my mind at once. I was irritated because I felt that my *step* family did not want Duane and I there to begin with. And from the looks of things, they didn't treat my father as they should have. I sat there listening to everything my uncle said, while seething inside. I knew my father was mistreated and was angry because no one helped him. After all he'd done for so many people, no one helped him. I heard some of the hints my uncle said throughout the eulogy. It hurt mostly because my father and I had just started getting along and he wanted nothing but the best for Duane and me, for some reason. I was furious because I knew my father worked very hard to provide for his children and there he was, a victim of maltreatment.

It was a hectic day and I was exhausted. Duane, his family, and I went to the repass to be with our *family*. We met some aunts, uncles, brothers, sisters, and other family members that day. I encountered a lady, who turned out to be my older half-sister. She looked very familiar and it seemed as if she avoided eye contact with me. I brushed it off because it wasn't important at the time. The women who made that crazy remark before the service started, approached me, and said she had not seen me since I was a small child— "I'm your aunt." She went on to say she *knew* Duane had a younger brother and used to ask her brother, my father, if I was still around. I confirmed, "Well, here I am" with a snide smirk. I excused myself because Duane called me to join him. I approached cautiously because he was accompanied by a man who resembled a Calloway. Duane introduced him as one of our older half-siblings, but I wasn't very interested because he was high. Then, it occurred to me who that young lady was. She used to be escorted out when I worked at Pathmark. Small world.

Duane, his family, and I stayed at the repass a while longer. I felt awkward because we were to ourselves most of the time. And if we weren't, one of us found ourselves in a precarious position. The older brother I spoke of earlier, he had the nerve to ask Duane for money, while I avoided my newfound aunt. We decided to leave because we were very uncomfortable. I wanted to go home and spend time with my family. I wanted to see Timothy. He had been asking my mother about me, so his mom made sure he was around for me to pick up that afternoon.

Seeing my little sister, Tihira, little brother, Roy, and Timothy was the highlight of this trip. My mom caught me up on how they were doing and asked me to pull Tihira aside when I had the chance. I did so immediately. Tihira asked how I was doing because she was worried about me. I assured her I was okay and noticed a tear in her eye. I hugged and soothed her because she became very emotional. Tihira said she wanted to share the details of the last time she saw my father. Tihira reported of seeing my father in bad shape and "he didn't look like himself." She couldn't finish because it was too painful. I told my mom what happened and asked her to tell me what happened. My mom said Tihira was present when she (my mom) tried to convince my father to stay with them a little while because "He was just that sick." My father promised he would go home and get some rest that day. My mom told me Tihira fell apart after he left. That was the last time they saw my father alive.

Duane and I were informed of a big snowstorm heading north. We decided to leave early the following day. I had to report to work that Monday (red flag one) after being given just a few days off (red flag two). I got on the road traveling on the opposite side of the storm. But, unbeknownst to me, the storm shifted direction and I drove straight into it. I struggled to make it through but ended up in a terrible car accident somewhere in Virginia. This period of time taught me several lessons that still holds true: 1) I rush for no one, 2) I appreciate family and true friends, 3) I am expendable in many positions in this life, and 4) I don't have an infinite amount of time to live. I was so worried about getting snowed in and missing work that I put my very life at risk.

I remember bits-and-pieces of what happened shortly after that car accident. I was an emotional wreck. I cried when they brought me into the emergency room and several days after that. The doctors had to sedated me in order to administer medical treatment. A Social Worker had to piece information and somehow contacted a family member. I'm not sure who was called first. It was a mess.

I was forced to accept my father's passing and my near-death car accident at the same time. And to make matters worse, when I called my supervisor to inform him of the car accident and hospitalization, he replied, "Do you think you'll be back in a couple of days?" What was he talking about? Again, I couldn't believe he would ask something like that? It was as if I said nothing at all nor informed him of my injuries that led to me being hospitalized. I do not remember what was said after that, but I do recall feeling angry because there was no concern about my wellbeing.

I was in the hospital for at least five days. I was alone, injured, and grief-stricken in a strange place. The first two nights were the worst. All I could do was cry, sleep and try to hold it together because I was afraid they were going to put me in the mental ward, but I later learned the hospital staff knew I was grieving and alone. They showed a lot of compassion toward me. There was this person (or persons) who visited me a lot. I cannot remember if it was a man or woman, or both, but they prayed for me, sat with me, and check on me. Once I started regaining my strength, the visits stopped. I shrugged it off and attributed it the pain medications they gave me. I asked one of the nurses if someone visited me when I was out of it. The nurse told me a couple of chaplains visited because they knew I did not know anyone in the area. I did not forget their presence and wanted to know more about their function.

I was on an emotional rollercoaster during my stay. I was sad, afraid, and angry, more of the latter. My supervisor's reaction led to me not speak to him during my three- to four-month convalescence. This was another time when I felt like a *thing*, a *commodity*, and a *service*. My supervisor was so focused on me getting home to meet my quotas that he showed no concern for my condition. I was one of his best workers and I usually met my productivity margins. But he did not give a damn if I had to use crutches or a wheelchair. All he wanted was for me to get my wounded ass back to work.

I spoke with the Director of our department regularly. She asked how I was feeling and encouraged me to focus on getting better. I voiced my concerns regarding my supervisor's behavior and indicated I did not feel comfortable with speaking with him any longer. The Director became my point of contact and asked me to call her in a couple of weeks after I rested.

My brother, Duane, lived in Virginia at the time and was very concerned because he did not know what my condition was and that no one was with me. He wanted to come to see about me right away but we decided he should wait until my discharge date, which was that Saturday (I believe). I had several emotional moments as my discharge date approached, and as Duane and I prepared to leave the hospital. I had to retrieve my belongings from my car. I wept when I saw the damage my car sustained. It forced me to grasp what happened, even though I did not remember what caused the accident. I was grateful I was not critically wounded or killed. Duane and I gathered my belongings and started on our journey to meet Willie, our eldest brother, at a halfway point somewhere in North Carolina.

The level of care I received from my support system in Atlanta (GA) was incredible. My friends came to visit and were so glad to see me I alive and in one piece. I am so grateful that I lived with Timothy and Tiyan Peterson at the time. It would have been very difficult for me to have recuperate alone. Terry and Keesha Walker, Jr., Charlene Sims, and the Jonathan and Sylvia Graham pitched in to ensure that I received what I needed, and appreciate all they done for me as well.

My church family were unaware of my father passing and me being involved in a car accident but pitched in as well. I went to church the day after my return. I was high on the pain medication. I stood up to ask for prayer and said a bunch. I don't know why I did that because those medications had me on another level. This is why I did not like to take anything stronger than Tylenol (Over-the-Counter).

Were Things Really Coming Together?

I started seeing direction in my life, even though the events leading to this revelation were painful, both physically and emotionally. My Program Director called to inform me of "triple good news": First, I would continue receiving a full paycheck. Second, my co-workers donated enough leave time to cover me during my convalescences and beyond. And third, I was offered a promotion to Program Manager upon my return. They also informed me of a new Program Administrator, who reviewed my resume,' and felt I would be a great fit for that role. I accepted the offer immediately. With this triple good news, I was able to focus on my recovery without worrying about my bills.

Learning to walk, drive and a number of simple things was painful. I had to build my confidence and strength in order to function more. I had a fractured pelvic bone around the socket area, shoulder bone, as well other fractures and bruises that were slow to heal. Some of the early days were the worst because the pain was intense, and no other narcotics were prescribed, except Tylenol III and OTC (Over-the-Counter). I pushed through the discomfort because my return date for work was rapidly approaching. I started walking around our apartment complex in increments until I was able to walk a couple miles a day. Although I was still sore in some areas, I didn't complain much because it was a part of the healing process. The pain began to lessen, but my doctor told me I was not quite ready to resume my usual activities yet. I was antsy about being able to function enough to return to work.

One day I decided to try to drive to the store. It was okay for the first few blocks, but when I had to break for the first time…! It felt like lightening shot through my pelvis. I decided to wait for the doctor to release me, thank you very much. When I went to the doctor, she was impressed by my progress and wanted me to continue walking around the complex, alternating longer strides with shorter ones. It was a difficult regimen, but it worked wonders because my legs needed to be conditioned again.

The Program Director called me a week or so before my return to check in on me. She advised me to check my email because a description of my new job was sent. I opened the email while we were on the phone so I could keep up with what was being said. I accepted this position because it gave me an opportunity to learn a new skill set as I continued healing. Program Director was happy to hear I was up for the task. She also told me about the managerial meetings and shared that it was traditional for the administrators to provide lunch. "I believe you will fit into this position well," the Director said. I had no questions or concerns. I went about my exercise regimen and rested as the days wound down.

When I did return to work, I received so much love from my coworkers. They draped a welcome back banner over my desk. One of my former supervisors, who had been promoted to another position in another department, stopped by to invite me to lunch that afternoon. I sent out an agency-wide message thanking everyone for their kind words, generosity and well wishes. I was happy to be appreciated and in others' thoughts and prayers.

I saw a few fresh faces here and there as I walked to my designated office space. It was good to know the new people were new workers and not replacements. My Program Director stuck her head in my doorway to tell me there was a short meeting with the new Program Administrator—"She's excited to meet you." I looked around the room and I noticed the other Program Manager, my old supervisor, was not there. My Program Director told me he would not be there for a few days, which was perfect because I needed time to get comfortable in my new space, which we shared.

The meeting with the Program Administrator was interesting because her leadership style was that of a "task master," if you will. If she gave you a project, she wanted to put her hands in it throughout the process. In some ways, that was not a terrible approach because in their minds, things are watched closely; however, it is not always prudent because it takes away people's confidence and can slow the project down. I began charting a plan right then and there. Apart from that, the Program Administrator seemed cool and was brought in because of their ability to expand programs and agencies. They invited me to be innovative in my duties and to share new ideas.

I left that meeting feeling good about what I was about to do upon. Having been a supervisor before helped a lot. The difference between this managerial position and supervising was I had to ensure things were moving aptly and solve those that were not. Supervision had to more with evaluating and assessing work performance but managing dealt with ensuring things went smoothly.

My Program Director asked me to step into her office for a moment. They wanted to advise me about my role. With a stern facial expression, she encouraged me to stay on top of *my own* responsibilities, and not get caught up in other things that were outside of my duties. I made a mental note and kept my eyes and ears opened.

I returned to my office and immediately began organizing my workspace. I knew a had a major advantage in this role because the people I was managing were my former coworkers. My team consisted of hard workers who were not afraid to pitch in to achieve the team's goal. When my promotion was announced in the monthly agency meetings (morning and evening), members from both teams agreed and expressed their willingness to get the job done.

Getting acclimated to this role did not take very long. I used a system that allowed me to see our productivity before the end of each week, and to identify who were the "top dogs" on our team. I noticed that my counterpart struggled at times, usually towards the end of the week. They started watching me and asking a lot of simple questions they should have known or figured out on their own, in my opinion.

One day, at a managerial meeting, the Program Administrator asked both Program Managers to present our weekly projections at that point of the week and the month. The Administrator called my counterpart to present his forecasts first. He stumbled through his report as if he was confused. The Program Director and Administrator glanced at each other before calling upon me. I was a little embarrassed because I had a clear report and was able to present without a glitch. Once again, the Program

Director and Administrator glanced at each other before moving on with the agenda.

One of the most important items on the agenda was the Annual Summer Camp. Traditionally, both Program Managers worked together to oversee its daily functioning. The Program Administrator announced I would spearhead this effort with my counterpart assisting. I was asked to remain seated at the end of this meeting to discuss Summer Camp in detail. I felt awkward because, as I said, both Program Managers usually worked together, sharing the load. My counterpart seemed a confused and avoided eye-contact with me. He lingered around at the end of the meeting, asking several questions. I felt bad for him because he was equally involved the previous year, and now he was only *assisting*.

The Program Administrator and Director thanked me for the hard work I put in up to that point. They emphasized not wanting to talk about Summer Camp in the regular meeting for various reasons to which I did not want to know. "A decision was made about camp this year, Kasim," the Program Administrator explained. "Your team is well-managed and is able to function independently for the most part. We want you to spearhead the Summer Camp, Monday through Thursday, and then, turn it over to your *assistant*," they said with the Program Director nodding in agreement. The Program Director chimed in, "That way there will be less confusion and things will get done." The Program Administrator continued on to say I would do the staffing interviews, ensuring all needed supplies were in place, as well as a number of other duties. There was a bonus that was usually a 50/50 spilt, "But this year you'll get 75% and your *assistant* will get 25%." I felt really uncomfortable by the end of this meeting because something didn't feel right between them and my counterpart, and

I did not want to be involved in whatever was going on.

Summer Camp went well but my counterpart seemed a bit resentful since the meeting before it started. I had to remind myself to be patient with him because he was most likely insecure for obvious reasons. I also had to keep in mind I was not there for three or so months and had no idea of what happened during that time. I ignored this behavior at first, but then, it started getting annoying because I didn't take this position for all of that commotion. Keeping up with my daily grind was enough. I started thinking about my next move. Somehow, I was told about a Chaplain Residency Program at Grady Memorial Hospital. I applied because I wanted to find out what Hospital Chaplains did after my experience during my hospitalization following the car accident.

I learned a lot that summer. I managed 30 to 40 people with only one incident the entire time. That was impressive. The greatest lessons I learned while functioning in that dual-role was time management, prioritizing, and delegating tasks and responsibilities to others. Everything I did was not to embarrass or outdo anyone. In the end, I asked my Program Director to give credit to both my *assistant* and me at the agency meetings. She laughed and agreed.

Being a Program Manager was a great experience but I missed working directly with the youths. I knew I could not risk being round them because of my physical condition, yet I wanted to go into field from time to time. My Program Director and Administrator told me I would not go back to my counterpart's team because it would be a conflict of interest. I agreed because of how he treated me while I was out.

Was I helpful?

After applying, interviewing, and waiting for a response, I was accepted into the Chaplain Residency Program at Grady Memorial Hospital in Atlanta, GA. But before I started this journey, there were a couple of matters I needed to settle before my start date—bringing my sister, Tihira, to Atlanta, and getting her settled in and registered for school. I knew this was a lot to handle but it was a sacrifice I willingly made. My mother and the states of New Jersey and Georgia deemed me fit to take custody of Tihira because I was no longer in school. The process started quickly because I needed to have things in place before school began in August of 2004. Within a matter of weeks, the court orders were sent by Federal Express and I was able to put things in motion. I secured an apartment, located in a school district, and started looked into various activities.

Things were rolling along when it dawned on me: *My sister was not a baby anymore.* I still had the image of the 9-year-old little girl stuck in my head. But I quickly realized she was a teenager with teenaged challenges, and mouth, to boot. I didn't let that worry me, because I had one (she was a mini version of me). I loved my little sister (and still do) and was finally able to bring her to live with me.

You see, the back story was New Jersey and Georgia would not allow me to take custody of Tihira earlier on because of my student status. I was considered "unstable." I didn't tell Tihira about it at the time because I didn't want to hurt her feelings, which was a mistake in hindsight. I should have said something. But, for the time being, I was so happy because Tihira had her own bedroom, her own space and was the only teenager in the household. Therefore, she had my attention without competing with others.

Tihira arrived in Georgia a month before school began, and my Residency started soon thereafter. She was enrolled in the legendary Benjamin E. Mays High School in Atlanta, GA. I intentionally moved in that area because Mays High School had a good reputation for its academics and a couple of teens from the Chapel were there as well. I wanted to help my sister receive not only a good education but a good high school experience. I knew it was going to be a lot of work because my Residency required that I worked crazy hours at times. However, Tihira was a trooper and hung in there with me. I was around a lot when school first started but it started getting crazy, yet Tihira quickly adjusted to this arrangement.

*****

I started my Chaplain Residency full of hope in knowing I was not only going to learn something about the hospital ministry but also make an impact in some way. I learned a lot about grief, compassion, empathy, human nature, and myself. I met my good friend and "Best Sis," Dr. O., in this setting. She and I saw one another when we were students at ITC, and she was finishing up her doctoral studies during this time and we bonded quickly. This Residency was emotionally and physically taxing. In hindsight, it was great to have someone to lean on throughout this journey, especially during group processing.

There were several memorable situations from my Grady experience. First, our group was a stark mixture of personalities, backgrounds, abilities, and shortcomings. We were divided into three factions most of the time. Next, the group comprised of three men (one Caucasian, Hispanic and African American) and four women including the Supervisor/Director (three African Americans and one Latina). And, lastly, the group processing almost felt like group therapy with the group acting as the therapist, while the individual presenting was scrutinized and *picked apart*. Keep in mind, everyone has their own issues and challenges in life, but many people do not seek professional help. Unfortunately, they do not wish to address their problems but are quick to point yours out.

The group process definitely had its advantages and disadvantages. I dreaded processing day because it was as if my cohorts were looking for something to point out or dread up. It was like sitting in a room full of tea bags. All of us had own flavors but did not want to be dipped in the hot water. Yes, hot water is scary because it is uncomfortable, but it brings out what was in us. I did not enjoy being interrogated and I certainly did not appreciate how some of those sessions went.

I thought of some positive situations to share and came up with a lot of circumstances where people were usually under pressure or the conditions demanded a lot from the Residents. I was scheduled for duty in the emergency room on March 11, 2005. The day started in its usual fashion. We, the Residents and Director, were getting ready for our morning briefings when our attention was brought to a television, where we first learned of the infamous Fulton County Courthouse shootings. The assailant was on the loose, and two Fulton County Sheriff Deputies were coming to Grady.

All of the Residents and Senior Chaplains were dispatched to the emergency room to provide support. It was a madhouse. Half of the hospital was cordoned off because no one knew where the shooter was, while the other half, where the ER was, had most of Fulton County Sheriff's Department milling around. At some point, someone from my church informed me that a Chapel family member was also admitted into the hospital. I took the information and planned to follow-up because the Deputy's mother was on the Mother's Board at my church, Mother J.

Being in that distressing situation taught me a great deal about remaining calm in the midst of chaos. The Director of the Chaplaincy Department was also present to serve, while a Senior Chaplain and I were points of contact. The Director worked with me and helped me to remain focused by exemplifying a relaxed demeanor. One of our assignments was to be present with the two Deputies' families—one who died of gunshot wounds and the other who was critically wounded. The Senior Chaplain took the decedent's family, while I took the other because of my existing relationship with that family—I was also their Youth Pastor. If my memory serves me right, the Chapel family member was in the Operating Room by the time I received my assignment. I went to check in with the family, letting them know I would be with them during that time, they had no clue of the calamity that was unfolding on the other side of the hospital and in the city. I let them know I would return once things settled down.

The hospital began to return to its usual function once the Sheriff's Department started leaving. It was not until the afternoon that we were able to take a break. The Director met with us to check in with before we went to lunch. We were tired because of the amount of energy exerted from being present during this ordeal. Our Director reminded us that our being in clear view for others to see served as a source of comfort for them. We shared some of our experiences before praying together and left for lunch in silence.

They say tragedy brings people together and/or strengthens bonds. I would say it was true for Mother J. and I. In a short period of time, we spent a lot of time sitting, talking, and praying together. I need to clarify that I spent a lot of time sitting at Mother J.'s feet, listening to her as she dispensed pearls of wisdom, some of which I hold dear to this very day.

Mother J. called me to her offspring's room for support one night. She looked at me and said, "You look tired, Reverend Why don't you sit down for a while?" Of course, I did as she suggested. Mother J. was one of the sweetest people I'd met in Atlanta. She wanted me to know how much I was appreciated "as our Youth Pastor and now our Chap." One time she brought in extra food to share with me: "I brought you something to eat 'cause you gotta eat." That was the type of person Mother J. was and I am indebted to her because of the things she planted in my heart and mind.

I want to share a story that Dr. O. and I still laugh at, even though it was not funny when it happened. I was on-call one night and it was absolutely tumultuous in that twenty-two people died that night. I did not have support from my colleagues, save for Dr. O. My pager chimed all night with different units requesting the on-duty Chaplain's presence. In this setting, being with families and friends when someone passed away was top priority. Clearly, I could not respond to the volume of requests on my own, so I paged the person assigned as my back-up. They did not respond to my pages, which were several. I was doing well at first because several people in the hospital pitched in to help—a few praying nurses and a security guard. I lost it when a young lady, who was born the same day as me, passed away.

I paged everyone on the list but no one responded. I called Dr. O. because I really needed someone to talk to. Dr. O. was on-call the night before and offered to come back to help. I declined because it was not her responsibility to do so. She prayed with me and encouraged me to help as many families as I could. I felt empowered to move forward and was able to be present with a large group who was not only grieving, but they were also in shock because their loved one died by hands of another family member; and then, *dumped* on the ambulance port, to boot.

I was furious the next morning when the rest of the group came in. Dr. O. saw my face and tried to catch me before the rest of the group came in. Nope! I let them have it. They repeatedly asked, "Why aren't you angry with O?" Oh, why did they keep asking that question? — "Because she's the only [bleeping] one who answered her [bleeping] phone!" 'Nough said.

There were times when we all worked well together, even in the midst of the factions within the group. A good example was when several large families/groups were present at the same time, either their loved had passed or was slipping away. I believe there were at least five families in different Intensive Care Units (ICUs) and others were in the emergency room. We went out by twos to serve those families—yup, just as Jesus sent his disciplines. Each case was emotionally taxing, and some were extremely complicated.

Two of those families stand out in my memory. A mother of two teenaged girls died a couple of hours before the family arrived. The youngest of the two was so distraught that she verbally attacked those who were trying to comfort her— "You got yo momma!" pointing at each individual as she repeatedly said this.

"Y'all got y'all momma. My momma dead!" she shouted. Not everyone present had their mother, and this effected Dr. O. because her mother passed away and this young person's words stung. Dr. O. and I continued providing pastoral presence and prayed with that family.

I checked in with Dr. O. before we moved on to the next unit, which was a tough one because the patient was a young person, who was randomly shot, for what seemed to be for no reason. Dr. O. and I paused for a moment because we were informed the family and friends were placed in a conference area, which told us it was a large crowd. As we approached this group, members of the outer group guided us to the nucleus, which was where the patient's immediate family was located. I remember feeling so drained. I imagined how Dr. King must have felt as he visited the families of the four girls killed in the 16th Street Baptist Church (Montgomery, AL) bombing in 1963.

Dr. O. and I were able to slip away to get something to eat because the patient was in surgery or something. We prayed with the family before leaving the room. Before Dr. O. and I could leave, I overheard someone say the patient had a toddler at home. It broke my heart to hear that, but I held it together in their presence because I needed to be able comfort them when it was time.

Dr. O. and I sat at our table in the cafeteria without talking very much. This had to be one of the quietest lunches we've had up to that point. We were able to finish most, if not all, of our lunch before my pager rang. It was the person's unit notifying us to report to charge nurse's station to meet the medical team *before* proceeding to the conference area. Dr. O. and I knew the patient had passed away and it was time to notify the family.

One of the aspects of this role I really didn't like was when I accompanied a medical team meet with the loved one's of the patient and someone yelled, "Oh no! Why is he coming." Well, it was the same with this group only this time the ripple effect was much bigger.

We reached the room where the immediate family was located, the patient's mother asked the doctors to wait a moment. She wanted me to stand next to her, to comfort her. The lead doctor tried to compassionately inform them that their loved passed away. The mother passed out immediately. The doctor was touched as he repeatedly said, "I'm so sorry." We prayed with the family before leaving the room. It was one of the most emotional prayers I had rendered in my life. This case touched me so because the person was a young man with plans for his future, and he had a young child, who was without their father.

One last situation that stays with me was when I was making my early rounds that Easter Sunday morning. I went to my assigned ICU and I noticed a woman standing outside one of the rooms. She waved for me to come to her. The woman had a huge smile on her face, which was a little odd for where we were. She told me her adult offspring was inside and they wanted to see me. That was a good sign because I visited this patient during the week, and they were not awake. The patient sat up as best they could and said, "I wanna accept Jesus as my Lord and Savior and do Communion." Oh, the joy that filled the room and at the nurses' station—they knew what he wanted. I told the patient I had to run down to the Chaplains' office to retrieve my Communion kit. Some of the nurses also wanted to partake after the patient was served.

It was a special event because as the patient repeated the "Sinners' Prayer," the sun began to rise as Communion was served. The patient thanked me several times and added that their mother had been praying for a long time, "but I just wouldn't listen." I stayed with them for a while longer before excusing myself to serve the nurses. I had to be present for the Chapel service that morning and made a mental note to follow-up later. I went to visit that patient a couple of days later and learned they passed away peacefully in the middle of the night. The mother left a thank you note at the nurses' station to which I held on to for a long time after completing this program.

My interest in completing the entire year began to wane. Going in everyday became a monotonous chore because it felt like I was constantly in battle with someone. Dr. O. started talking to me about pursuing a doctorate degree, but I was a bit hesitant because I hadn't been out of school an entire year yet. It did have an appealing ring to it, even though I gave a few excuses. Dr. O. was persistent and when I offered my last excuse—I'm going to wait until I'm 35. "You'll be just about finished by then," Dr. O. retorted. This gave me something to think about. I prayed about the concept of pursuing another degree. I talked it over with Tihira to see how she felt about it. Tihira said, "Do it! Do it! I'll have a big brother who is a doctor!" Done deal. It set me on the path of achieving what spoken over me by Drs. Toby and Proctor during my undergraduate years.

I planned to call Dr. O. to tell her my decision, but she called to tell me she was done with the Residency Program and was submitting her resignation. It turned out that the demands were proving to be too much, and it was no longer a priority for her. I promised not to say anything until it was announced.

It felt very strange being there without Dr. O. When it was finally announced to the rest of the group, some members were upset as if someone violated them, personally. A few questions came my way as if I had something to do with Dr. O.'s decision to leave, which I did not. I finally said, "Maybe this is not where her heart is anymore." That was like blaspheming. One of the other male members had a weird look on his face to which I took note of.

I sat with that male member in the cafeteria and we talked for a while. After a few awkward moments of silence, he said, "You're next." I was thrown off a little because I had not given much thought to leaving the Chaplaincy program at that point. There were things brewing in the background of my life beyond this program, which I had to balance some things before I could start making moves.

A lot can be said about God's timing, but I will say God's timing is perfect. It was time for me to move on. I started searching for a job when someone told me the child protective agency was conducting a mass hiring and where to apply. This was great because I needed to be able to be around for my sister more. I updated my resume' and applied for one of the positions and waited to hear from them. I didn't try to overdo it by applying to multiple agencies because my schedule was already tight, and I didn't have time to run all over Atlanta for interviews. I knew what I needed to do and why it had to be done.

Meanwhile, I submitted my admission's application to begin my doctoral studies that summer. I was really excited by the prospect of starting this program because it would allow me to participate in an area I was interested in, Pastoral Community Counseling. I also felt it would serve as a good example for Tihira and others.

Things were in motion. I had to allow them do what they were supposed to do. I was accepted into the doctoral program, and was offered a position in the Department of Family and Children's Services (DFCS) in Fulton County (GA) to which I accepted. The pieces were coming together. I left the Chaplain Residency Program a month or so early. My mother decided to move to Georgia to be closer to Tihira. My mom and eldest brother made the arrangements for this move before the school year started for my younger brother and sister: Roy and Connie. Tihira was excited because this gave her a chance to see mom more often. I started training for my new position before my mom and the younger siblings arrived. We were able to move into a better apartment in Cobb County, GA. Tihira was able to see mom biweekly or more if she needed/wanted to, and she was in a new area.

Not long after moving to Cobb County, I decided to move into a townhome in Paulding County (GA), in a quieter area, because I grew tired of the congestion of inner city life. I had to drive more because of the type of work I was doing. This moved help me to avoid sitting in traffic during the rush hours. The bonus of this move was the peace and quiet I needed to study. But the main reason for this move was to give Tihira a better opportunity to live and learn in a different setting. She seemed a little hesitant at first but started making the needed adjustments.

I cannot remember the exact reason, but Mom and my two youngest siblings moved to Paulding County to be with Tihira and me. It seemed like a promising idea at first, but some days seemed off as time moved on. I tried to put my finger on the problem and had to consider some of the struggles and discussions Tihira and I had before and after this move.

One of the revelations Tihira and I discovered was we could not fix the past. We had problem after problem, and we could not seem to work them out no matter what I tried. Tihira challenged me on just about everything I asked her not to do. I could not understand why this was happening and why. One night, after learning that an adult female had been filling Tihira's head with a lot of foolishness about she (Tihira) not having to listen to me because *I was only her brother*. I not only confronted Tihira but that adult as well. I wanted to know what their angle was (motivation) and how splitting my sister away from me would benefit her. I'll have to admit, I didn't put up with a lot of bullshit when it came to my little (baby) sister, whether Tihira agreed with me or not. A number of times people saw my dark side when they should have left it asleep. Needless to say, I didn't have any more problems with that person because I didn't believe a word that came out of their mouth. I let it be known, in not so gracious terms, I wasn't with the tomfoolery. PERIOD.

I sat down with Tihira to see if we could straighten some things out. Tihira finally told me she was angry because "You left to come here [GA]." This was my opportunity to explain what I tried to do and what stopped me from achieving it. But Tihira didn't want to hear my explanation because she was irate. She asked why I didn't bring her back to Atlanta when I went home for my father's funeral. I explained I did the best I could after the accident and was relieved she wasn't in the car at that time because she would have gotten hurt as well. "But we're here now. Why can't we move forward now that you've told me what's really going on?" I asked. Tihira paused for a moment and said, "But I'm not finished." Oh boy, I thought. She was about to let me have it and I knew it because our personalities were so much alike, and she wasn't going to let this opportunity go without speaking up.

I was not ready for what Tihira had to say. "You left me…" was repeated several times as I sat there listening. "First, you left the house. And then, you left the state. You didn't care about me because you didn't tell me you were leaving until the last minute," she declared. Without going into too many details, I felt like Tihira wanted me to suffer as she suffered. I understood why she felt abandoned and cast aside by someone she really loved. By the end of that night, Tihira was still angry. I gave her space, but she never recovered, I believe.

The last move I made was transferring to Paulding County for work, so I could be closer to home. My relationship with Tihira was (and is) not the same and there really wasn't much I could do about it. I did everything I could to bring us to a place where we could restore our sibling relationship someday. My primary responsibilities at that time were to keep Tihira safe, to teach and help her as best I could. I learned the hard way, parenting your siblings is risky business. You have to take the good with the bad and pray for the rest.

It really hurt when Tihira decided to leave home. I punished myself for several weeks because I felt as though I failed her and made her life miserable. I respected the fact that she chose to leave home. This was when I started learning about causing offense to others because my expectations of them might not match those they may have for themselves. To my chagrin, I would have to see this several times before I was able to stop placing expectations on others because *I* ended up disappointed.

* * * * *

The next few years were challenging for me in that I was working full-time, going to school full-time, helping to rare my younger siblings, looking out for others, serving as Youth Pastor, and trying to have a "social life." Something had to give. I was spread too thin, and it was showing. Once again, my focus was not geared toward the latter. Whenever I did go out it was usually for someone's birthday or a special occasion. My life was full yet empty in many aspects. I became jaded towards the concept of dating and what people *really* wanted out of a relationship—was it love, companionship or just help. I became frustrated and really did not see the need to waste my time and energy, which were already stretched thin, and engaging in empty, senseless relationships.

Walking in various roles wasn't a problem for me, it was having to conceal a couple of them—namely my marital status and the fact that I was doctoral student. This hiding caused me the most grief. Unfortunately, my job and church were the two places I could not openly discuss my statuses because either someone felt "some kind of way" or they wanted me to do something. Either way, it was a-no go.

Unfortunately, it was made clear as to why I could not talk about school openly at work. I worked in a county that was still considered rural and European Americans were the majority in terms of population. A lot of my colleagues held college degrees, with the highest being a master's degree. I observed what happened when people discovered a couple of my coworkers were in school. One was pursuing a Master of Social Work degree, while the other was pursuing a dual-master's degree in social work and psychology. One was given "special provisions" to adjust how their duties were carried out, while the other was left to figure it out on their own. At first, it appeared that the dual-majored student was not advocating for themselves. That was far from the truth according to them.

I learned more about the minute details of the work-place discrepancies without asking. A co-worker came to talk to me about the program I was in and how it was going. I did not give any indication of what level I was studying on nor my actually progress therein. They commended me for going back "to get that master's" and encouraged me not to expect too much support from "the higher ups." I was curious so I asked what was meant by that statement. I was reminded of the vast practice of favoritism that was clear and widespread in that agency. I took heed to this warning and held onto my status for as long as I could.

It was not a good time for me when the administrative team finally discovered I was pursuing a doctorate degree. I went to Florida for an on-campus class and somehow my status was revealed. Once that happened a lot of transgressions occurred, and no one did anything about them. I had been approved for this leave months prior to its date and I was careful to satisfy my responsibilities before I left. I was also transitioning to another unit and could not leave things undone before then. I received a call regarding work while I was away. This was unusual but I answered the call, anyway. I indicated that my work was completed, and that was the end of that call. Yet, I received another call stating I did not do so.

Things were really shady when I returned to work. Folk welcomed me back and smiled in my face, without say a word. The agency was switching information systems and a lot of work had to be done. Each worker had to manually enter each client's information. I spent four to five days doing just that. I was caught totally off guard that Friday morning.

As I said before, there was no indication something was wrong nor that I was in trouble. But I was so wrong. The administrative team hatched a plan to get rid of me for something I had no control over—a "supervisor's" actions or lack thereof. I was called into a meeting with two supervisions (my new supervisor and current supervisor), a lead worker and the administrator. I was thrown off because this meeting took place in the middle of the morning and no one said anything prior to me being called into the office. Needless to say, I was immediately told: "You neglected your duties before you left." I was confused at first because I did what was required. Not doing so would have placed people at risk, and that wasn't something I did. Afterall, this was not my first trip to Florida to attend classes. I was always mindful of important dates and kept track of them on a chart. I was told steps were taken to have me terminated. I froze for a moment before asking the reason for this decision. Once I was told, "dereliction of your duties," I went the hell off. "So, this decision was made before I questioned?" The administrator snapped they didn't have to "because the documents weren't filed, and that was your responsibility." I was flabbergasted and knew nothing I said would have mattered at that point. I asked to be excused to retrieve my laptop to show them when those documents were last accessed, to whom they were given to for approval, and what day the said documents were submitted to my supervisor. None of this seem to matter.

This meeting was not going right for me. Once I tried to clear the air as far as my so-called "dereliction of duties" were concerned, it pretty much gave me permission to let loose. "Well, if I'm going, I'm taking some [people] with me," I announced. "You can say many things about me but calling me liar for something I did not do is something I will not stand for. I told you what I did before I left and now I'm left holding the bag?" I asked. I was given no response. "But oh, you don't think your precious Supervisor would've never missed something like that," I said as sarcastic as I possibly could. Silence. "But they did!" I snapped.

I turned to the new supervisor and asked, "Was that the reason for your call when I was away? The other supervisor didn't tell you anything, did they?" That supervisor was beet red in the face and just stared at me. I warned her about the blatant favoritism that had been all but ignored for so long— "Check out how the cases have been distributed on the unit you're inheriting."

I turned my sights onto the administrator and said, "Ma'am, you do what you feel you must do, but I'm telling you right here and right now: I love a good fight, especially when I did nothing wrong. No one thought to go over to the court to check if I submitted those documents? No one thought for just *one* moment that my former Supervisor was negligent and did not tell someone about the court date and where the court documents were?" Once again, silence. I asked if they were done with me "because I'm going to go get copies of the documents as soon as I leave this meeting." Everyone's face was beet red because I was telling the truth and intended to stand on that truth. The administrator said an investigation was underway and a decision would be made upon its completion. "You will continue to work those cases, along with your new ones, until this is straightened out," she snapped.

They watched me walk to the next building where the court clerk was located. I retrieved the stamped cover pages of the documents in question and brought them back to the administrator, who took them without saying a word.

Situations like that demonstrated what my family meant when they said, "Leave them white folks alone," each time I came to Georgia as a child. I felt tension in the office because the new supervisor started sniffing around her unit. She saw the discrepancies in how cases were assigned and redistributed them in such a way that was fair and balanced. However, this supervisor was overheard saying something foul about my studies to which they later denied. The new supervisor told me they admired my guts "to stand up for yourself like that. Glad I'm not a target." I assured them they were not there for the moment. They almost swallowed their tongue.

Sometime later, the Administrator called me into their office again. I was instructed to give my old cases to the new supervisor and staff them with the new case manager. They never told me the outcome of the so-called investigation nor apologized until years later once we both left the agency.

A couple of weeks later, I found a typed note in my chair saying, "The documents were found in a box left in the supervisor's office." I knew, immediately, what box this note was referring to. I thought it was funny because that box also contained other documents that were left behind. I never received an apology or a "my bad" from anyone. I just kept on doing what I needed to do and watched out for other opportunities.

My time with this agency was winding down and there was no way around it. I knew my next move had to be within the mental health/counseling field because I was so disconnected from the child protection system and was doing the bare minimum. One of the mental health providers was making their rounds, updating case workers on the services they were providing to our clients and families. On this particular day they saved me for last, which I didn't think much of because they were providing services for several of my colleagues and me.

They approached me with a big smile, saying, "Boy do I have something for you." They asked to speak to me in private, which I agreed to this unusual request. They asked about my educational background and some of my professional goals. Once they heard my explanation, their face lit up with excitement. They told me about their agency and how my expertise would be a viable asset. They invited me to join their agency. I clarified that I did not want to do case management stuff anymore and asked for more information about this position before I accepted/declined their offer—I wasn't about to leave this stable job without another one lined up. They told me they would get back to me in a few days.

A few days came and gone without a word from the person from that agency. I didn't think much of it, only that "they're full of it." Another day or so went by and that agency representator was back making their rounds. Same as before, they saved me for last and we stepped outside, again. They asked me if I had a chance to consider her proposal to which I did and shared that I was ready to do something to advance my career. I asked what this proposed position entailed. They excitedly stated they brought the description this time, which included in their offer— "Oh yes, we want to compensate you as well as supervise for your licensure." They explained what the position was, CORE therapeutic service, my role on the team and its requirements, my pay, and my caseload. They asked me to think about this offer and get back to them.

I considered this offer prayerfully and decided to give it a try, because it seemed to be a step toward building my counseling skills and obtaining my licensure (Licensed Professional Counselor or LPC). I took a leap of faith, accepted the position, and then submitted my resignation to the child protection agency.

*****

I learned a lot in that next year or so. I went from one agency to the next that provided both CORE/IFI, which stands for Community Outreach Routine Evaluation and Intensive Family Intervention. As all this was happening, I was finishing my doctoral program and traveled to Florida several times in the process. Not only did I successfully complete my classes, but I also finished my doctoral dissertation. Writing and defending my dissertation was an eye-opening experience. My Dissertation Committee pushed me, while they dealt with turmoil within their group. One of my chairpersons encouraged me to focus on writing as they worked out the kinks. I did as I was advised and reached a place where I became frustrated and angry because of the information I discovered as well as the political climate at that time. I decided to sit out one term as I got my head together. In the end, I dealt with my irritations by refocusing my energy, while compiling and presenting the information I gathered as best as I could.

Although I had never done anything like a dissertation before, the process was not only interesting but grueling to say the least. Apart from the numerous rewrites, I started seeing what each of the Committee Members wanted in their particular areas of expertise. There were several layers to this process and I knew I had to work hard in order to be successful.

The first level I had to pass was the Dissertation Prospectus. This phase served as the roadmap to the rest of this journey. Although it was not absolute in that it could change as I continued writing and researching, it was still a vital step of the process. My Committee Members had to agree and approve it before I could move forward in this process.

Once I was finished drafting my Dissertation Prospectus, I had to pass what is called a Proposal Defense. In the Proposal Defense process, and the document itself, you must include a brief Literature Review and state how you intend to complete your testing as well as have a full understanding of the problem you are analyzing. This portion was critical because it helped me to remain focused on my topic. I was informed of a new Committee member coming aboard and was introduced during our monthly teleconference. It turned out that this member was an expert in the methodology portion of this process and was labeled as "thorough and resourceful." My Prospectus Defense was scheduled to take place in Sarasota, FL.

I was somewhat nervous because I had no idea of what was to come. My Committee Chairpersons were wonderful and very supportive. The first Chairperson, who was with me before this leg of this journey began, assured me that I was ready because I "already know your stuff (information)." Both Chairpersons told me how this defense would go. They also assured me that they would not have scheduled it "if we thought you weren't ready." This helped me immensely.

On the day of the Prospectus Defense, I was ready to get over it with. I had written several drafts and felt I couldn't do much more until I passed this defense. I focused on relaxing. The

Committee was waiting as I entered the room. I was formally introduced to the new third Member. We quickly got into the defense. The Chairpersons asked several questions and I answered as best I could, being that this defense dealt with things that were future oriented. Then, to my surprise, the third Member took control of the Defense. He peppered me with a plethora of questions that required detailed responses regarding the theories that were to be used in my dissertation. The entire process lasted an hour and thirty-eight minutes (a number I still remember). My Prospectus was approved. Then, I was off to begin the writing portion of my dissertation.

* * * * *

I left the child protective agency in May of 2010 to join a new mental health agency because it showed great promise, at first. It wasn't until I was all the way in that I started seeing inconsistencies and contradictions as to how things really worked in comparison to what I was told. For starters, I did not have a full caseload, even after the first month. And then, a question about my money came up. In hindsight, I should have done this part-time at first. But I was over the *hustle* of two and three jobs at that time. I did that when I was younger and felt that my experience and education should have influenced my compensation.

A lot was learned during this time and I discovered, the hard way, how people will use you for what you have (your credentials, etc.). There was a core group of us who earned so much money for this agency and were willing to work long hours as well. It became clear that leadership did not know what it took to sustain and grow an agency. The owner began showing signs of greed and desperation once the heat started to increase from the state. An audit of our notes was conducted, and we failed miserably. It turned out we were not taught how to document properly and the owner was the one who taught us how to do so. In the end, many of us were abruptly "let go" as if it was our fault.

Things took a turn from bad to worse. My last day at this agency was February 10th, 2011, and I was hired by a reputable agency that had been around for many years, soon after. This agency hired me to do more clinical work, and I earned more money doing so—almost twice as much as the former agency. I had a wonderful supervisor who supported and encouraged me to grow as a clinician. I was assigned to provide therapeutic counseling with children/youths and their families, assessments, and other services as well. I was constantly busy, which was great because I was making a difference in people's life. However, I was not aware of the trouble this agency looming over the horizon.

There was a change in leadership as I was coming aboard. Unbeknownst to me and many others, this leader's role was to close up shop, smoothly and quickly. A number of my teammates and I were classified as "money earners" because we were conducting at least three to four assessments every other week in addition to our regular caseloads. Full assessments were 25 to 50 pages long, and the templates we used were not complete because every family's situation was different. The most that was provided were general subheadings. Each assessment, regardless the type, meant nice bank. But when the walls begin to shake, they crumbled quickly.

Meanwhile, I was diligently at work on my dissertation. My Dissertation Committee and I worked tirelessly to ensure that I was working efficiently. Coming off the heels of a successful Proposal Defense, I felt more confident in the work I was doing. My

Committee grew more and more impressed with the material I presented. This caused them to start giving me additional information to absorb, which excited me because I was (and still am) an avid reader and did not mind doing what they suggested. I did not try to restrict the amount of information I read because the Committee Members made sure I did not go into "information overload."

    I had only one instance where I did not make the connection with a repeated directive: Include the second, Pastoral Counseling. I knew from the beginning I would be working with two theories, but I forgot to include the second one as I continued writing. The Members reminded me to incorporate the second theory before I could move onto the next chapter. I kept submitting drafts to which were "kicked back" with the repeated theme: "You're missing information. Please complete before resubmitting." I couldn't catch on to save my life. "That's it!" I declared as I sat straight up in my bed and rushed to my computer one night. I worked on incorporating the second theory for about a week or so before submitting it once again. My Committee was pleased with the information submitted, and then instructed: "Save this draft and cut it down." I had no problem with that directive and happily chopped it down.

    The final phase was the most demanding part of my doctoral journey. My Dissertation Committee and I meticulously combed through my work to ensure that I did not miss anything based on my approved Prospectus. I had written and submitted countless drafts and had grown tired of this process. You could have knocked me over with a feather when my Committee finally told me it was time for my Final Defense. But that did not stop the readings and rewrites, though. "It's not final until we sign off," the

First Chairperson cautioned. The date was about month out and I was so ready to get it over with. I was not nervous about the content because I read and re-read it so many times that I couldn't help but to know it. There was one last directive given before the Final Defense: Send it to an editor. My good friend, Glennisha, took the helm and finished it in about a week or so. She did an excellent job and anxiously waited for it to be accepted along with me.

As the appointed day drew closer, I checked and rechecked my hotel reservations, calculated and recalculated monies needed for this trip, and scheduled a check-up with my auto mechanic a couple of days before my departure. I recall being on edge most of the time. I knew the information but it was in the dark as to what was going to happen during the Final Defense. Anticipation had mounted and I had to let that go because I had no way of determining what the Committee would do or ask for.

On the day I was preparing to drive to Sarasota, Florida, I was restless, but still had an enormous amount of energy. Many things went through my mind as I checked and double-checked my to do list. My mom and others were praying for my success since I had been distracted as could be.

I left Hiram, GA at nightfall. I was excited like a child on the last day of school before summer break begins. I called one of my classmates, Dana Taylor, whom I now call my "Precious Doctor Sister" or PDS (and I'm her Precious Doctor Brother or PDB), for encouragement and prayer. PDS said, "You got this! Just think of it as you are crossing the burning sands of a fraternity." I got excited again and drove on through a rainstorm not worrying about anything.

I arrived in Sarasota in enough time to check into my hotel, grab a bite to eat and rest for a while. Sleeping was out of the picture because I was too revved up, even after that 10-hour drive. I worked on calming my nerves or at least presenting as composed. It was a long, painstaking two to three hours of waiting. I set my alarm for 45 minutes before I had to be on campus and laid down with my eyes shut.

It was time to get up and do what I had been preparing for five long years. My moment of truth was quickly approaching. There was a lot of self-talk going on as I dressed and causally strolled to my car. It took approximately ten minutes to get to the campus, but it seemed as if I drove for hours, although I laterally did.

Once I arrived on campus, I quickly recognized there was a game of "hurry up and wait" occurring. I walked into the designated office and the secretary greeted me with a smile. She asked for my name before glancing at her calendar. "I see, you're here for you Final Defense. Congratulations!" she said. "Are you excite or nervous?" I told her both. She assured me I would be fine. "You're here. So, that means you're ready," she said in a supportive tone. She went on to say she had seen me around campus and I seemed to be "a serious student." She offered me something to drink because, "You'll either relax or go to the restroom," she laughed, which made me laugh. I was given a cup of coffee and a bottle of water—the coffee was decaf but accepted it despite the fact that I loathe decaffeinated coffee. I sat there ready to go. I had my PowerPoint on my jump drive and quietly practiced the tone of voice I would use. The secretary got a kick out of all this as I tried not to focus on her. I could hear the clock as the hand ticked to mark each grueling second that went by.

I started watching the clock because it was approximately five minutes after my scheduled time. The first Chairperson appeared and informed me that the Committee was finishing up a few things and needed little more time. I agreed even though I thought it was odd. I sat back, tried to relax, and did not look at the clock again. Moments later, I was summoned to follow my first Chairperson, who was in his usual jovial mood, into a room in the back of the office. I was given some time to set up my PowerPoint presentation as my second Chairperson informed me of the third member was present via phone conference. It didn't matter to me because he was still able to participate.

I was ready once my PowerPoint was connected. The first Chairperson assured me that my presentation did not have to be very long. Trust me, I remembered that as I outlined the important points of reference. I did my thing and took my seat. I was expecting to be interrogated as I was the first time around, but the room fell quiet for a few moments, and the "hurry up and wait" game continued. The next thing I knew, we were engaging small talk related to my dissertation, upcoming vacation plans, and where I lived. A few questions were asked here and there as I waited for the onslaught to begin. It never came. Finally, my First Chairperson asked me to step out of the room as the committee deliberated.

I took the same seat I'd sat in before. The secretary remained quiet for the first few moments before asking, "How do you think you did in there?" I swallowed hard and shrugged my shoulders. She giggled and waved her hand, while saying, "You got this because you knew your stuff." I agreed with by saying, "Yeah, you're right." But how did she know I really knew my stuff or not? She wasn't in the room, so how could she'd known? I sat there wondering what was going on in the other room.

The air grew more and more tense as each moment passed. Somewhere between the silence and the deafening tick-tocks of the clock, I felt as if I was in the twilight zone. My eyes repeatedly went from the clock to the hall from whence I walked a moments before. I heard laughter a couple of times but wasn't sure if it was my Committee or not. I tried not concentrate on reasons I could be rejected, because I'd heard of people being turned away. I began to hum "We Come This Far by Faith," and heard my mother's voice in my ear—"Everyday I'm leaning, leaning on the Lord." Suddenly, my first Chairperson appeared again with a grim expression on his face. He didn't speak but only motioned for me to follow him to the room, again. It was like walking their last mile.

I was invited to "Have a seat," once again. The room was somberly quiet. The Second Chairperson asked me to comment on how I thought my Defense went. I did not anticipate this question but said I didn't know. The Third Member, who was on the phone, posed a question regarding the demographics of the county used in my study. Once I answered this question the room became quiet again. My First Chairperson broke the silence by asking how this portion of my journey felt. "Painful." I declared. "Good," as he rubbed his beard.

The suspense was killing me because I didn't know what was going on or what was coming. I answered all questions briefly at first, and then, was told I could express myself freely, "The Defense is over." I talked for a few more moments because, quite frankly, I was sick of this belaboring stuff. I observed the two Members as they nodded their heads while presenting flat facial expressions. I couldn't read them to save my life.

After a few more minutes, which felt like hours, both Committee Members stood in unison, still not saying anything as they glared at me. They looked at one another for a second. "On behalf of my colleagues..." the First Chairperson began saying, and blah, blah, blah is what I heard thereafter. "We want to extend a big congratulations to you, Dr. Kasim Ali Sidney Jones, you have successfully passed your Final Defense!" All I could think of was: *Damn, he used my whole gov'ment name.* The Third Member said, "You're quiet! What's happening?" That's when I realized I did it— *I successfully wrote and defended my dissertation!* I froze for a few seconds because I didn't know what I was supposed to say or do. "Dr. Jones, did you hear what I said?" First Chairperson inquired. I saw them smiling with extended hands. I thanked them and shocked their hands. They all laughed and assured me it would sink in at some point. I remembered the gifts I had for them, and, to my surprise, they also had a gift for me. It was book on the history of Africa with their signatures.

In shock, I drifted past the secretary, who yelled congratulations, and lingered in the parking lot before getting in my car. My cell phone rang, snapping me back to reality, somewhat. It was my PDS calling to check up on me. "Is Dr. Jones in order?" she asked. "I think so. The Defense is over," I numbly said. I ended up in a local supermarket. I had no idea how I was there or why. I left the store with a six-pack (of beer) and a sandwich. PDS advised me to go back to my hotel room, have a beer, and then, call her back "Because I think you're in shock, Dr. Jones," and laughed before disconnecting.

I found myself driving in circles. I could not remember how to get back to the hotel. I called my best friend, Minnettia, to ask for directions. She laughed and told me she could not help me. "Did you pass? Are you a doctor, yet?" she pressed. Then, it occurred to me, "Yup, I'm Dr. Jones now!" The next thing I heard was screaming: "You did it! You did it! I knew yo ass had some brains up there!" We chatted for a while before I realized I had to call my mom to tell her the good news. My mom was elated! She dropped the phone as she screamed, "That's my baby!!! I'm so proud of you" she repeatedly yelled. I started crying tears of joy because it was finally over. My mom went into "Momma Bear" mode: "Did you get some sleep? You sound tired. Did you eat?" I had not slept in the past day or so, and I wasn't hungry. I agreed to try to eat and get some sleep, but I eventually checked out of the hotel early and went home without going to sleep.

*****

My family and I traveled to Florida to attend the graduation ceremony two months after my Final Defense. All of my hard work had finally paid off. This meant no more drafts to submit and no more defending. All that was left was the formal ceremony. I didn't want to participate in the ceremony at first because I was done with the Pomp and Circumstances. I just wanted it to be done. I decided to do it for my family and friends. They beamed with pride and was happy to that I completed this trying journey. I prayed about it and was convinced when three of my high school seniors at my church said they couldn't wait for us to take pictures together in our regalia. I became excited with them. Afterall, I did work hard for this moment.

Apart from my mom, my younger siblings, and other family members, my best friend, my Pastor and his wife, attended this ceremony as well. This was an occasion of occasions! I was thrilled that my younger sister, Tihira, was also there to see it through to the end. My uncle with whom I stayed with several times during this journey, he and his family was also present.

Everyone beamed with pride. But I was in a haze the entire weekend. I was happy to have achieved such an enormous feat but was somewhat saddened because my father and dad were not physically present to see me walk across that stage. My Pastor's wife asked why I looked so down. I told her I was happy but saddened by the absence of my dad and father—"This was something they dreamed of, one of their children earning a doctorate degree." She hugged me and said, "They are with you and will walk with you across that stage." Her words helped immensely. I listened for my name to be called before I stepped on the stage with my head held high. I was hooded by this woman with a gentle spirit. I did not know who she was at that moment. She whispered, "Congratulations. You've done well, son." I smiled for the rest of the ceremony. I later learned that woman was the University's President, Dr. Sandra Wise.

*****

My graduation euphoria did not last long! Just when things appeared to be on track, professionally, the bottom fell out. I had a huge increase in pay coming because of my recent educational attainment, which was also another incentive for me to complete my clinical hours and testing for the Georgia Licensed Professional Counselor (LPC) credential.

I was so energized and thought things were heading in a positive direction. Boy was I wrong! I returned to work that Tuesday and the vibe did not feel right, and no one was saying much. There was a looming reality headed our way: This agency is about to fold! I ran into my supervisor in the hall. They congratulated me on graduating the past weekend and reminded me about our Team/Clinical meeting the following day. I saw all of my clients and I planned to work on two assessments before this meeting.

It was a weird time because there were a couple of emails that stated all of our assessments needed to be finish within the next 48-hours. That had never happened before. So, I stayed home and worked on finishing all of my assessments, which was okay because I didn't schedule a lot on meeting days. My supervisor also sent out a message notifying us that the Director of the agency was going to make an appearance in our meeting. I didn't think too much of that. I was preoccupied with the task at hand, and I needed to use those few hours wisely.

By the time I was ready to get dressed for my Team/Clinical meeting, I could feel something was happening. I didn't know what it was, and I didn't spin my wheels on it too much because I already had a slight headache. Riding to this meeting calmed those thoughts a bit. I really enjoyed the work I was doing and the families I served. I stopped speculating for the time being and paid attention to the road because it was almost time for the afternoon rush hour.

The parking lot was full when I pulled up to the agency, which was not usual. It took a few moments for me to find a parking spot. I entered the building and had a sinking feeling again. I proceeded to my supervisor's office and took a seat. My supervisor started the meeting by announcing my recent accomplishment and congratulated me before my peers.

My Supervisor reminded us that the Director of the agency was going to pop in to update us on some developing issues.

Everyone around the table appeared unfazed by this and focused on the agenda. My Supervisor asked for the status of our assessments and what was happening on our individual caseloads. The Director entered the room as one of my peers was talking about a case. Everyone stopped to look as they took their seat.

My Supervisor broke from the agenda to hear from the Director. I don't recall how it was worded, but we were told the agency was closing in approximately 2 weeks—September 1, 2011. Everyone was startled because this was the first time we heard of the agency being in trouble, but there we were being told the agency was closing. The Director informed us that services were to cease the week before the closure date so we could focus on paperwork that was due the following week. That was the end of that meeting.

We were shocked by what was meted out moments before. No one had questions in the moment and my supervisor said they were going to meet with the Director to find out what was going on, because they didn't' know what was going, either. I thought this situation was crazy. Keep in mind, this agency had been around for quite some time and was highly reputable for the quality of service they provided. So, what the hell happened and why were things moving so swiftly?

Sometime after that meeting, I found out the State had been cracking down on agencies providing both CORE and IFI services because most of them were poorly managed. I didn't know what that meant at first because of the vague details most of us were given. On the flip side, both services required a certain level of structure and accountability for the notes, bookkeeping and accreditation. A lot of oversight and time was needed on a weekly, if not daily basis. I was later told by a state representative it was best practice for an agency to provide one or the other, "That way it is more manageable." That was enough for me.

I was both aggravated and outraged. Just as I was making plans for my household financially, the rug was jerked from under me. I worked very hard to not only provide the best services I could to my clients, but I worked diligently to earn my keep. All of a sudden it was over.

I finished my last assessment, and CORE notes, submitted all of them before the deadline. The accountants promised I would be paid for the work I rendered, which was about five thousand dollars. When I went to pick up my check on payday, I was shocked, and then, pissed off because I received less than half of what I'd earned. The accountant gave me the Director's number and email address to contest my earnings. The Director did not respond to my emails and calls at first. I saw them when I went to the office for something. They said they were working on compensating me for the work I'd completed. It turned out that most of the missing money was from the assessments I completed, which was $1,200.00 multiplied by three.

Weeks went by and still no money or anything. Suddenly, the email addresses and phone numbers were no longer in service. This agency not only closed its doors, but they owed so much money to over half of the staff. I had to face the fact that I was not going to see the rest of the money owed to me. I could not believe this happened again.

*****

I was presented with another opportunity to continue providing therapeutic services to children/youths and their families not long after this fiasco. My former Supervisor called me and asked me to join his team at another agency. I was apprehensive because I had been burned twice in the past year and wasn't in the mood to go through it again. My supervisor told me they would call me the next day so I could check the agency out. I gave it some prayer and thought.

I decided to accept my former Supervisor's offer because I trusted them based on my experience at the other agency. "I promise to keep you in the loop if something starts happening," he vowed. I came aboard and was assigned a full caseload almost immediately. And just as I begun catching my rhythm, my supervisor said, "Heads up." Not long after this warning, strange things started happening. First, there were problems with my notes. Then, problems with my caseload. And, finally, my checks started coming up short. It turned out that this agency was providing FI and CORE services. I had enough of being robbed. So, I interviewed with the child protection agency again and accepted a position on an intake unit in Fulton County, GA. I was going to do this temporarily, until I found another position as a therapist.

*****

The years went by quickly. I realized I had been with that child protection agency another five years. This bothered me because nothing changed for me since I graduated five years earlier. I wasn't working towards my goals, even though I managed to complete two books. I spent a lot of time helping others, while putting my dreams and goals on hold. This was something I never set out to do but there I was doing the very thing. Some might say it was a blessing to be a blessing to someone else. Yes, that may be true;

however, it does not negate the fact that I oftentimes regretted being a "blessing" in a number of situations I entered wide-eyed, bushy-tailed, and most of all importantly, willingly. I didn't mind at first, but it started bothering me in due time because of a few ungrateful souls. I had to pray about my willingness to say yes so often. We all have assignments we must carried out. I had to learn there is sacredness in not being accessible to everyone, all the time. I, eventually, learned there is a place and purpose for us, and every person and/or situation is not for us to take on.

Arriving at this place mentally, emotionally, and spiritually was not easy. I endured a lot of hardships and heartache. I faced unemployment several times, near homelessness twice, I lost or gave away almost everything I had, and have to scramble to get back on my feet. God brought me to a place where I had to do some real, deep self-evaluation, and introspection, which goes beyond shallow self-adjustments. God literally took me out of my confront zone before God would even speak to me.

Of course, me being human, I was frustrated, angry, and sad all at the same time. I couldn't understand why these things kept happening to me. The last set of events that sent me into my "2nd wilderness" experience, which angered me most because of how I was treated by others, really opened my eyes to a number of things. I went to work for one of those agencies that provided both CORE and IFI services. I took the job out of desperation. I was doing well but the red flags were there from the start.

I submitted my resume and all the other needed documents to this agency and received a call a few days later. The caller stated they wanted to schedule an interview with me by phone, which was odd being that the agency was within driving distance. On the appointed day and time of this interview, I received the call and proceeded with the question-and-answer portion with the person conducting the interview. I was told I should receive a decision within a few days. I asked the interviewer for their name and title to which they freely stated they were the owner. All of this took place that morning. I received another call before the end of the day offering me a position as a clinician.

Again, I must emphasize: There were signs of distress within this agency from the very beginning. I went through a rigorous training, which was lengthy and without pay. The following week I attended an all-day conference, and again, without pay. Some of the things said during this conference really caught my attention. The owner, for example, made comments like: "So what things aren't going the way some of you want them to go" and "If some of you want to be mad at someone, be mad at me." Those words were odd, and I didn't catch the context to which brought them out. I looked around to gauge other people's reactions. Some were a little put off, while others seemed unphased.

In the days following this conference, I started receiving my caseload drip by drip. Although my clients were over 15 miles away, I didn't mind because driving because it cleared mind between appointments. However, the problems began when I wasn't being paid for the work I was putting in with one client/family. I would visit them two or three times a week plus several phone calls. I expressed concerns regarding my compensation and was told the client's reauthorization was underway— "Continue seeing them and keep the notes updated."

I learned I was the only one consistently working with this family when there should have been a fully licensed therapist on the case, but they only went out every now and then. Things got worse when some of this agency's key personnel began behaving erratically. They perpetuated some of the most despicable acts towards hard working people, who tried to make an honest living. They stopped paying us on time, if at all. I kept meticulous records and, once again, I lost money, again. I did all that I could to recoup monies owed to me. I ended up losing my apartment, car, and income. I was distraught and wanted to lash out but there was no time for that. I had to scramble fast to figure things out. My god sister, Keesha, and her husband, Terry, opened their doors to me, and I ended up staying with my eldest brother, Willie, for a few months. God had other plans for me. Willie repeatedly said, "Fight your battles on your knees." It took some time and humility for me to get there, but this was at the beginning of my second "wilderness season."

One of my daily chores while living with my brother was job searching whenever I was not working as a substitute teacher, working with others in completing their dissertation, or finishing my third book. I delivered pizza when school was out and didn't care because it was honest work. In the meantime, I interviewed for an interesting position at the Veteran's Health Administration. My family and I prayed about this opportunity because I was at a point where I needed to do something different from what I had been doing. It was time for me to relinquish control over the things I had no control over to begin with. I was offered and accepted the position before I fully understood it meant relocating to another state and another region all together: Kansas. As a matter of fact, I didn't know exactly where Kansas was. I didn't care because I had been trying to get into the Federal System for years, and now I was responsible for only me. So, on the appointed day, I packed my things in my van and headed for Topeka, Kansas.

God gives us what we need, when we need it, and how we need it. I had never been far away from my family and friends for an extended amount of time. In fact, I had never lived anywhere other than the east coast. But God had a plan. I had to go to a strange place, work with a different group of people, while learning who I was and trusting God, completely. It was a strange adjustment for me because my closest relative lived in the next state, east bound.

I managed to make it through the holidays without a drop of homesickness. But tragedy visited my family on February 2nd 2019, when one of my nieces died (see the Dedication page). I was suffering from a severe sinus infection that was spreading throughout my sinus cavity towards my left ear. My doctor prescribed strong antibiotics and placed me on a "no travel" restriction before I learned of this situation. My brother, Duane, notified me of Desre's passing, while speaking from a 3rd party viewpoint. I was going to go back to Georgia, but Duane insisted that I stayed in Kansas because he didn't want me to put my health in jeopardy. I didn't like it but I remained in Kansas.

I wanted to return to Georgia, or at least the east coast, when I started missing events and situations—like illnesses and funerals within my family. The straw that broke the camel's back was when I could not get to my mom when she was very sick. I asked God to show me if it was time for me to go home. I could not make decisions based on emotions. I had to wait until my time had come.

I appreciated Topeka, KS because it was a good place for me to get myself together. I learned how to focus on caring for myself, stick to God's plan for my life, and the things that interested me. I was able to publish my third book, and paid off all of my Georgia debt. But I had to wait for conformation from God because I didn't move without hearing from God first. There were two opportunities for me to apply to the Atlanta site, but the first one wasn't my time. When the second one came, I jumped on it and headed back to Georgia at the end of June 2019.

Once I arrived in Georgia, I found that some things and people were no different from when I left nearly a year before—11 months and 4 days, to be exact. I had at least three reasons why I returned to Georgia. One of them didn't work out almost immediately. However, my mom and I were getting along great, which was the main reason for my return.

I had to work extra hard not to fall back into my old behavioral patterns. I had to set and maintain boundaries, which took some time. Many times, I found myself coasting back toward the things and people I worked so hard to get away from. But, eventually, I came to a place where I grew weary of believing in people and their ability to change, although I still believed in the possibility for change. I found myself gravitating toward my own need to heal. I started putting in the work that was necessary for my growth and elevation.

Part Three:

Redemption

"Shattered like safety glass but not shard."

Anonymous

Chapter Seven:

How Is It Done?

Now What's Happening?

"We're living in needed times," my elders would say. There were several things going on around the world as I wrote this and the following chapters. First, we had a pandemic that was killing thousands, if not millions of people worldwide. It's called COVID-19 or the Coronavirus. COVID-19 was much deadlier than the flu or the common cold. Public Health and the Center for Disease Control (CDC) implemented a number of safety precautions to reduce the number of people falling victim to this virus. There was a lot of controversy regarding these measures, and how this situation was being addressed. But that's a story for another day.

Then, there was the Black Lives Matter movement and racially charged civil unrest protests and riots in cities not only in the United States but around the world. What sparked these activities was the death of an unarmed African American man, named George Floyd. Mr. Floyd died by the hand of a police officer, who dug his knee in Mr. Floyd's neck, while three officers stood by and did nothing to stop it. As Mr. Floyd cried out to his deceased mother: "Momma, they're going to kill me," and "I can't breathe!" as heard on the video that a brave teenager recorded.

This event, as well as other activities that followed, not only triggered reactionary responses from people of color, especially Black people. I was also affected by these events. I could not talk about what was going on very much or watch the news. Winters

(2020) called what I was experiencing "Black fatigue," and described it in the following manner:

> ...I define" Black fatigue" as repeated variations of stress that result in extreme exhaustion and cause mental, physical, and spiritual maladies that are passed down from generation to generation. It is a deeply embedded fatigue that takes inordinate amounts of energy to overcome—herculean efforts to sustain an optimistic outlook and enormous amounts of faith to continue to believe "we shall overcome someday... (p. 33).

And, lastly, I was going through a bitter break-up with a woman I had been involved in an on-and-off-again "relationship" for roughly three to four years. Her exploits not only left deep scars, but a bitter taste in my mouth in terms of romantic relationships. I decided to take a break to heal following that break-up because it was acrimonious at best. I took myself out of a toxic situation after I finally arrived a place where she was no longer on my mind constantly (obsessively). Even though it hurt, I did not allow her to consume my thoughts, my emotions, my energy, nor my moods after my departure from that relationship.

It's ironic how things seem to work out the way they should, especially when we're not trying to control every aspect of our lives. I told a close friend I needed to spend time getting to know myself and communing with God more before COVID-19 reached the United States. I did not make those things happen. It seemed as if distractions popped up a lot (or I allowed them to), which led to me focusing on what others deemed urgent. But then, COVID-19 came along with its restrictions and isolative measures—wearing masks, social distancing, limited contact with others, telehealth, and teleworking.

To a great extent, those precautionary methods made it easier for me to concentrate on myself. I started working from home and only went outside for essential activities—grocery store, pharmacy, doctors' appointments, and an occasional ride just to get out of the house. I was a homebody long before these restrictions, but it gave me a reason to be alone with my thoughts, prayers, and this project. I had very few interruptions because I lived alone. Turning my ringer off on my cellular phone had not been an issue for a long time but it became necessary. I pulled away from many situations and people, focused on writing, and observed myself as much as I could. I also had the chance to evaluate a number of relationships to determine their place in my life and what needed be done about them moving forward.

Some of the things I observed during this time had been in front of my face for a long time, but I chose not to deal with them until they caused great consternation. I noticed how much effort I was putting into maintaining some relationships that were truly past their prime. I was reaching out a lot, trying to keep the lines of communication open when they should have been closed. Calling and texting people first, for example, became a chore. It was a clear problem when I felt tinges of vexation when people were slow in responding, if at all. Then, there were those who reached out only when they wanted/needed something.

Stopping to evaluate those behaviors as well as my reactions to them was essential because I had to develop and maintain boundaries in order to hold onto my sanity. I picked up what I'd started in Topeka, KS: being mindful of my needs, wants and dreams/goals. My priorities shifted from others being first to caring for myself in a way that enabled me to address my needs/wants sooner rather than later. I, then, began to learn how to lend my time and energy when it was necessary for me to do so, and not because I was *obligated to do so*.

My emotional responses, or lack thereof, ranged from intense displeasure to hardly moved, and the fact that racial tensions/protests were going on for a few months, I felt overwhelmed to numb at times. But what annoyed me the most was two-pronged: many people voiced strong opinions without practical solutions, and views were based on feelings not facts. I also noticed enormous amounts of energy, time, and attention was exerted almost 24-hours a day. Yes, protesting and making our voice be heard is essential because it has been an effective method used to effect change. However, not having a resolute solution only deepens division and injustices in this country.

I really didn't talk about the racial injustices a lot because these was too much going on, too many events that occurred, and it was so overwhelming for me. What's more, I had to listen to other people's opinions and tirades when I went to work and endured a plethora of racial slurs to boot. My anxieties began to escalate until I realized I didn't have to agree or disagree with anyone nor give my two cents. This made a significant difference because I was able to say, "I don't care!" and mean it.

I was asked if I cared about the plight of the Black man in America, "because you are a Black man." I immediately recognized questions/statements like that were provocations for me to engage discussions that really didn't lead to a productive end. In the time I spent in introspective mode, I learned not to respond to everything because a lot of it does not required a reaction.

Discernment, the ability to see what it is, is a viable tool. Every agenda is not mine—meaning, I have to accept the fact that all things and people are not healthy, good, or beneficial to/for me. Therefore, it's not necessary for me to exert energy to something that is not my concern.

As far as me being wounded by my ex-girlfriend, the one I genuinely believe is a sociopath, she exasperated the situation even more when she tried to provoke me into reacting in my usual way—arguing and playing tic for tact. I worked hard to break free from her grip. I stopped speaking to her on January 1st, 2021. Months later, something came up that required us to communicate to my very chagrin! When we spoke to one another, I had to be on my best behavior to avoid feeding into her insatiable need for conflict. I was mindful of this because, even though she deserved a little venom, which I dished out in very small increments, I would have been blamed for what was said or done. Although it wasn't pleasant for me, I knew it would serve me best if I spoke to her face-to-face.

True to fashion, this woman exhibited many signs of her usual abnormal behavior, which was flat affect as if I were not speaking to her at all, and making statements she thought would invoke a negative effect. She made attempts to deflect and irritate me with provocative statements and/or responses. I did not appease her by sticking to the purpose of why I met with her. This did not come from a bitter or angry place, because, like a blood hound, she would have picked up on it. It was purely an *information only* discussion to which we both needed information from one another. One of her statements almost caused me to lash out: "You need to just forgive, forget and move on." I calmly let her know I had already forgiven her, "but I will not forget." I walked away because I saw what was gearing up for useless banter to which I no longer needed to her. I was over her, her manipulation, and the extra drama she brought with her.

All of these situations helped me make one key point clear: I needed to put some work into myself. This does not mean things will not happen or my life lessons will cease. Not at all! As long as I live I will continue to learn and be tested. However, I must continue striving to be the best version of me that I can be. This entails learning who I am today and finding ways to move forward with living a healthier, productive life.

What's the Question?

"Is It Just Me or am I making too much out of all this?" I've asked myself countless times throughout my life. There were times when I could have been *over dramatic* and blew things out of proportion, according to my self-critic. But some of my observations were on point. I realized it was self-doubt trying to convince me to dismiss and/or discount what I saw and felt.

As I continued working on this project, I referred to the information I'd read, people I talked with or observed, it wasn't just me. Some of my experiences, feelings, thoughts, and behaviors were _not_ unique to just me. Many things are a part of life and there's no getting around it. But what a revelation to finally see! Coming to the awareness that a lot of the information that had been under my nose, meaning books, other materials, and experiences, contained keys to my resolve and my healing.

Based on this information, which is available to us all, especially to African Americans and people of color, there are sound connections to our experiences. There are a number of ways to describe this phenomenon; yet there are no easy, clear-cut way to address them. Therefore, I will do my best to bring some of this information together in a way that we, African Americans and people of color, can eventually help ourselves answer the question: *Is It Just Me?*

* * * * *

As I contemplated the direction of this book, I was prayerful that my efforts were in order. I checked in with my mom, who encouraged me to "get it, baby," to make sure I would not offend her. I shared my desire to look at how trauma was passed down in our family as well as other families, because I came across concepts that said trauma and other things *are* imprinted in our DNA and can be inherited (Baack, 2016; DeGruy, 2017; Eyerman, 2001; Jimerson, 2016; Van Der Kolk, 2014; Wolynn, 2016).

I was fascinated when I read these words: "During pregnancy, nutrients in the mother's blood nourish the fetus through the wall of the placenta. With the nutrients, she also releases a host of hormones and information signals generated by the emotions she experiences" (Wolynn, 2016; p. 27). I related to this statement because, according to the stories surrounding my conception and birth, my parents faced a number of stressful circumstances and had to make decisions that would have impacted their lives as well as the lives of others. I can only imagine how being in that position could have caused an enormous amount of pressure, which affected the baby (me) inside my mother's womb. Wolynn went further on to say:

> …These chemical signals activate specific receptor proteins in the cells, triggering a cascade of physiological, metabolic, and behavioral changes in the mother's body as well as in

> the fetus. …Chronic or repetitive emotions like anger and fear can imprint her child, essentially preparing or "preprogramming" how the child will adapt to its environment… In that sense, a child who experienced a stressful in utero environment can become reactive in a similarly stressful situation (p. 27).

This made sense when my mother told me I had always been an anxious person, even during childhood. Can you imagine how far back in my family's succession anxiety and other behavioral conditions had been present? When I looked at my siblings, my aunts and uncles, and others, I saw it for what it was.

Now, think for a moment. Can you imagine how many conditions were passed down from generation to generation? This is not just in my family. It is present in all of our families. Some would argue those "traits" are learned behaviors, but for the sake of time and debate, they may have a good point. But for now, take greatness, for example. It is said to be in our DNA (Jimerson, 2016). I'm with that because it's true. But what about the not-so-great traits? Aren't they a part of our DNA, too? But resiliency is another characteristic that can be found in our DNA, but how or why do you think this is so? Trauma and other ordeals had to occur in order for resiliency to be acquired. So, let's explore this concept further.

Many researchers and writers have investigated the meaning and the effects of trauma and resiliency within people of color, namely African Americans. For starters, Willis (2020) defined trauma in the following terms: "Trauma is usually a violent injury caused by an external physical, psychological or spiritual assault, force, event, or experience. This trauma can upset one's balance and sense of stability" (p. xxi). This definition is clear and covers a myriad of areas. DeGruy (2017) asked and answered the question of trauma in the ensuing fashion:

> So, what is trauma? Trauma is an injury caused by an outside, usually violent force, event, or experience. We can experience this injury physically, emotionally, psychologically, and/or spiritually. Traumas can upset our equilibrium and wellbeing. If a trauma is severe enough, it can distort our attitude and beliefs. Such distortions often result in dysfunctional behaviors, which can in turn produce unwanted consequences. Since even on traumatic experience can result in distorted attitudes, dysfunctional behaviors, this pattern is magnified exponentially when a person repeatedly experiences severe trauma, and it is much worse when the traumas are caused by human beings.... (p. 8).

Wolynn (2016) also explained what happens when a traumatic event occurs: "... [Trauma causes] our inability to articulate what happens to us. Not only do we lose our words, but something happens with our memory as well. During a traumatic incident, our thought process can become scattered and disorganized in such a way that we no longer recognize the memories as belonging to the original event" (p. 15). Menakem (2017) described trauma as a reaction: "Contrary to what many people believe, trauma is not primarily an emotional response. Trauma always happens *in the body*. It is a spontaneous protective mechanism used by the body to stop or thwart further (or future) potential damage" (p. 7). The fear or a threatening situation causes the body to react. Menakem continued onto explain:

> Trauma is not a flaw or a weakness. It is a highly effective tool of safety and survival. Trauma is also not an event. Trauma is the body's protective response to an event—or a series of events—that it perceives as potentially dangerous. This perception may be accurate, inaccurate, or entirely imaginary. In the aftermath of highly stressful or traumatic situations, our soul nerve and lizard brain may embed a reflexive trauma response in our bodies. This happens at lightning speed.
>
> An embedded trauma response can manifest as fight, flight, flee, or freeze—or as some combination of constriction, pain, fear, dread, anxiety, unpleasant (and/or sometimes pleasant) thoughts, reactive behaviors, or other sensations and experiences. This trauma then gets stuck in the body—and stays stuck there until it is addressed (p. 7).

Wright (2011) wrote, "Trauma is the response to any event that shatters your safe world so that it's no longer a place of refuge" (p. 189). A lot of trauma takes place in spaces we consider safe havens. Yet, Wright clarified,

> Trauma is more than a state of crisis. It is a normal reaction to abnormal events that overwhelm a person's ability to adapt to life—where you feel powerless… As a result of trauma, something happens in your brain that affects the way you process information. It affects it overrides your alarm system (pp. 189, 192; containing T. A. Rando's (1988) *Grieving: How to Go on Living When Someone You Love Dies*).

Therefore, one of the characteristics of traumatic experiences can lead to is resiliency, the ability to bounce back when people survive what they've experienced, no matter how injurious they may have been. Willis (2020) asserted the following statement regarding the fortitude and toughness, if you will, of African Americans through the years:

> The Black story represents one of the greatest survival stories of Earth's history. For us to experience the cruelty, brutality, and wickedness we encountered, and survive the experience with any amount of collective or individual sanity is a near-miracle. However, that survival experience did not occur without its consequences... (p. 2).

As we move on to discuss Post-Traumatic Slave Syndrome (PTSS), there are other key factors germane to our understanding of some behaviors and/or attitudes as well as their lineage/legacy amongst African Americans and people of color. There is a growing discussion regarding DNA and how behaviors, actions, and other traits are passed down from generation to generation.

It is believed certain characteristics and experiences (reactions) are imprinted within our DNA. Well, a number of writers, scholars, and researchers started discussing this information more openly in the recent years. DeGruy (2017) stated, "Recent research in the field of epigenetics has revealed that trauma can actually impact an individual's DNA, and the manifestation of the traumas experienced by prior generations can be passed along genetically to future offspring" (pp. 8 – 9). Other theorists named this phenomenon differently but they are essentially the same. Another writer asserted these words about passing trauma along to the next generation:

> ...Tragedies varying in type and intensity—such as abandonment, suicide, and war, or the early death of a child, parent, or sibling—can send shock waves of distress

cascading from one generation to the next. Recent developments in the fields of cellular biology, neuroscience, epigenetics, and developmental psychology underscore the importance of exploring at least <u>three generations of family history</u> in order to understand the mechanism behind <u>patterns of trauma and suffering that repeat</u> (Wolynn, 2016; p. 17, underscores mine).

Explanations such as these hit close to home because a certain pattern of trauma and suffering occurred in my family-of-origin, repeatedly, which tweaked my curiosity. So, I started looking at some behaviors and family stories without involving my mom right away. The amazing thing about my discovery was I observed a trait several years before this book, and the details were not shared with me until years after the fact. I thought it was strange but, now that information regarding its existence is becoming more available. This information was applicable to my family's situation, and it surely applies to the African American experience.

There are several conditions I'm speaking of is Post-Traumatic Slave Syndrome (DeGruy, 2017; Jimerson, 2016; and Willis, 2020), Inherited Family Trauma (Wolynn, 2016), Generational Trauma (Baack, 2016), as well as other enduring legacies. Being that this book is a part of a series, I will provide a brief overview of the African/African American experience, especially within families. I will also focus on some challenges, namely sexual trauma, and some of the effects on African Americans' overall well-being because it will add to what has been written thus far. So, let's start by looking at a statement Menakem (2017) avowed:

Trauma or no trauma, many Black bodies don't feel settled around white ones, for reasons that are all too obvious: the long, brutal history of enslavement and subjugation; racial profiling (and occasionally murder) by police; stand-your-ground laws; the exoneration of folks such as George Zimmerman (who shot Trayvon Martin), Tim Loehmann (who shot Tamir Rice), and Roy Bryant and J. W Milam (who murdered Emmett Till); outright targeted aggression; and the habitual grind of everyday disregard, discrimination, institutional disrespect, over-policing, over-sentencing, and micro-aggressions (p. 15, note: Micro-aggressions are relentless things people do to insult or dismiss us or deny our experience or feelings….).

How Did It Get This Way?

One of my favorite songs from the late 1990s is Lauren Hill's "X-Factor" (1998). I played it a lot when a young lady and I broke up back then. We really cared for one another but could not work out our differences. One of my favorite lines was: "Loving you like a battle and we both end up with scares….." As mentioned earlier, I was dealing with an ex-girlfriend, who was dragging an issue out for God knows why. Since our break-up on New Year's Day 2021, I've learned how to *handle* her better whenever she shows up. But the fact is, she knew how to get under my skin and tried several times after my departure. Like Lauren said, "I keep letting you back in (You back in). How can I explain myself? (I don't understand why). As painful as this thing has been, I just can't be with no one else. See I know what we've got to do (Yeah), you let go and I let go too (and I'll let go). Cause no one's hurt me more than you, and no one ever will…"

In a nutshell, we had been on an unhealthy, turbulent, emotional rollercoaster ride, which happens to be another great song, for three to four years. I finally made the decision to leave this noxious cycle and limit our interactions to a need-to basis. Sometimes people are not aware of how their brokenness affects them and others. And based on our last contact, no dealings with her is the appropriate response.

As I focused my attention on something more productive, my thoughts came to these questions: Why is it so hard for an eligible Black man, such as myself, to have meaningful relationships with Black women? Does being sexually assaulted years ago still affect me or cause problems in my life? Is it my fault it seems as if I cannot maintain a long-lasting, meaningful union? I grew tired of talking about this and was fed-up with kicking myself over it. So, I resorted to the best way I knew how to deal with tough questions: I prayed and read as much as I could about it. Much of my readings for this project increased my knowledge, my ability to forgive myself, and my willingness to strive to be the best version of me I can be.

*****

Let's begin with these questions: How did so many relationships amongst people of African descent in the United States of America become so thorny? Why does it seem as if a *good thing* ends so venomously and hurtful amongst African American and people of color? Although there are tons successful African American relationships, a lot of time and attention is diverted to those that are unhealthy—like a source of entertainment for some. There are countless African Americans, both men and women, who have been patiently waiting while still believing in Black love.

I don't intend for some of these questions and statements to be overgeneralized or wide sweeping because it certainly does not apply to everyone in the African American community. However, there are far too many codependent, toxic, unhealthy, emotionally enmeshed relationships wreaking havoc in a great number of lives, homes, and communities. Such relationships have cast Black love in a negative light not only amongst African Americans themselves, but for the world to see. Take some of these "reality TV shows," featuring African American couples, for example. As entertaining as they might be to some, they do several harmful things to our image and authenticity: 1. They portray Black love and relationships in a trivial light, 2. They give everyone, including African Americans, something that might confirm suspicions and/or views about Black love, 3. They teach our children, teens *and* adults how to mistreat, disrespect, and denigrate one another, 4. They lower the expectations and standards regarding Black love and relationships, 5. They keep a vicious cycle going, and 6. They teach others how to treat ourselves.

In his book, with a provocative title, *Why Black Men Love White Women*, Persaud (2004) wrote an insightful commentary with the hope that this *dysfunction* can be addressed and rectified in time. But for now, this author made the following observation:

> From the inception of slavery, blacks have been driven toward a visceral dislike for one another as well as themselves. And after four hundred years of oppression, repression, and exploitation, it is still prevalent in the black community. This dislike can best be described as a form of insanity or even disease, and there is a good argument for both (p. 49).

In a sense, this *dislike* was planted in our ancestors' minds in the way they were managed, treated, handled and controlled by others during and following slavery. In other words, these devastating ideas were forced upon them by others. It was advantageous for most slave masters/owners to cause our ancestors to feel discombobulated in order to create a false sense of insolence and contempt toward themselves, individually and as a group. Willis (2020) supported this position when he wrote, "Slavery put the finishing touches on the degradation and dehumanization process. Some social scientists say that slavery scarred and marred Black Americans and was the most defining experience in America for Blacks. ...Slavery had the greatest effect on disunity in Black families in America. We are still experiencing the effects from this situation" (pp. 31, 32).

    Our ancestors oftentimes used aspects of this "degradation and dehumanization process" to protect themselves and their children from threats and impending danger. Adult slaves had to resort to tactics that made the younger slaves seem less appealing to the predatory predilections of some white people around them. DeGruy (2017) shared a story of how a slave mother downplayed her daughter's blossoming physical beauty in order to shield her from their slave master's gazing (or grazing) eyes. In the end, "The mother's denigrating statements about her daughter were spoken in an effort to dissuade the slave master from molesting or selling her, and of course, no one would fault her" (p. 9). In that situation, the mother's words were made out of desperation because it was all she knew to do for the safety of her child. In a sense, the very act of demeaning her own child in of itself must have been sickening to her, but it was something she felt was necessary. "For hundreds of years," DeGruy wrote, "enslaved mothers and fathers had been belittling their children in an effort to protect them. "Yet what originally began as an appropriate adaptation to an oppressive and danger-filled environment has been transmitted down through subsequent generations" (p. 9). Think about that the next time you call your child out their name or degrade them. When we know better, we do better.

Many slaveowners and masters used sex as a means to control, intimidate, and dehumanize our ancestors into doing their bidding because many of them (our ancestors) did not simply go along with everything they were told to do. In other words, a lot of enslaves people of African descent did not roll over and comply without resistance or something, and the slave masters/owners knew this. Enslaved African and African American, both male and female, were sexually violated in many ways, and for many reasons. For starters, it was utilized to damage, dismantle, and compromise African/African Americans' sense of self in order to mold and control them; otherwise, it was to satisfy the reprobate minds of numerous individuals.

These vile acts were designed to ruin our ancestors' psychological, emotional, and spiritual foundations. For example, the phrase "young buck" was used to describe a healthy, strong, resistant African/African American young male. The "breaking of a buck" was a way to make that individual into a workable, obedient slave by demoralizing and conditioning him. Brown (2009) articulated the rationale for this practice in this way: "The humiliation our ancestors suffered was to demonstrate to the other captives what they would get if they rebelled, and to display the power the captors now had over them; to break them down mentally and physically...." (p. 21).

Certainly, we know there were countless methods that slave owners/masters used to suppress and inhibit our ancestors, but they used something that was revered to force them to do what they wanted them to do: They either used the act of sex itself or they damaged reproductive body parts of our ancestors. But this author went on to illustrate the depth of depravity some slave masters/owners carried out upon our ancestors in order to break, program, and dominate our ancestors, and/or to simply entertain and/or satisfy themselves:

> They [the African/African American men] would be sexually tortured with whatever object the tormentors could find lying around in the jungle or in their possession. Perhaps fire would do the job. Light a match to the private parts of the men or little boys to prove a point... These activities were the first part of the brainwashing of our ancestors to show who the superior and inferior race was.
>
> During the hike to the ships the crew had to stop and rest if the journey was too long. The slave ship crew would stop and some would sleep, some would eat, and others would take girls, no matter the age, and rape them, torture them and beat them just for fun, and not outside the presence of his comrades... But not just the girls were in danger of the perverted appetite of the captain and his crew. Little boy suffered the same fate... "...In addition, the rape and sexual abuse of African men and boys would also be a frequent occurrence. You can be sure that over the tens of thousands of days and nights of the Slave trade, no demented sexual fantasy was left untried upon the bodies and souls of the African Captive." He further states, "Rape, public and private, gang and individual, was *a primary form of*

> *disempowering a powerful and proud people*. It was usually the first act after all were rounded up and shackled and yoked. African men shackled, yoked, held at gunpoint could only look on as their mother, daughter, sister, wife, relative, friends were put through some of the most degrading acts a human could do to another. Children were sexually violated in the most brutal ways, often leaving them bleeding to death or racked with trauma… not to mention syphilis or gonorrhea (Brown, 2009; pp. 21 – 22, 23; includes an assert from S. E. Anderson, 1995; emphasis mine).

Keep in mind, these acts were employed to tear down the mind, body, and spirit of our ancestors in order to mold them into the ideal slave they wanted. Some slave owners/masters went on to destroy another important institution our ancestors valued: the family—which was another "…step toward successful conditioning of a slave was to break up the family," Willis (2020, p. 23) explained.

It's been said one of the ways our ancestors attempted to protect any semblance of family was not showing emotional attachments in the slave owners'/masters' presence because they "were separated and not allowed to develop a concept of family in most cases; [and] there was absolutely no respect for the emotional existence of the black family" (Willis, p. 26; Persuad, 2004, p. 18). This was mostly due to the slave owners' ability to sell members of a family for several reasons (debt, profit, loss, spite, etc.) and at any given moment. Stewart (2020) wrote the following in this regard:

> …Slavery's racial logic brought Blackness into existence as a human identity at the same time it brought forbidden

Black love to the African captives and their descendants exclusively adorned by its chain and whips. ...Experience of prohibited love are indeed legion across America's temporal and geographic landscapes of slavery, reminding us that, for nearly 250 years, enslaved African descendants in America, who Whites bought, sold, mortgage, gifted, and inherited as moveable property, had no legal rights, essentially—and certainly no right to pursue love, coupledom and marriage based upon their own somatic desires. ...love for them and their kinfolk was directly or indirectly *forbidden* through the often combined factors of sexual and reproductive violence and control, "misogynoir" jurisprudence and legal transactions, and the domestic slave trade and family separation (pp. 18 – 19; containing A. Kaye's (2007) *Joining Places: Slave Neighborhoods in the Old South*).

Gutman (1976) proclaimed some slave owners did recognize marriage amongst enslaved people of African descent, while others maintained control over the outcome of such unions:

> ...the sale of a spouse beyond a distance of thirty miles "was considered by the clergy equivalent to a divorce because the husband could not walk to his wife and back between Saturday at sundown and Monday at sunrise..." The separation of slave family members by sale or for other reasons led some sensitive owners to encourage contact between them (p. 287).

The latter sentiment was held by some slave owners, which was few and far between because, at the end of the day, it was about their economic bottom line. In fact, Brown (2006) asserted this statement about our ancestors' emotionality:

> …the slave master would deter any emotional involvement between any of the childbearing parties so that no bonds or feelings of protectiveness would occur within the men because then they would feel an obligation to try and protect his family. The slaves masters knew that if this were to happen, the strength of the could destroy control…" (p. 30).

In other words, some slave masters did not care about emotional bonds amongst the slaves because economics superseded emotive expressions and they didn't want to deal with an impudent male as he sought to protect his family (Brown, 2006; Willis, 2020).

To further demonstrate slavery's diabolical means to ensure that the African American family remained weak, vulnerable, fractured, and unstable, Brown (2006) posited: "By removing the African American male from the strong family structure, the family begins to break down. Just as a house with no foundation crumbles, so does the African American family" (p. 33). Does any of this sound familiar? Some slave owners' primary concerns were economics and control over their "property." Yet, Willis' (2020) depiction made this point abundantly clear when he wrote:

> Neither men nor women had the authority to make decisions concerning the family. Blacks learned to depreciate family life and family relationships, their families were broken up, and Black men were used as studs and sent from plantation to plantation. Slaves were even forced to have sex with each other for the purpose of producing babies, who were then snatched away and sold.

Black men learned to see their women as objects and to use for sex only. It was all slaves could do. Women saw men for a similar purpose. Those Black families that did exist were considered temporary, for any member could be sold away at a moment's notice... The practice of slave breeding often prevented Blacks from creating permanent relationships. Men and women were matched together for the purpose of producing offspring for the market... Slavery removed the sacredness of the sex act altogether (pp. 27, 28, 29).

If you see a decline in or a shortage of Black love, and/or an increase of other behaviors that some African Americans display, one cannot or should not help but to say, Ah ha! I'm not necessarily speaking from a judgmental or snobbish position because there are differences in each individual's perception of morality. However, when one stands in judgment of others, they cannot see things objectively, or clearly assess the situation to see where these actions/attitudes came from and why. Sadly, many sexual behaviors and other lifestyles can be traced back to not only the American chattel slave system but beyond.

How Was It Used?

Although I discussed some of the methods that numerous slave owners/masters used to condition our ancestors, let's explore sexual exploitation and abuse a further. There were some monstrous agendas many slave masters and other Caucasians held for our ancestors. First, they wanted to teach them *morality*, because "for many slaves, sex was a natural urge frequently fulfilled in casual liaisons" Blassingame (1979, p. 154) wrote, as if these "natural urges" were exclusive to "many slaves." Eventually, some slave masters and other Caucasians gave into their lust-filled, dissolute thoughts and *urges*, and carried out their sexual desires upon our ancestors. This author continued on to write:

> The white man's lust for black women was one of the most serious impediments to be development of morality. The white man's pursuit of black women frequently destroyed any possibility that comely black girls could remain chaste for long. Few slave parents could protect their pretty daughters from the sexual advances of white men. This was particularly true when the slaves belonged to a white bachelor or lived near white bachelors… Often through "gifts," but usually through force, white overseers and planters obtained the sexual favors of black women. Generally speaking, the women were literally forced to offer themselves "willingly" and receive a trinket for their compliance rather than a flogging for their refusal and resistance (p. 154).

Unfortunately, this type of behavior was common practice among many Caucasians. Sadly, as Persaud (2004) asserted, "Her humanity had no value, but her vagina often carried a high value—especially since it was unlimited" (p. 22). Not only were these forms of exploitation rough on our female ancestors, but they were also disrespectful toward the males slaves as well. Persaud wrote:

> …Entering slave quarters, the white man would walk past the black man and his children and defile any black female at will. The female could even be a child and often was. He would also warn the black man that the experience had better be good; and oftentimes the black male would pledge that it would be good, as if to provide the rapist a sexual guarantee. On the way out, the rapist would arrogantly

acknowledge that it was good and rub the black man's head. ...Indeed, not all whites owned slaves, so many whites did not have this evil, licentious luxury; still, one did not have to own slaves to be perversely nourished by the nectar of the black woman. Quite the opposite became true. Slave owners were known to lend out their 'girls' to friends and relatives. (p. 18, 21).

Sexual exploitation of our female ancestors, and oftentimes males, became sources of trade/commerce. Several Caucasians—slave masters, owners, and common folk alike—saw this as an opportunity to reduce our ancestors' precious bodies to things to be used as commodities, such as credit, settling debts, prostitution, and brothel house workers. It was what we call sex trafficking today. In fact, Jones-Rogers (2019) contended: "Historians of the southern slave market view it as corrosive, corrupting, sexually charged, and brutal, and many claimed it was considered too abhorrent a place for white women to visit" (p. 82). What was the outcome? Jones-Rogers explained: "...But [white] women chose to hire, buy, or sell enslaved people in or near their homes and beyond the formal marketplace...." for the use of prostitution or to service in "Negro brothel houses" (pp. 82 – 83). She also made this point: "Such incidents made it clear that the social and sexual disorder that characterized southern slave markets also pervaded slaveholding households" (p. 83).

Of course, we cannot ignore the degenerate desires that some of the white women held for our male ancestors because, they too, took advantage this "peculiar institution." Genovese (1974) illustrated this type of phenomena when he wrote:

> According to legend, antebellum miscegenation coupled white men and black women, and occasionally black men and poor white women, but rarely if ever black men and white women of the planter class… Despite the legend, white women of all classes had black lovers and sometimes husbands in all parts of the South, especially in the towns and cities…. (p. 422).

Other sources are now providing information indicating some white females saw our male ancestors as they were passed around as reproductive "studs" and wanted a piece of the action for themselves—like seeing candy being passed around while having a sweet tooth. Trying to imagine how white women were able to take advantage of male slaves was a stretch for me, at first, but one writer declared: "White women derived power from a variety of social and culture mechanisms including courts" (Foster, 2019; p. 78). Utilizing coercion, influence, and/or threats to get what they wanted were powerful tools they wielded. These methods made our ancestors fearful for their physical wellbeing, their lives, and the possibility of being separated from their families and loved ones. However, Foster continued on to explain this condition in the ensuing manner:

> White women of the planter-class were certainly able to wield power over black men—although all white women could coerce enslaved black men, given the legal and social settings in which they lived. Planter-class women might more easily and more believably have persuaded the community to view them as innocent victims of their sexual contact with black men. …Even women who may have been physically smaller and weaker than their victims may have wielded a powerful threat. The recruiter [of Black Union

soldiers] testified about "a young girl" who "got him (a Black male slave) out in the woods and told him she would declare he attempted to force her, if he didn't have connection with her" (p. 79).

Sexual exploitation of our female ancestors may have been more flagrant than their male counterparts, or at least that's how it appeared until recent publications were made available. The evidence shows that we should not minimize our male ancestors' sexual trauma and/or exploitation by the hands of whites, namely white females. One writer highlighted an explanation as to why this phenomenon occurred: "Some sources come to us from white men who had personal motives for characterizing white women as having engaged in aggressive sexual behavior with enslave men..." (Foster 2019; p. 70). Jones-Rogers (2019) wrote the following:

> The slaveholding household was a place of coerced production and reproduction, racial and sexual exploitation, and physical and psychological violence. It was a place where white southern women grew accustomed to the violence of slavery, contemplated the sale and purchase of slaves, and used the bodies of the enslaved people they owned in ways that reinforced their pecuniary value. The household became an extension of the slave market, and white women capitalized upon their access to both... (p. 83).

Many sources illustrate how young white males were groomed to carry-out deplorable sexual acts upon the Black female body. Huggins (1977) postulated, "White males were reared to be free sports: they were expected to sow their oats... most would admit the Southern white boy found his first sexual experience with a black woman" (p. 141). Point taken!

It was believed, and I emphasize *believed*, having sexual with enslaved people was not accepted in a number of social settings: "While sex with black women was frowned upon, and any man who had a reputation for *frequenting* his slave cabins was likely to encounter some social ostracism by his white neighbors..." (Huggins, 1977; p. 141). However, this feeble deterrent proved fruitless because the practice of *frequenting* the slave cabins was so extensive, which was evidenced by the number of mixed-race children present.

Back to how the young white males, most likely the master's sons, exercised "power" over our female ancestors. One would think these youngsters would have lusted after the female slaves their own age, but these little boogers' attention was geared toward the adult females, who were probably old enough to be their mothers. Huggins (1977) described this occurrence this way:

> The young white boy, beyond the first aches of puberty, having played his games of peeping at women in the outhouse, having played with himself despite the pain of it, would be possessed by his fantasies. His lust would be for a grown woman, not a frightened child like himself; a mother, not a sister. In the corners of the kitchen or the rooms of the house, he would pester her while she did her chores. There would be games of teasing and flirting. She played with him; he was such a baby, how he used to trouble her he was little. Thus, she could prick his soreness. It could be amusing to toy with the white boy and privately pleasing to know someone so seemingly helpless ached so much, to dominate youthful dominance. In time, the game

would play out, and she would take him to her bosom—or allow herself to be taken—it did not matter. There would be little tenderness to follow. He would walk away as most child-men do, feeling self-satisfied that a mark had been passed to make him a man-child…. (pp. 142 – 143).

Let me stop here and put "political correctness" aside. You mean to tell me our beautiful queens not only had to care for the slave masters'/owners' household, look after the slave owners' children, and then, stop what she was doing for couple minutes so Junior could get his rocks off! Wow! But wait for the kicker: Junior does this crap, walks away like he really did something, and she had to let him believe it. But oh, the writer continued on to say:

…a mark had been passed to make him a man-child. Yet he would harbor the faint suspicion that he had been mastered, and he might have a slight taste of shame because of that. She might keep the amusement alive for a while, but in time it would fade even if she stayed in the same household or bore the boy's first child (Huggins, 1977; p. 143).

The amount of debasement our ancestors, both male and female, endured to survive is incredible. Gratifying this "man-child's" lustful urges was only a part of the ill-treatment they braved in order to make it from one day to the next.

Even when someone did attempt to stand up for them, it really didn't matter nor did it make a difference. Genovese (1974) elucidated that "The frequent charge that slaveholders and overseers seduced or forced most of the young, sexually attractive slave girls appears to be a great exaggeration and an injustice to blacks as well as whites" (p. 422). In a sense, this was a way to introduce and spread another illogical rationale to support the thought of our ancestors being less than human—mere property. Genovese (1974) added:

> The sexual exploitation of black women, however outrageous, will startle no one. The problem is to explain why it did not go much further. The resistance of the women and their men, important as it was, does not provide a full explanation, for the restraint shown by so many whites must be also accounted for (p. 423).

I included this exert because I wanted to show why I repeatedly emphasized *some, a number of* and *many* whites' actions were deplorable and reprehensible because many white people did dislike these activities. There were white people who saw and acknowledged our ancestors' humanity.

Yet, more evidence is becoming available supporting the likelihood that our male ancestors were sexually exploited more than was reported in the past. "Wives and daughters of planter who formed these sexual relationships took advantage of their position within the slave system" Foster (2019, p. 83) wrote. But like countless young white males, many white females used their status to get what they wanted from our male ancestors. Foster wrote:

> …Daughters of planter could use enslaved men in domestic settings, however, retain their virtue, and maintain the appearance of passionlessness and virginity while seeking sexual experimentation. In other words, one of the ways that some southern women may have protected their public virtue was by clandestine relations with black men. …even suggesting that young women imitated the behavior of their brothers (p. 83).

This cycle of abusive behavior went on and on. White people of both genders helped themselves to human beings they "possessed." White females, both young and older, observed their fathers, husbands, brothers, sons, and I would add other females, taking advantage of our ancestors and used them at will; so, countless women did the same. Foster (2019) also included the accounts of former slaves to support this point:

> Hinton explained that some daughters of wealthy individuals on the American frontier, where interactions with male suitors were also relatively limited, as they were for planters' daughters, given social constraints, "knew that their brothers were sleeping with the chambermaids, or other servants, and I don't see how it could be otherwise than they too should give loose to their passions. Another man reported that the conditions of slavery not only brought about the "promiscuous intercourse among blacks, and between black women and white men" but also created a context that encouraged white women to be "involved" in the "general depravity." Harriet Jacobs wrote that daughter "know that the women slaves are subject to their father's authority over men slaves" and therefore "selected" and coerced certain enslaved men to be sexual partners. Although Hinton and Jacobs perhaps could not conceive of women taking the initiative on their own and understood them as following the example set by their fathers and brother, we should not that daughters seem to have engaged in the same behavior as fathers and sons, if not perhaps as many. Although clearly from Jacob's testimony, field hands were abused, we should not also note that house slaves, given their closer proximity to white women, would have fallen under special control (p. 83).

Other accounts revealed, "Many ex-slaves told stories about the seduction and rape of black women; others insisted that their masters permitted no such non-sense and that the black women lived without dread of white sexual violence" (Genovese, 1974; p. 422). Not only were our precious foremothers and forefathers used and abused, but they were also labeled animals, and oftentimes forced to *agree* with their corrupt slaveholders because they may have believed they could benefit somehow.

African/African American slaves were also viewed as "hypersexual," to boot. Harris-Perry (2011) illustrated the incongruity this label added when she discussed the absurd rationale used to explain or validate the perpetual abuse/misuse of African/African American women:

> **HYPERSEXUALITY** was more than a demeaning and false stereotype; this inaccurate portrayal was intentional. Myth advances specific economic, social, and political motives. In this case, sexual lasciviousness was a deliberate characterization that excused both profit-driven and casual sexual exploitation of black women. Emancipation did not end the social and political usefulness of this sexual stereotype. White men's "right" of access to black women's bodies was an assumption supported both by their history as legal property and by the myth of their sexual promiscuity. This myth meant that neither the law nor social convention allowed that black women might be victims in this arrangement. The rape of black women, like the lynching of black men, was both a deep personal violence and a form of community terrorism that reinforced their vulnerability and lack of self-ownership... The mythology of black women as promiscuous was important

to maintaining the profitable exploitation of slave society (pp. 56, 57; emphasis mine).

Many times, as we oftentimes see today, the perpetrators tried to say *she wanted it*, or *she liked it*. But Harris-Perry (2011) addressed this so-called hypersexual issue or promiscuity with a bit of history:

> The promiscuity myth has roots in Southern slaveholding society, which operated by a gendered social and moral code… African American women's lives and labors in the antebellum South contrasted sharply with this iconic womanhood. Black women were subjected to forced nudity during slave auctions. They often labored in fields with skirts hiked up. They were punished on plantations by being whipped in partial or total nudity. They were banned from legal marriage. The myth of black women as lascivious, seductive, and insatiable was a way of reconciling the forced public exposure and commoditization of black women's bodies with the Victorian ideals of women's modesty and fragility. The idea that black women were hypersexual beings created space for white moral superiority by justifying the brutality Southern white men… Not only were black women described as animalistic and aggressive, but they were also sometimes cast as vile seductresses who lured white men away from their chaste fame counterparts (pp. 55 – 56).

This label, hypersexual, was pinned on our male ancestors as well. Foster (2019) made this point clear when he wrote: "While the objectification of enslaved men's bodies could appear to some as a harmless appreciation for the beauty of some enslaved men, overall, the same impulses that gave rise to eroticizing enslaved men's bodies fueled the forces of enslavement that were held in place by physical abuses and exploitations" (p. 17). Once again, we have to take note of who controlled the flow of information. White men did not want to be seen as unable to manage their own household or protect their image. Foster insisted:

> Many of the sources that allow us to recognize the troubled nature of intimate relations between white women and enslaved black men are problematic. Some of these sources come to us from white men who had personal motives for characterizing white women as having engaged in aggressive sexual behavior with enslaved men: divorce cases filed by angry [white] husbands and sexual assault cases provide commentary bout white women's sexual agency in a manner that was designed to attack their character in order to skew the outcome against the women (p. 70).

As we consider the treatment of our male ancestors, let us not forget the mindset of some slaveholders—slaves were property, much like cattle. So, we must also accept that male slaves were frequently violated, too. Foster (2019) explained it this way in regard the male's slaves' "manhood":

> The bodies of enslaved men were sites of contestation over the definition of black manhood recognized by white men and women, as well as enslaved people. Masters and overseers punished those bodies in sexualized ways, violating private dignity and emasculating men trough public exposure. Physical tortures also damaged the men's bodies and rendered them less physically able to enact

manly norms of capability. ...Enslaved men's bodies were sexually violated, exploited, and abused, but that would only deepen the physical ways in which manhood could enacted. Bodies were sources of intimate pain, but... they could also continue to be associated with pleasure and power.

Winthrop Jordan notes the conflicting messages embraced by Anglo-American culture as it sought control and circumscribe the bodies of enslaved men and women, on the one hand, voicing repulsion for Africans, framing them as beastly, ugly, and unappealing, while on the other hand, viewing them as hypersexual. Anglo-American culture had a long-standing view of black men as "particularly virile, promiscuous, and lusty" (p. 30; containing Jordan, 1968; p. 151).

A disparaging impression of this entire situation is what Persaud (2004) called "the soiling of the black woman." I would also say this had a devastating impact on relations between male and female African/African Americans. Although the following quote sends pangs through my being, it is something that has to be shared in this context:

> This was the beginning of the soiling of the black woman in America. It was especially devasting when seen through the spectacles of black men. The experience painted an unflattering picture of her that has remained in the mental albums of black men. She was reduced to a sexual brood mare to increase the slave population, which helped to create the enormous white wealth that further empowered the colonizers, as well as satisfy the slave population, as

> well as satisfy the slaver's salacious sickness, degenerating her to an ejaculatory dumping ground for the grotesque pleasures forced on the conquered... Dirt floors, barns, cotton fields, slave houses, back porches, bathrooms, outhouses, and any place one could imagine served as the theater for the slave master's pornographic exploits. Not only was the black woman brought down, but she was now dirty, used, abused, passed around, and been around (pp. 15 – 16).

Although this "soiling" primarily had its fingers in finances and the grimy urges of others during this period, it still has long reaching effects on generations much later. Brown (2009) wrote the following passage to give us an overview of the male slaves' condition:

> We find in slavery that men were powerless. That slave masters used them for work and procreation or breeding in order to make the slave master more prosperous. They would mate the slave males with whichever females were thought to be able to bear the strongest children (multiple women in a short span of time). At the same time, the slave master would deter any emotional involvement between any of the childbearing parties so that no bonds of feeling of protectiveness would occur within the men because then they would feel an obligation to try and protect his family (p. 30).

"We could not be fathers to our children or protectors to our women," Willis (2020, p. 25) accentuated. Our male ancestors had to not only standby and witness this type of abuse, but he could not say or do anything about it. What was more devastating to our male ancestors was he had no say over his own life, let only his family members' lives. This author continued on to express the following: "Slave men were used as studs and mainly kept on the move from plantation to plantation… Some slave masters would mate a strong, healthy 'buck' with a strong, healthy female to produce an offspring that might be strong and healthy for work in the fields" (pp. 25 – 26, 28). Sounds familiar?

I think it is clear, our male ancestors were used for their physical, brute strength in performing the manual labor, but they also suffered tremendously as their humanity was unceasingly challenged. Their mental, emotional, and psychological constitutions were nefariously compromised and reconditioned. Willis (2020) insightfully wrote a powerful statement regarding the male slaves' psychosocial fitness during those times:

> The slave master ensured that the Black man wouldn't be able to maintain his dignity and self-respect because of the slave master's treatment. The slave could not defend, protect, or be responsible for his family. The slave master could have sex with the slave's woman or abuse his woman or children—both physically and mentally. The [male] slaves were incapable of defending their young daughters from assault. Many of them were raped by the slave master… It left the author irate to think how destructive is must have been for the Black man's self-esteem, not to be able to exercise the same territorial prerogative that even lower animals in the animal kingdom are able to exercise: to defend and protect the family. The slave master could go out to the slave's cabin, have sex with his woman, and there was nothing the slave could do. It's my understanding that in some cases the slave would be forced to watch activities. It was difficult to maintain families since slaves were

considered property and could be sold at any time (p. 27).

To add even more insult to injury, some slave masters encouraged our female ancestors to be promiscuous because, in most cases, it benefited them financially. "Masters who prized prolific Negro women not only tolerated but sometimes came close to promoting sexual promiscuity among," Stampp (1956/1984, p. 247) wrote. Slave masters basically granted female slaves the ability to be loose and available because if and when they became pregnant, it added to the slave owners'/master's wealth. Yet this author went on to say, "A few [slave masters] sanctioned the breakup of marriages when one or the other partner gave evidence of sterility" (pp. 247 – 248). Again, this shows dubious disregard of slave marriages and families. Yet,

> A slave woman could have six children on one plantation and sold to another slave master and breed six more. She could then be sold and breed more children. In turn those children, who all related through the mother could be sold off and on and on the cycle goes… (Brown, 2004; p. 29).

As you can imagine, some slaveholders' *handling* of female slaves added to the strain on the African/African American family. Not only did some slaveholders' rape and violated African/African American females, but they did so in the presence of their male counterparts and children. African/African American males could not do anything about it because "Any sort of defiance would result in the death or further dehumanization of any or all involved in such action" (Persuad, 2004, p. 18). Of course, because the evidence shows our male ancestors were used in a similar fashion, our female ancestors could not do much about that neither; for as Foster (2019) noted: "White women's sexual exploitation of enslaved men may well have led to marital tensions among enslaved couples (p. 83). Stewart (2020) wrote the following in this regard:

> …Slavery's racial logic brought Blackness into existence as a human identity at the same time it brought forbidden Black love to the African captives and their descendants exclusively adorned by its chain and whips. …Experience of prohibited love are indeed legion across America's temporal and geographic landscapes of slavery, reminding us that, for nearly 250 years, enslaved African descendants in America, who Whites bought, sold, mortgage, gifted, and inherited as moveable property, had no legal rights, essentially—and certainly no right to pursue love, coupledom and marriage based upon their own somatic desires. …love for them and their kinfolk was directly or indirectly *forbidden* through the often combined factors of sexual and reproductive violence and control, "misogynoir" jurisprudence and legal transactions, and the domestic slave trade and family separation (pp. 18 – 19).

Our ancestors learned to adjust to survive these inhumane acts against them. Many also discovered advantages within these harsh conditions and used them to their advantage. However, many of these so-called *gains* caused a greater rift between African American male and female, which lingered on for generations.

And This Means What…?

After being mistreated, used, and diminished in the most heinous ways, it's no surprise to see numerous African Americans continue to struggle in some of those ways today. Earlier, I shared my difficulties in engaging in meaningful, long-term relationships with Black women. Well, I forgot to mention I did have some great ones that left me hopeful. Therefore, my goal is to participate a relationship absent of mental and emotional abuse, manipulation, and exploitation. What does this mean?

In reading some of the historical evidence to which our African Americans predecessors experienced, I discovered a lot of behaviors that are still present today. Unfortunately, I had to go through a lot to see the correlation between the past survival tools and behaviors within the African American communities. Therefore, it is my hope that some of this information will shed light on the way people of color think, treat, feel, and relate to one another.

I took a long, hard, and painful look at myself during this process. Although there were a number of rough spots along the way, I came to a place where I wanted more out of life. I was not satisfied with repeating the same ole song and dance, and I had to hold myself accountable for a myriad of decisions and actions so far. After all, I *am* in partnership with God regarding my destiny and I am responsible for how I pursued it. So, I'm encouraging you, the reader, to either examine yourself, or at least give some thought to examining yourself because you are worthy of such consideration.

* * * * *

One of the characteristics I observed during my time of reflection and introspection was my willingness to help others, even when it was to my detriment. I watched my parents, siblings, and extended family help people whenever and however they could. So, in a sense, helping people came naturally for me.

When I was younger, some people thought I was mean and unapproachable. In a way, I was because I really didn't trust a lot of people—and still don't to a certain extent. Yet when someone needed my help and I could support them, I would. True to my zodiac sign's symbol, the Libra scales, I was unpredictable in that my moods shifted according to the vibes, energy, and attitudes I felt or received from others. I became more patient as I matured and more sociable, and allowed people to take advantage of my "giving spirit," a lot. I would forgive people, and, most likely, be taken for a ride, again.

I genuinely believed in the "forgive and forget" philosophy most of my life and tried to live by it. Unfortunately, it spilled over into other areas of my life that was debilitating. I had to check myself because I knew it was a source pain and resentment. I grew sick and tired of being taken advantage of by those who did not have my best interests at heart. I had to repeatedly say to myself: "You cannot take on projects (people) that were not assigned to you. Everybody's problems are not yours to solve!" In a word, I had to reel my "savior complex" in and concentrate on myself. Not to make it seem like my thought process had shifted to self-centeredness because I am not that type of person. However, I had to come to see how people were abusing my kindness or seeing it as a weakness.

It was time for me to get out of God's way and let God work on us all. However, letting go when it is time was another challenge to work through. I had to relearn the concept of *forgive and forget* because I do feel that forgiving is necessary, but the forgetting part is pure non-sense. I don't even know if it's possible purposely forget the discomfort experienced by the hands of someone else. Where did this way of thinking come from? I believe I inherited this benevolent quality from my parents based on their experiences as children and adults, and how they adapted based on what they endured.

My father was the oldest of his siblings. Resources were scarce throughout his childhood. Since then, he was expected to do and be a lot of things to many people, especially his siblings. My father had several children of his own to which he provided for. I believe, according to some of the stories I've heard before and after his passing, resources being scarce when he was a child impacted him, which affected him for the rest of his life. I'm not sure if my paternal grandparents experienced similar circumstances, but this is what I know about my father's charitable disposition.

As for my mother, she is the eldest child of her mother and one of the oldest of her father. I learned that my maternal grandmother was a teenager when my mom was born, so my maternal great grandfather adopted my mother. My mom grew up as an only child in that household and was loved and cared for by her grandparents. My mom was aware of her younger siblings from her father and was able to be around them. I believe my mom wanted to relate to her siblings, so she gave a lot of herself to compensate for distinct reasons. My mother also had younger siblings from her mother, but they were separated for varying periods of time, and she did the same with them. So, my mom became a giver.

My dad was pretty much the same as my mother and father. He taught my siblings and I to help those who try to help themselves. My brothers and I watched my dad do things for others that not only helped them in that moment but showed them how to get it the next time. All of these acts made a huge impression on me;

but then again, were they learned behaviors, or did they come from a deeper place for me?

With that being said, let's jump into the effects of trauma and other circumstances that are believed to be inherited or imprinted within our genes. I shared definitions of trauma earlier in this chapter, which were appropriate for our discussion on the American chattel slavery experience.

Let's examine the effects of trauma and other occurrences as they shape who we are as well as previous generations. Let's start with defining and discuss Post Traumatic Slave Syndrome (PTSS). DeGruy (2017) posited that PTSS "is a condition that exists when a population has experienced multigenerational trauma resulting from centuries of slavery and continues to experience oppression and institutionalized racism" (p. 105). This definition revolutionized the field's attention toward how people of African descent in America have been affected by their experiences in this country. DeGruy continued on to say:

> Added to this condition is a belief (real or imagined) that the benefits of the society in which they live are not accessible to them. This, then, is Post Traumatic Slave Syndrome: Multigenerational trauma together with continued oppression and absence of opportunity to access the benefits available in the society lead to...Post Traumatic Slave Syndrome.
>
> A syndrome is a pattern of behaviors that is brought about by specific circumstances. The circumstances that produce PTSS are outline above—multigenerational trauma and continued oppression, plus a real or imagined lack of access. What is the resulting pattern of behavior? There's not a

single pattern of behavior. There are many. I have identified three categories: vacant esteem, ever-present anger, and racist socialization (p. 105).

DeGruy's powerful insight helps other writers, scholars, and researchers of the African American experience to include African Americans in the context of existing and developing theories and methodologies. Jimerson (2016) said this about PTSS: "Science has identified that memories, phobias, anxieties and post-traumatic stress disorders, like PTSS, are passes down from previous generations through DNA held in our brains" (p. 9, containing Kase, 2015).

Willis (2020) emphasized, "Slavery initiated stressors that were devasting, creating a sore on the Black American's psyche that continues to raise its ugly head" (p. xxii). Menakem (2017) asserted the following concerning trauma being kept within a group: "When trauma continues for generation after generation, it is called *historical trauma*. Historical trauma has been likened to a bomb going off, over and over again" (p. 39). And Baack (2016) discussed a concept called "Inheritors of Trauma," which are "the generations of people who, consciously or unconsciously, have thoughts and feeling about devastating events that happened when they were very young or before they were born, or that may even go back to earlier generations" (p. 3). I'll have to admit I was a little skeptical about all this talk about DNA and trauma but relied on my training and discipline to dig a little deeper to gain more insight. My first question was: What's the basis for these concepts? And how do they apply to African Americans and other people of color today? Allow me to share the rest of Jimerson's (2016) input before moving on:

Genetic memories of past lives are imprinted in the DNA helix. The DNA is the blueprint for what each organism becomes contingent upon environmental influences. These unconscious memories are necessary for survival. They are rooted into our primordial existence. These voices, sights and experiences of our ancestor are always with us and may serve as either the root of our constructive or unconstructive behavior. If Black American do not recognize PTSS rooted in their DNA and affecting our conscious behavior than it is more likely that they will on an individual basis be overcome by it... We must then stop modelling our oppressors, devaluing out own in the service of the dominate culture, and began to replicate the greatness of our ancestors... (p. 9, 10, containing Hammon, 2016).

As I continued reading and thinking about this information, I observed a concept called Epigenetics. What in the world is this? How does it relate to me and other generations? Wolynn (2016) offered this explanation: "Epigenetics is the study of heritable changes in gene function that occur without a change in the sequence of the DNA. On one hand, this is good news. We're born with an intrinsic skill set—an 'environmental resilience,' as Yehuda calls it—that allows to adapt to stressful situations. One the other hand, these inherited adaptations can be detrimental" (pp. 29 – 30). In other words, these traits can help us in certain situations but can also be a hindrance in others. Fight or flight, for example, may not be the best reaction in a calm setting, but it may be effective in a threatening situation.

Menakem (2017) added that "The transference of trauma isn't just about how human beings treat each other. Trauma can also be inherited genetically" (p. 39). Is this the same as unresolved issues or disturbances? "Unhealed trauma acts like a rock thrown into a pond," Menakem explained, "it causes ripples that move outward, affecting many other bodies over time" (p. 39). This is a prime example of how and why therapeutic intervention is so critical following traumatic incidents. But this author goes on to write:

> After months or years, unhealed trauma can appear to become part of someone's personality. Over even longer periods of time, as it is passed on and gets compounded through other bodies in a household, it can become a family norm. And if it gets transmitted and compounded through multiple families and generations, it can start to look like culture... What we call out as individual personality flaws, dysfunctional family dynamics, or twisted cultural norms are sometimes manifestations of historical trauma (p. 39).

This exert is amazing in that it helps clarify many things I have observed not only in my own family, but in other families and groups as well. When I was providing individual and family counseling in the community—with children and teens as the focus—my frustration came when the focus made progress one week, and then was back to the same behaviors the next. This happened because the family dynamics do not change nor did the focus' surroundings. So, if cussing, for example, was the problem and everyone in that household cussed, it is likely that the focus will continue to cuss. The same occurs with traumatic experiences. Baack (2016) said it this way: "Ours is a kind of second-hand story, and it pervades our lives like deadly second-hand smoke. And like second-hand smoke, it has been invisible, often unacknowledged, but it has grievously betrayed our ability to be whole" (p. 3). Well said.

Getting back to Epigenetics and how many writers and researchers are making this connection between legacy and trauma. My first word of caution is some of this information gets a little deep. So, we'll have to journey together on this one. In his prodigious work entitled, *The Body Keeps the Score*, Van Der Kolk (2014) unveiled:

> Recent research has swept away the simple idea that "having" a particular gene produced a particular result. It turns out that many genes work together to influence a single outcome. Even more important, genes are not fixed; life events can trigger biochemical messages that turn them on or off by attaching methyl groups, a cluster of carbon and hydrogen atoms, to the outside of the gene (a process called methylation), making it more or less sensitive to messages from the body. While life events can change the behavior of the gene, they do not alter the fundamental structure. ***Methylation patterns, however, can be passed on to offspring—a phenomenon known as epigenetics.*** Once again, the body keep the score, at the deepest levels of the organism (p. 154, emphasis mine).

Amazing! So, not only can our genes be affected certain events and/or circumstances, but they can also be passed down to our offspring? But it gets better! "As new discoveries in epigenetics are revealed," Wolynn (2016) said, "new information about how to mitigate the transgenerational effects of trauma could become standard practice" (p. 39). This is awesome news because it informs us of how we act or react. "Researchers are now finding that our thoughts, inner images, and daily practices, such as visualization and meditation, can change the way our genes express [themselves]..." (p. 39), Wolynn concluded. With that being said, let's look at a summary of what's known about trauma, genes, and DNA so far:

- A fetus growing inside the womb of a traumatized mother may inherit some of that trauma in its DNA expression. This results in the repeated release of stress hormones, which may affect the nervous system of the developing fetus.
- A man with unhealed trauma in his body may produce sperm with altered DNA expression. These in turn may inhibit the healthy functioning of cells in his children.
- Trauma can alter the DNA expression of a child or grandchild's brain, causing a wide range of health and mental health issues, including memory loss, chronic anxiety, muscle weakness, and depression.
- Some of these effects seem particularly prevalent among African American, Jews, and American Indians, three group who have experienced an enormous amount of historical trauma (Menakem, 2017; p. 40).

This information is very interesting because it really brings the effects that trauma could have on our genes. With all that has been said, the basic question can be: How can Americans of African lineage still experience Post Traumatic Slave Syndrome even though slavery ended so long ago?

Before we move on, allow me to state my position regarding some "inherited behaviors": some modes of survival that were used by our ancestors are still around today, but may look differently and used for several reasons. I've heard and said this axiom at least a thousand times: "You cannot thrive if you're constantly trying to survive" (Unknown source). I've known so many people who lived this way — in constant survival mode — and seemed to be okay with it. But the question becomes: Are they thriving or merely existing? I had to step back and look at their family-of-origin to gain some idea as to why this was happening. There may be deeper meaning behind this lifestyle underneath the surface. As discussed with a good friend, this may be an acceptable characteristic on a sub-cultural level. However, and let me be clear, it could also be based on personal choices and/or trauma. I appreciate how Willis (2020) shared his perspective when he wrote:

> My contention is that pre-slavery, the Middle Passage, slavery, post-slavery, and modern-day conditions all had dysfunctional effects on my family, and so many other families... I realize that you can't blame every Black family's problems on these conditions, but I can't but believe that this situation was contributory to my family's dysfunction. Some individuals choose to blame every problem in the Black family on history (p. xvii).

I know that was a mouth full, but it certainly shined a light on his family. I'm a firm believer that each person has an opportunity to make decisions for themselves, especially when it comes to familial patterns of behaviors. Yes, I do understand there are many circumstances, arguments, and rationales to explain different occurrences.... I still believe we have the ability to look at various situations and make choices for ourselves.

Returning to Post Traumatic Slave Syndrome or PTSS as well as other conditions that impact people of African descent in the United States of America. Hearing statements like, "You should just get over it," "It wasn't me or you," and "I think it's good that you guys are standing up for yourselves. I would do the same thing," can sometimes set my nerves on edge. Sometimes it isn't so obvious, but the tone and/or timing of statements like those may be in poor taste, revealing the person's real intent or sentiment. These comments are notable examples of *microaggressions*. Yes, some could say these comments are not so bad based on the context they were made... Um, um. Most of the time we are cognizant of the negative connotations they carry.

In most instances, African Americans and other people of color may not be in a position to respond the way they would if similar comments were made in a social setting. We lack the *privilege* to do otherwise. We simply do not respond in an abrupt manner, especially in the workplace, because we do not want to be labeled angry, aggressive, hostile, to name a few. Micro-aggressions or slights, jabs, etc., are leveled by those who are favored, or at least think they are. Unfortunately, it is another form of "keeping us in our places" without being so obvious. Please note you do have those who don't care about social or profession decorum. These and other slights as well as blatant injustices are contributors to Post Traumatic Slave Syndrome.

On an interpersonal level, some of the survival tools our ancestors used to make it through were passed down to ensuing generations and might present today. To the untrained eye, a lot of these behaviors may appear to be antisocial behaviors or personality disorders; and they very well may be. With that noted, these "disorders" and/or behaviors may be survival tools, coping skills or protective, substantive measures to protect or sooth themselves.

Yet some of these survival tools may be used for selfish gains, or to prey upon others. I'd like to call this "faces of the same coin." When people act certain ways, there are people on the receiving end, creating a givers and takers dichotomy. Take for example, Huggins (1977) wrote of how some of our female ancestors used their male slave masters' lust-filled desires as a "one up" on them when he wrote:

> Sex too might seem a means of manipulation, a means of giving stability and weight to one's life. It is not a peculiar vanity which assumes that the comfort and love the body gives can make one special in another's eyes. There is a kind of security in the consciousness of one's beauty and the pleasure it gives another... ...She was the only woman to give him real comfort, to understand what he really was and what he really felt. He would care for her, and free and their children in time. That was the bargain she held to, that generated her life, that was he calculation. Occasionally, she was right (p. 143).

Our ancestors used their bodies to provide not only a sense of security for themselves and their families, but a way to entice their slaveholders into granting them special favors. Stampp (1984) concurred while entering another point of view in this regard:

> Slave women did not always regard a sexual contact with a white male as a privilege which was in no case to be rejected. Many whose sexual behavior was altogether promiscuous doubtless gave their favors without restraint to whites and Negroes alike. Others who were less promiscuous and would have rejected most whites, out of sheer opportunism willingly submitted to the master or

overseer with the hope of that special privileges—perhaps even freedom—would be their reward…. (p. 359).

But to balance his assertion, Stampp (1984) also stated: "But some women, because of devotion to their husbands, or because of a belief that it was morally wrong, or for some other inhibiting reason, did not voluntarily have sexual relations even with their masters. If they submitted, it was only under coercion" (pp. 359-360). Berry and Blassingame (1982) made an interesting point as they explained the irresistible lure of our ancestors:

> Until the last decades of the twentieth century white men, often suffering from puritanical and psychological inhibitions and taught that sex was somehow sinful and unnatural, put up many barriers to interracial sexual contacts. Yet, blacks fascinated them. Many of the white man's sexual fantasies, dreams, and desires that he considered sinful were projected onto blacks. The fantasies appeared most clearly in the myths about black women. The image of the black woman was that she was the most sensuous, exotic, mysterious, and voluptuous female in the world—the embodiment of passion. …By creating a mythological black Venus and a white Virgin Mary, the white man dehumanized both… (p. 115).

But, still, our ancestors were reduced to mere objects, either by others or themselves, to serve many slaveholders because "Seldom did female chattels disappoint their owner. After all, sexual promiscuity brought them rewards rather than penalties…" (Stampp, 1984; p. 248). What were the rewards? They gained trinkets, advantages and/or a sense of security. This type of exchange can be seen today but from a slightly different angle.

Many of the exploitative practices leveled upon our ancestors set in motion a number of lascivious behaviors amongst our people. A number white people had the nerve to label them lewd and other degrading appellations. Jones-Rogers (2019) helped make this point clear when she wrote: "Slave-owning women who set enslaved women to work in their 'negro brothels' also benefited from their engagement in slave-market activities, and their livelihoods brought the markets in slaves and sex together" (pp. 146 – 147). So, as we consider some of the behaviors we view as "immoral" and promiscuous among some African Americans, remember the evidence shows that many of these actions were set into motion by force many years go. But, oftentimes, we believe the white male slaveowners were the only culprits of the foul treatment of our ancestors, but there is information that indicates white female slaveowners were just as ruthless, as their male counterparts:

> In the early- to mid-nineteenth -century South, courts charged many women with crimes *related* to prostitution, such as "keeping a disorderly house," but prostitution itself was not a crime. Thus, slave-owning women's sexual exploitation of enslaved women often remains invisible. …The slave market offered a range of possibilities for white women, and until now these women have been among the slave trade's best-kept secrets. But white women's invisibility within southern slave markets has little to do with their avoidance of or aversion to the commerce that took place there. In fact, white women were ubiquitous in slave-market dealings. …Yet every time a white woman chose to buy and sell slaves, provide a slave trader with goods or services, or prostitute the bodies of the enslaved females she owned, she contradicted the sentimental or

maternal view of white women's relationships with slaves and the institution as a whole.... (Jones-Rogers, 2020; pp. 148, 149 – 50).

Researchers, such as Brown et al. (2013), wrote about the image of women of African descent when they asserted: "African American women, as well as other women of color, have been subjected to a form of oppression that researchers have termed 'gendered racism' in which they experience negative, sexualized stereotypes (e. g. Jezebel and Sapphire), or sexual scripts, that attack both their gender and racial identities" (p. 525). And then, Harris-Perry (2011) addressed the so-called "myth of the black woman" as some whites attempted use to justify their unscrupulous behaviors: "…The mythology of black women as promiscuous was important to maintaining the profitable exploitation of slave society. …The idea of black women's sexual wantonness was important to late nineteenth- and early twentieth-century *nation-building efforts*" (p. 57, emphasis mine). Yet Stephens and Phillips (2003) added:

> Beliefs and attitudes about African American women's sexuality appear to be sanctioned by a culture that continues to embrace stereotypes about race and sexuality. This is made especially clear when one scans media models available for women. The good, innocent, virginal girl continues to be an idealized image for womanhood associated with white females, but unattainable for African American females. …this socially constructed image of white womanhood further relies on the continued production of the racist/sexist myth that African American women are not and do not have the capacity to be sexually innocent (p. 4, contains insert from Brown and McNair, 1995).

Brown et al. (2013) agreed as they wrote this: "... [Black women are] portrayed by stereotypical images that depict them as oversexed, promiscuous, angry, and loud" (p. 525). A number of our male ancestors were viewed/treated in the same manner as their female counterparts. Foster (2019) asserted:

> As an alternative to or in conjunction with threats of retribution, some white women may have wielded the purse as a means of coercing enslaved men to have sex with them. That is to say, following the custom of occasionally tipping enslaved men for services to white women. ...Enslaved men, like enslaved women, may well have turned opportunities that sex under slavery presented them to their advantage. For men, this would have posed a paradox: the wages could provide a measure of manly independence while also potentially emasculating them as sexual subservient (p. 80).

Persaud (2004) noted how our ancestors used the same "opportunities" following the Emancipation Proclamation, "...others had to hustle the only thing they had, and for black women it was their bodies. ...Hunger became the black woman's new pimp further dulling her image in the eyes of the black male" (pp. 29 – 30). Unfortunately, this motivation and practice are still around today. Harris-Perry (2011) agreed when she wrote: "After slavery ended, the myth of lascivious, wanton, and sexually available black women could not alone support a system of domestic labor... ...A seductive, exotic wench would threaten the stability of white families, but an asexual, omnicompetent, devoted servant was ideal" (p. 71). All of this further added to stereotypical myths and image of women of African descent.

On the other hand, other salacious means of acquiring resources were present and are seen to this very day. It's almost as if they are taught and/or encouraged in some circles. Persaud (2004) wrote:

> "Dancer" is now the first job experience that many young black women obtain. This paradigm further allows the black woman to become increasingly limited desirability. Interest, respect, and concern are halted at her loins. Throughout America, many black men are putting dollar bills in the drawers of black "dancers" and not a dime on the dinner table of those who mothered their children. Soiled again (p. 30).

"This ("dancing" among other things) is a standard behavior with this current generations (Millennials and Generation Z)," someone said during a private discussion. But according to epigenetics, can it be more to this story? Brown (2009) offered a historical context to which a lot of these practices derived along with the benefits: "Those cast-off objects of the slave masters gave the slaves temporary satisfaction, enough to take their minds off their misery for a brief moment" (p. 99). In other words, the slave masters provided distractions to divert our ancestors' attention away from what really mattered—figuring out how to survive and thrive on their own.

Willis (2020) revealed something that was methodically instilled in our ancestors when he declared, "Since the demise of slavery, the African American's experience has been filled with many dilemmas. Only now are we beginning to sense the burden placed on African American children by a nation which does not want them to grow into mature men and women" (p. 51). Yet

Brown issued a clarion call that will not sit well with some, but oh well. Constructive criticism doesn't always feel great and speaking truth doesn't always stroke the ego. But like a seasoned prophet, proclaiming judgment upon her people, Brown (2009) wrote concerning vast number of behaviors and motivations:

> ...Instead, African Americans are focused on money and fame, jewelry, cars, and material possessions. Less and less of us are focused on real life and how to obtain happiness; we are more focused on material gain. Children no longer want to become doctors, they aspire to become rappers because they see the money and how its depicted in the videos. They see all the materialism and how important money is in society. They see all the bad things money can do but those things are overshadowed in the presentation because they focus on the material aspects of what they could buy. We have made money more important than the quality of life and life itself. We have given material objects power over our lives. We buy our children material things to keep them occupied instead of giving them our time, talking to them and being there for them when they need us...

> ...We revere the oppressor and place them on pedestals and offer them to our children as saviors, like God and Santa Clause while shooting each other in the streets in the name of prosperity, while offering African American womanhood up as sex objects, nasty, vile creatures whose only purpose is to please men (or any man) sexually; no love involved. You only need to have cash to get what you want out of them and you can discard them after that like trash on the street and African American women are offering

themselves up by the truckload to portray themselves as whores with no regard to personal dignity or pride and certainly no regard or respect for motherhood and African American womanhood/femininity... (pp. 100, 101).

Although Brown had much more to say, I stopped there because these points demonstrated the decadence and depravity many in the African American community have fallen into as a means of *existing*. To be fair, when you are constantly worrying about where your next meal will come from or paying your basic bills, survival mode is most likely where you'll function. When you lack the ability to earn adequate wages to provide for your family, you turn to what you know. When the odds are stacked against you, where do you turn? You rely on what you know, your hustle.

*****

Let's begin our discussion of individuals who have challenging personalities as they might relate to genes and trauma. Many writers and others have different names for people with difficult personalities; namely narcissists, sociopaths, psychopaths, or "difficult to deal with" personalities. (Disclaimer: Although I have knowledge of these personality types, I do not go around diagnosing or labeling people. Not my role, and I'm not getting paid me for that.) Once again, it is fitting to start with brief descriptions of said personalities, starting with the more colorful ones.

Eddy (2018) rendered a fair assessment in his description of "high-conflict personalities" when he wrote, "...Unlike most of us, who normally try to resolve or defuse conflicts, people with high-conflict personalities (HCPs) respond to conflicts by compulsively *increasing* them" (p. 6). These are people who thrive in the presence of unsettledness and discord, even when it appears as if they did not start it or are directly involved in the dispute. But where there's strife and conflict, they seem to be somewhere around. Eddy went on to drop hints as to how you spot HCPs:

> They usually do this by focusing on *Targets of Blame*, whom they mercilessly attack—verbally, emotionally, financially, reputationally, litigiously, and sometimes violently—often for months or years, even if the initial conflict was minor. Their Targets of Blame are usually someone close (a coworker, neighbor, friend, partner, or family member) or someone in a position of authority (boss, department head, police, government agent). Sometimes, though, the Target of Blame can be completely random (p. 6).

Wolhandler (2018) discussed an interesting personality type called, "Emotional Predators." Yup, these characters are just as they are named, predators—"It's a person who exploits other people by manipulating them and preying on their emotions and does this without restraint from conscience or the negative impact on others of their own toxic behaviors" (p. 3). This depiction captures the same group of personalities whom are considered High-Conflict Personalities (HCPs). Yet these folks, Emotional Predators, can be coning in their efforts as they set out to achieve what they want. Wolhandler said, "...typical Emotional Predator behavior includes omitting relevant facts to hide the truth, ignoring rules, denying facts, being indignant and bullying when called on bad behavior, blaming their target, being hypocritical, refusing to inconvenience themselves or change, being indifferent to their negative impact on others, playing the victim, and manipulating emotions with melodramatic tones and words" (2018, p. 3). WOW!

The personality types discussed above are good ways to define various personality types but let's look at them individually. Eddy (2018) succinctly described five personalities who he believes "can ruin your life" in following manner:

- **Narcissistic HCPs:** They often seem very charming at first but believe they are hugely superior to others. The insult, humiliate, mislead, and lack empathy for their Targets of Blame. They also demand constant undeserved respect and attention from everyone.
- **Borderline HCPs:** They often start out extremely friendly—but they can suddenly and unpredictably shift into being extremely angry. When this shift occurs, they may seek revenge for minor or nonexistent slights. They may launch vicious attacks against their Targets of Blame that involve physical violence, verbal abuse, legal action, or attempts to destroy their Target's reputations.
- **Antisocial (or Sociopathic) HCPs:** They can be extremely charismatic—but their charm is a cover for their drive to dominate others through lying, stealing, publicly humiliating people, physically injuring them, and—in extreme cases—murdering them. Antisocial HCPs are remorseless and are said to have no conscience.
- **Paranoid HCPs:** They are deeply suspicious and constantly fear betrayal. Because they imagine conspiracies against them, they will launch preemptive attacks against their Targets of Blame, hoping to harm them first.
- **Histrionic HCPs:** They can have very dramatic and exciting personalities. They often tell wild and

> extreme stories (which are sometimes totally false). Over time, they can be very harmful and emotionally draining to those around them, especially their Targets of Blame (pp. 6 – 7).

I shared this information because it's helpful to know, and it will make more sense in a moment. But for now, the same author added: "Not everyone with a personality disorder is a high-conflict person, because not all of them attack Targets of Blame…" (Eddy, 2018; p. 7).

Now let's look at the other side of this proverbial coin, the givers/scapegoats. These personalities can be prone to codependent behaviors. They take a lot of abuse and punishment in order to feel needed or secure in a situation they call a relationship. One might call this group decent folk, good natured, kindhearted, and/or the unsuspected victim. But beneath it all, this group may have needs/issues (or whatever you choose to call them) that compels them to behave the way they do. Some of these challenges might derive from past trauma, abuse, neglect, or maybe all of the above.

On the other hand, some of these behaviors can be based on fears, weather they are real or imagined. A big culprit of this side of the proverbial coin could simply be a lack of boundaries. What are boundaries and how can they serve me? one might ask. Birch (2014) explained it this way: "Boundaries protect you and everything you hold dear—your dreams, your goals, your values, your time, you autonomy, your money, your self-worth, your emotional well-being, your physical health, your safety, and your self-respect. ***Boundaries keep you intact. They allow you to live your life the way you want to live it.*** Boundaries are invisible and are held in place by your decisions and actions" (p. 15, emphasis mine).

There are other means that drive "decent folks" to people who abuse and exploit them. People with deficits such as insecurities, issues with self-esteem and self-worth, lack of purpose, vacant esteem, low to no motivation, and/or limited life experiences are most susceptible. Figuring out the impetus of such behaviors can be exceedingly difficult because some are well-meaning people, trying to make a difference in this world, but end up in the sharks' tank.

I worked with a young adult a few years ago, and their "go to" was "I never did anything wrong to anybody, but this shit keeps happening to me!" The more I dug around in their background, the more interesting things became. It turned out she was groomed to think of themselves this way. In other words, she was prepared to be prey, the victim, and whatever other illustrations that can be used to explain them—vacant esteem. Some folks seem to dwell in or become content with living in the victim's role, and predators can sense it and they pounce! DeGruy (2017) discussed vacant esteem this way:

> Vacant esteem is the state of believing oneself to have little or no worth, exacerbated by similar pronouncements of inferiority from the personal sphere and larger society. Vacant esteem is the net result of three spheres of influence—society, community, and family... When these influences all promote a disparaging and limiting identity to which we believe we are confined, vacant esteem can be the result. It is important to note that vacant esteem is a belief about one's worth, not a measure of one's actual worth. ***Vacant esteem, being a symptom of Post Traumatic Slave Syndrome, is transmitted from generation to generation through the family, community, and society*** (pp.

108 – 109, emphasis mine).

There are so many scenarios that could fit to this description. However, Skeen (2014) suggested that "core beliefs" shapes a person's disposition in that "Our core beliefs serve as a predictor even in the absence of all the information" (p. 12). Therefore, core beliefs began to take shape during childhood or based on the person's environments or life experiences—we'll talk more in a moment. Skeen further discussed core beliefs as they relate to the fear of abandonment. In fact, five types, including abandonment, are listed below:

- **Abandonment**: is a core belief that is formed as the result of physical or emotional loss, a lack of emotional support or connection; or an unstable or unreliable environment. ...*People who love me will leave me or die. No one has ever been there for me. the people I've been closest to are unpredictable. In the end I will be alone* (pp. 13, 15).
- **Mistrust and abuse**: is a core belief formed in childhood from experience that involve abuse (verbal, physical, or sexual), betrayal, humiliation, or manipulation. The individual with this core belief expects others to hurt, abuse, humiliate, cheat, lie, manipulate, or take advantage of him or her. ...*I always get hurt by the people close to me. People will take advantage of me if I don't protect myself. People I trusted have verbally, physically, or sexually abused me* (pp. 13 - 14, 16).
- **Emotional deprivation**: the core belief that others will not adequately meet one's desire for a normal degree of emotional support. ...*I feel lonely. I don't get*

> *the love that I need. I don't have anyone in my life who really cares about me or meets my emotional needs. I don't feel emotionally connected to anyone* (pp. 14, 17).

- **Defectiveness**: the core belief that causes people to feel like they are defective, bad, unwanted, or inferior in important respects, or that others would find them unlovable if their "flaws" were exposed. These flaws may be private or public. ...*If people really knew me they would reject me. I am unworthy of love. I feel shame about my faults. I present a false self because if people saw the real me they wouldn't like me* (pp. 14, 18).

- **Failure**: the core belief that causes an individual to feel like he or she is inadequate or incompetent and will ultimately fail. When compared to others, this person feels like a failure. Any successes the individual has make him or her feel like an impostor. ...*Most of my peers are more successful than I am. I am not as smart as other people in my life. I feel ashamed that I don't measure up to others. I don't possess any special talents* (pp. 14, 18).

Linking these core beliefs to how givers and takers coexist, especially in romantic relationships, is quite interesting because so many parts come into play; yet it could be quite puzzling because their relationship may be co-dependent in essence. But one thing we can say of these types of situations is they will most likely turn out to be a highly toxic and/or abusive, where someone usually ends up deeply wounded.

Keeping in mind that the givers/scapegoats' behaviors might be indicative of some sort of deficit or core belief, usually linked to their childhood or traumatizing experiences, while the takers/perpetrators, who seek to dominate and/or control, function from the same source. Skeen (2014) said this about the former group, but could also apply to the latter in some ways: "You may find yourself drawn to similar relationship dynamics and environments that you experienced as a child... Your core beliefs have you trapped in emotions, thoughts, and behaviors that are hurtful, and they are denying you the happiness and healthy, loving relationships that you desire and deserve" (p. 8). As I said, the above quote can also apply to takers but it might read like this: Your core beliefs have you trapped in remorselessness thoughts and actions that are harmful to others, and they are blocking you from happiness and healthy, loving relationships, absent of harm, you desire and deserve. Either way, when things go south, it can get really ugly really fast, even deadly in some cases. MacKenzie (2019) had this to say (excuse the length, but it's necessary):

> People coming out of cluster-B relationships (with sociopaths, narcissists, borderline or histrionic personalities) carry a misery about them that no one else seems to understand... Instead, it's like they've been disconnected from the things that make life worth living. Their natural joy and love has disappeared, replaced by constant anxiety and self-doubt.
>
> These relationships start out better than anything you've ever experienced. This disordered individual seems to love and needs you more than any partner you've known. They latch on, mimicking your hopes and dreams, even mirroring your vocal and texting mannerisms. Of course, you don't know this is happening, because you don't know what cluster-B disorders are (yet). You're just freely falling

in love, grateful to have found this amazing "soul mate."

But inevitably [and they always do], things take a turn for the worse. This person becomes controlling, manipulative, critical, dismissive, and unfaithful. They do hurtful things and then blame you for reacting. You desperately keep trying to re-create the original perfect dynamic, wondering where in the world that person went. You are punished with the silent treatment and other painful behaviors. Every time you're feeling ready to leave, your partner swoops back in with promises that remind you of the person they used to be (pp. 39 – 40).

You can imagine how this "relationship" might end. The person on the receiving end of this foul treatment ends up, as they say, buked and scorned. To make matters worse, the "issues" they had before meeting that difficult personality might become even more pronounced, causing them to go on the defensive or maybe withdrawing. Or, even worse, they might convince themselves that it didn't matter or they were not affected by it. Oh but, MacKenzie (2019) explained a phenomenon that shows up when people are deeply wounded: "When our true selves are rejected, betrayed, or abused by a trusted loved one (usually parent or partner) and we don't yet have the emotional tools to heal, it's common for a protective self to form" (p. 21). I was thinking, "Merciful God, teach us!" the first time I read this. But it gets better:

> The protective self sees itself as separate from others. It became more of an observer of the world, rather than an authentic participant. The protective self is usually seeking external validation for proof of its worthiness. ***To save or be saved***. To fill a void it cannot express, to meet an old unmet

need. It is largely based around control. ...The protective self has probably had the reins for a long time. It's your natural way of thinking at this point. It is [or became at some point] "who you are." You can't work on something that you're not even aware of. The protective self convinces us there is nothing wrong with us, that we've figured it all out... It is often disguised in an innocent, childlike, confident, cheerful, victimized, or heroic way. ***This illusion keeps us stuck in the same patterns.*** While it's true that there's nothing inherently "wrong" with us, the protective self is blocking us from experiencing the wounded feelings that actually need to hear that message... The wound is unfelt, blocked by the protective self. It takes an incredible amount of energy to maintain this makeshift solution. (One more) ...the protective self [is] growing stronger and stronger, as the wound fades into a numb obscurity, an invisible status quo (pp. 21 – 22, emphases mines).

I can go on and on sharing a lot more of what I've absorbed, but I'll bring it around to the relationships African Americans tend to have with one another. You may have noticed I have spent a great deal of time discussing the treatment of our male and female ancestors. Now is the time to begin examining some of the effects on Black/African Americans in the next chapter.

*****

A follow-up to the introduction of this chapter. One day, I was in a situation where I had to listen to (and not agree with) a person complain about Black Lives Matters and other "banter" regarding the racial injustice protests, and the incidents that ignited riotous acts at various times, historically. This person angrily declared,

"Black people need to let that shit go! Ain't nobody alive today participated in slavery. *Those* people need to let it go and move on with their lives…" Everything inside of me wanted to scream, but because of the position I was in at the time, I held it in because it would have been "inappropriate." So, I half listened. Once this person noticed my quietness, they went on to the next subject that was on their feeble mind.

I thought I was in the twilight zone because this person failed to mention that people of color were/are being gunned down at ridiculous rates, for little to no reason. They forgot to look at the way people of color are and have been labeled and treated as threats, even when they present themselves in a non-threatening manner. And they neglected to mention that too many people of color are still being denied access to necessary resources. This person did not want to talk about these things because it would have stolen their thunder. And finally, this person did not realize their way of thinking was contributing to the ongoing racial "problem" that has a cold grip on this nation.

This person continued on to rant about being "anti-racist" and "anti-reparations," because they felt that everyone had "an equal footing on a(n) equal playing ground." Oh but, they added: "None of this shit has anything to do with us!" I clarified because I needed to know who the "us" was. They said, "Hell, all of us." All I could say was "Oh." I was annoyed because folks, both people of African descent and European Americans alike, were spewing opinions like these based on faulty information or their own beliefs or feelings. But then, this person said something that made me cringe: "You don't see the Indians [Native Americans] or the Jews crying like babies at the slightest whim, do you?" Following protocol and my patience meter, I ended this discussion.

Comparing one group's atrocities to another is not okay nor is it acceptable because how do you place value or intensity on unjustified cruelty? How do you say someone's misery is worse than another's sorrow? *You cannot!* It sounds as if the old "keep them blind" mentality still exists, and no one should fall for it because it is a form of oppression.

Everyone should look into their own history no matter how dark and difficult it may be. "…We are reminded of the period in our history when Black men were lynched," Winters (2020) wrote, "put on public displays as a means of terrorizing and controlling. These recent deaths are examples of modern-day lynching" (p. xi). These and other accounts are indicative of this country's shame-filled history in terms of race relations. Some people, who have not tasted the bitter elixir of such treatment are left oblivious as to why events have unfolded the way they did. Winters continued on to state what is almost expected:

> With the Black community already at a heightened level of stress from dealing with the multiple disparate impacts of COVID-19 on Black people, these all-too-familiar racist incidents were the proverbial straw that broke the camel's back. They sparked monthlong fervent protests by people across the spectrum of diversity who globally denounced police brutality and demanded racial justice. These rebellious, mostly peaceful, signaled new movement against anti-Black racism that proclaimed, enough is enough. We are exhausted from dealing with racism and violence against Black people. Symbols of racism such as confederate flags and other historical monuments were dismantled forcibly, and in other cases, lawmakers decided to remove them (p. xii).

As I prepared for this book, I came across something very interesting that seemed to not only explain some of these microaggressions (because that's what they are) voiced by some, but also those on the receiving end of such statements. Eyerman (2001), in his discussion on "cultural trauma," said the following lengthy citation:

> Resolving cultural trauma can involve the articulation of collective identity and collective memory, as individual stories meld through forms and processes of collective representation. Collective identity refers to a process of "we" formation, a process both historically rooted and rooted in history. While this reconstructed common and collective past may have its origins in direct experience, its recollection is mediated through narratives that are modified with the passage of time, filtered through cultural artifacts and other materializations, which represent the past in the present. *Whether or not they directly experienced slavery or even had ancestors who did, blacks in the United States were identified with and came to identify themselves through the memory and representation of slavery. This came about not as an isolated or internally controlled process, but in relation and response to the dominant culture. The historical blackness came to be associated with slavery and subordination.* A common national history was ascribed and inscribed as memory, as well as indigenously passed on, as groups emerged out of protective necessity and/or collective solidarity. In this sense, slavery is traumatic for those who share a common fate, not necessarily a common experience. Cultural trauma articulates a membership group as it identifies an event or an experience, a primal scene, that solidifies the group, must be recollected by later generations who have had no

experience of the "original" event, yet continue to be identified by it and to identify themselves through it. *Because of its distance from the event and because its social circumstances have altered with time, each succeeding generation reinterprets and represents the collective memory around that even according to its need and means.* This process of reconstruction is limited, however, by the resources available and the constraints history places on memory (pp. 14 – 15, emphasis mine).

I included this extensive quote to show that we, African Americans, as well as other people of color, are and will be affected by this country's most reprehensible period in history. To tell someone to "Just get over it" can and should be countered with "You should too," because those who were oppressed way back then left a legacy with those who dare utter such stupid shit now. This is why I mindfully said: "…both people of color and Caucasian alike, are spewing positions/opinions like these based on faulty information or their own belief systems, or feelings." Yes, in times like these, emotions can run high and get the best of both sides. HOWEVER,…! Someone has to slow down and "fact check" what's being said.

As a psychologist said, and I cannot recall her name right now, "This is a wounded country because of its checkered past. We all need healing in order to move forward as one country under God." What this person was saying, in my opinion, all of us suffer, in some way, from the American chattel slavery experience, whether your ancestors were slaves, slave owners, or simply living in the United States of America, before and after its inception. To some degree, your ancestors had some involvement in this dreadful system, whether they participated in it directly or indirectly. If my understanding of the "Good Samaritan" rule is accurate, watching something harmful go down and not stepping in to help stop it carries as much culpability as those who are actually doing it. Yet Eyerman (2001) ordered this stance as he discussed the effects of trauma has on successive generations:

> The generational shifts... ...can be said to structure temporally the formation of collective memory, providing a link between collective (group) memory and public (collective) memory. *Groups of course, are public, but a particular group's memory may not necessary be publicly, that is officially, acknowledged or commemorated.* If a collective memory is rooted in a potentially traumatic event, which by definition is both painful and open varying sorts of evaluation, it may take a generation to move from group memory to public memory; sometimes it may take even longer, sometimes it may never happen at all. The case of American slavery is an example. As Ira Berlin notes in his introduction to *Remembering Slavery* (2005), slavery is remembered differently in the United States depending upon which time period and which racial group and regional location one starts from (p. 15 and Berlin, pp. xiii – xiv; emphasis mine).

I said all this to make one point: Change in this nation, and in this world, for that matter, starts with individuals,' groups' and society's willingness to heal themselves. This will never be accomplished by utilizing a one-sided, blaming-the-other approach. Everyone must do their part. If not, we'll all be stuck in the same disease-ridden position. It is time for us to heal thy self in order to come together and reconcile the past.

Chapter Eight:

Can We Heal Together?

What's Bothering You?

I wondered if my past sexual assault still had its nasty grips on my life, even years later, several times before and during this process. In my heart of hearts, I knew the answer, but I didn't want to accept it. I knew there were some things I could have addressed, but my questions were more along the lines of how I could make positive, impactful changes. I prayed about these things because I believe they may have been out of my hands. As I continued preparing for this chapter, I came across something that confirmed what I was thinking and prayed for:

> Each one of us has a destiny in this life determined by God, but unhealed damage can steal the fullness of His [God's] purpose in us. If we don't understand how we have been damaged in our lives and don't understand God's way of restoration, this can be a barrier to us appropriating (accepting and receiving) God's pardon, freedom, and healing (Cross, 2006; p. 8).

It's amazing when we find ourselves in a dilemma, big or small, and deny knowing how or when we got into that situation. It is also interesting to know we're in a precarious position, and yet, we act as if we don't know how we got there or why. Sometimes we know the issue/challenge, but do nothing about it. Accepting our challenges for what they are and figuring out how to find a suitable route. Not being able to act is one thing but *choosing* not to when something can be done says a lot about your condition. Let's continue.

For me, naming my issues was the easy part, believe it or not. I didn't have to look very far because they were in my face. No, it wasn't being home a lot more because of COVID-19 restrictions that caused the problems. It was not due to the racial injustices, nor a woman. All of those things did not bring about my unsettledness because my issues had been there for quite some time. However, I recognized there was something deeper, something beyond me and pass the physical plane. One thing lends to the other. Mentally, emotionally, and spiritually, I knew I had to work on setting and maintaining boundaries across the board, which the lack thereof led to repetitive behaviors, situations, and outcomes. "Why do these things keep happening to me?" the young woman asked. I am a firm believer that things, similar or the same, repeatedly occur when there are lessons to be learned. Still, I wondered why some people, especially survivors, tend to draw unsavory people and circumstances into their lives.

With that thought in mind, I planned to focus on the African American family unit in terms of relationships, marriage, or lack thereof, and the barriers that persisted for quite some time. I sought this information for myself as well as others in the African American community. I prayed that my "lil brah" and I were wrong and that some of this information will reach someone because they took the time to read it—contradicting the old adage that "If you don't want Black people to know something, put it in a book." I am hopeful this information will be received whether it's in book form, on a computer, tablet, phone, or audio device.

The time is now that we do something different to affect change. In fact, Carmichael, and Hamilton (1967/1992) prophetically offered a solution to help us achieve pure liberation in the following terms:

> …Black people in the United States must raise hard questions, questions which challenge the very nature of the society itself: Its long-standing values, beliefs and institutions.
>
> To do this, we must first redefine ourselves. Our basic need is to reclaim our history and our identity from what must be called cultural terrorism, from the depredation of self-justifying white guilt. We shall have to struggle for the right to create our own terms through which to define ourselves and our relationship to the society, and to have these terms recognized… (p. 35).

This quote covers not only equity and equality, but also how we address our own conditions. Willis (2020) wrote of a major obstacle that persistently block our progress, "Trans-generational adaptations associated with symptoms of the post-trauma of slavery and on-going oppression," (p. 77). In this, Willis listed several indicators:

> 1). Low self-esteem; 2). Undermining behavior; 3). The setting of unrealistic limits; 4). Poor self-image; 5) Self-hate; 6). Fear, anger, grief, and hopelessness; 7). Loss of dignity and identity; 8). Destroyed bonds and relationships; 9). Feelings of inferiority; 10). Inability to unify as a family; 11). The assumption of failure; 12). Lack of self-confidence; 13). Poor parenting skills; 14). Lack of pride and respect for one's self and others; 15). The tendency of the father to abandon

the family; 16). The tendency to see other males and females as the real men and women; 17). Ever-present fear and rage; 18) Lack of feeling secure about self and others; 19). Paranoid against the system; 20). A belief that we have limited choices; 21). Plague by doubts about one's self and others; 22). Limited view of one's potential; 23). Aloofness and instability; 24). Lack of self-worth; 25). Lack of aspirations; 26). Fatalistic attitude; 27). Often self- and other-destructive; 28). Identifying with the oppressor; 29). Belief that Black human characteristics are inferior and that other groups characteristics are superior; 30). Belief that other groups are intellectually superior; 31). Adopting other groups standards of beauty and material success, as well as violence and brutality; 32). Denial that racism exists; 33). Glamorization of lack of education (pp. 77 – 78).

Not all of these characteristics are applicable to all African Americans, however, a pattern can be seen and has been present for a long time. You see, when we learn to do better, then we ought to do better for not only for ourselves and our direct descendants but for generations to come. Willis (2020) went on to render the following characteristics regarding our children:

1). Die at a disproportionate rate; 2). Negative habits of all types; 3). Don't know who we are; 4). Internalize negative images in the media; 5). Internalize and adopt negative stereotypes; 6). Discord between you men and women; 7). Expectation of failure; 8). Internalized shame and humiliation; 9). Orchestration of the demise of other Blacks; 10). Hypersensitive to disrespect (p. 78).

Having heard "sexual abuse happens more often than we know," or "sexual abuse is something that runs in my family," especially within Black families, motivates me to not only learn more about this problem, but to seek feasible solutions to combat it.

I thought about the impact of being sexually assaulted as a young adult has had on me. The shock and trauma that resonated in a number of areas in my life, I now realize the importance of God's timing in my healing process. Trusting the process is key and it can only happen when I am open to being set free from what happened so long ago.

Realistically speaking, the aftermath of traumatization must be addressed. Distressing experiences can have life altering effects, namely on how we see ourselves. This may also include our purpose. For a while, I felt like a piece of meat because that's what my assailant said to me as she violated my person. Although I did not continue behaving that way, I still felt and thought of myself as such on a deep level of my consciousness. I now know those feelings/thoughts were tied to shame. My ongoing struggle with shame brought on feeling of unworthy of truly living the life I was destined to live. Yet even when I did attempt to live, I felt guilty and engaged in self-sabotaging behaviors, which led to additional disappointments and heartache. Once I knew I was not defined by my past state of affairs, almost twenty or so years later, I'm working towards change in my self-image and in my life. I know God never intended for me to be limited as I sought out my destiny. I can redefine myself, reinvent who I am and reauthor what I see and believe myself to be.

Can We Get to the Bottom of This?

My worldview began to shift drastically because my thought process and sentiments have changed. Without an abundance of distractions or influence, I started embracing the experiences I've had, both good and bad, bitter, and sweet, as a means of coming to a place of peace and fulfillment. Understanding that there were elements of my life *I* needed to recover from, because *I* didn't realize they were hindering me from becoming who I was created to be. I ceased from doing certain things, being around specific people, looking at things in a particular way in order to center myself and get back on my square to restore my relationship with God and myself. I had neglected my end of this relationship as I continued being contrary and obstinate. Therefore, many things had to be settled so I could realign myself with what I desire and who I am destined to be. I could not deny or avoid what it was any longer —unresolved issues.

* * * * *

I decided to dedicate this chapter to relationships, healing and changing patterns of behaviors that did not work for me. I saw there were a number of things I could work on. There were certain situations I needed to avoid as I looked at a number of aspects of my life; and then pushed myself to modify them. I had (have) a lot of work to do. First, I examined how I related to Black women, and do my best to figure out how to amend that. I had to comprehend and accept this, especially after being angry for such a long time. However, I had to stop blaming others because it took two people to be in a relationship in the first place. So then, my work entailed getting to know myself more. It was the only way I would be able to engage in a healthy, loving relationship with the woman God created just for me. Therefore, I picked up where Chapter Seven left off, the historical rift between African American men and women.

I don't believe I was made to be alone, even though I enjoy having my own space for now. I am a natural introvert who learned how to be sociable when it is called for. So, it's not a question of my ability to get out and about. It's about deciding to do so. Next, I had to acknowledge the fact that a number of my past romantic relationships contained crucial lessons needed for me to achieve my relationship goal(s). I want a healthy, functional, long-lasting relationship with an African American woman with whom I can heal and grow together. I must thank my most recent former "girlfriend" because she helped me to see how noxious we can be toward one another when we are hurting. This caused me to see my own woundedness, and my need to mend before moving onto someone else. One writer described what happens when we do not take time to heal when she wrote:

> For [African American] men and women who consider themselves martyrs of the Uncivil War, anger has become their battle armor. It protects them from openly and honestly feeling and expressing the hurt of betrayal, the pain of unfulfilled expectations and dreams and the grief of love lost. The victims wear their armor wherever they go, and especially when members of the opposite sex are present. Like a medal of honor, this anger is clearly visible. It can be seen and heard in their body language, their eyes, negative comments, and tone of voice. ...As a result, the angry person concludes that their difficulty in meeting and attracting new people is confirmation of their own negative perceptions of the opposite sex, when in reality it is their repugnant anger that is more likely the cause of their

troubles (Washington, 1996; pp. 29 – 30).

It took my last relationship for me to see that my challenges in relating to Black women started with me. I could not take all of the blame for these relationships' downfall. I'm mature enough to take responsible for my actions and reactions. When certain things were triggered within me, I lashed out. Those actions ultimately brought out anger and pain to both parties.

I had to stop long enough to say to myself, "You *are* hurt because of the betrayal, unfulfilled expectations, and losing yet another relationship." Duplicity and unfulfilled hopes hurt the most because of how *we* treated one another, which ultimately led to bitterness because of the disappointment of my believing we could have gotten past those issues and/or disagreements. But, hurt people, hurt people.

Yet some people will go onto the next person, while harboring poison from unaddressed issues from previous relationships. They do not take time to heal or recover before moving onto someone else, which is a disservice to all parties involved. I decided to take a break to be by myself for a while. I acknowledge my need to lick my wounds, recover, and rectify some stuff. In fact, Washington (1996) discussed how not doing so affects us:

> When an angry black man or woman enters into a new relationship, they often do so consumed with skepticism and acrimony. This, of course, greatly increases the likelihood that the relationship will fail. And again, the blame for the relationship's demise will be undoubtedly assigned to the "enemy," or the opposite sex. Consequently, this same man or woman will drag even more pessimism

and hostility into their next relationship, with it, too, doomed to fail. The vicious cycle continues (p. 30).

I emphasized some negative aspects of Black love before but I would be remiss if I didn't talk about some positive outcomes — you know, when grandma and grandpa stayed together for 40 to 50 years. Although I saw this a few times in my life, I do believe there were many African American couples who manage to stay together in spite of rocky times along the way. I can confidently presume they were willing and able to work through their trials, even if they were immensely painful. "Few emotionally healthy people want to spend their valuable, quality time with someone who radiates hostility toward them" Washington (1996, p. 30) wrote. In other words, those Black couples took the time to work it out, for the sake of their love. However, this writer expressed an aspect of generational obstacles as the following:

> …Young people often do not get to know their grandparents and older aunts, uncles, and other relatives. As a result, the years of experience and valuable insights these have to off is unavailable to far too many African American men and women. …Without knowledge of the lessons learned and the strategies used by older family members to build and maintain relationships, many African Americans have little practical knowledge from which to evaluate potential partners. Nor do they have the experience or insight necessary to respond appropriately to situations and crises that occur within their relationships (Washington, 1996; pp. 177 – 78).

I concur. A lack of elders' presence can be a disadvantageous, especially during our formative years, because many behaviors can develop due to a "trial and error" foundation. I would also add that the lack of respect of those elders who are around is even more unfortunate. Yet information can also be obtained from unreliable sources, such as the streets or peers. This would be an appropriate place to discuss codes of conduct on the streets because they are germane to the overall subject matter and our understanding as to how we, African Americans, and other people of color, relate to one another within the context of sexual and romantic relationships.

Anderson (1999) and Harding (2010) conducted studies on life in the inner-city. In *Code of the Street*, Anderson discussed what he called "Sex: The Game and The Dream" wherein "To many inner-city males, the most important people in their lives are members of their peer groups," (p. 150). Anderson continue on to explain the importance of conduct and acceptance within these male peer groups:

> They set the standards for conduct, and it is important to live up to those standards, to look good in their eyes. The peer group places a high value on sex, especially what middle-class people call casual sex. But though sex may be casual in terms of commitment to the partner, it is usually taken quite seriously as a measure of the boy's worth. A young man's primary goal is thus to find as many willing females as possible. The more "p**y" he gets, the more esteem accrues to him (p. 150; slang word for vagina was altered by this author out of respect).

At the same time, Anderson (1999) addressed inner-city girls' aspirations of finding their dream lover or "prince charming":

> ...The popular love songs they listen to, usually from the age of seven or eight, are imbued with a wistful air, promising love, and ecstasy to someone "just like you." This dream involved having a boyfriend, a fiancé, or someone or a husband and the fairy-tale prospect of living happily ever after with one's children in a nice house in a good neighborhood—essentially the dream of the middle-class American lifestyle, complete with nuclear family. ...Many girls dream of becoming the comfortable middle-class housewife portrayed on television, even though they see that their peers can only approximate that role (pp. 151 – 52).

Anderson (1999) wrote of how the game is played: "When a girl is approached by a boy, her faith in the dream clouds her view of the situation" (p. 152). In other words, the girl's perception can be obscured by her hopes of finding the man of her dreams, her knight in shining armor, who would come to rescue her from her current situation. To be sure, Anderson went on to say:

> ...A romantically successful boy has a knack for knowing just what is on a girl's mind, what she wants from life, and how she hopes to obtain it. The young man' age—he may be four or five years older than the girl—gives him an authoritative edge and makes his readiness to "settle down" more credible. By enacting this role, he can shape the interaction, calling the resources he needs to play the game successfully. He fits himself to be the *man* she wants him to be, but this identity may be exaggerated and temporary, maintained only until he gets what he wants. Essentially, he shows her the side of himself that he knows she wants to see, that represents what she wants in a man. For instance,

he will sometimes "walk through the woods" with the girl: he might visit at her home and go to church with her family or even do "manly" chores around her house, showing that he is an "upstanding young man." But all of this may only be part of his game, and after he gets what he wants, he may cast off this aspect of his presentation and real something of his true self, as he flits to other women and reverts to behavior more characteristic of his everyday life—that which is centered of his peer group.

At times, however, a boy earnestly attempts to *be* a dream man, with honorable intentions of "doing right" by the you woman, of marrying her and living happily ever after according to their version of middle-class propriety. But the reality of his poor employment prospects makes it hard for him to follow through (pp. 152, 153).

In essence, Anderson (1999) described the game as "…a contest going on between the boy and the girl even before they meet" (p. 150). I would even venture to say, this contest starts during the socialization stage in that the boys and girls learn "the ropes" by either observing older people around them or they are taught how to "get over" and/or "finesse" their way into getting what they want. Although Anderson described the boys as the "players," there are a large number of girls who are quite skilled in the game as well. However, for now, Anderson went on to say, "…To the young man the woman becomes, in the most profound sense, a sexual object. He body and mind are the object of a sexual game, to be won for his personal aggrandizement…" (p. 150).

In his book, *Living the Drama*, Harding (2010) focused on how inner-city boys as they navigate the rough and tumble elements within their urban surroundings. In the discussion of sexual behavior, this author spoke of the culture in which those young boys participated in the game. Harding said this of the young boys: "His 'tool kit' simultaneously contains another competing model derived from his dealings with peers: he can be freely arranged outside of a long-term relationship and without commitment…" (p. 12). Within this model, the boy picks up "tips" from his peers and from his own experiences with girls. "The beginnings of this script are visible to anyone…" Harding wrote, "…as young men practice 'hollering at girls' or 'spitting their game' in full public view and as girls compete for the public attention of boys" (pp. 162 – 63).

This is where the guidance of the elders could be usefully beneficial to teenaged boys and girl. But from my experience, the elders are counted as "out of touch" and "don't know what's up." However, the game hasn't changed, only the players. There is something to be said about those who reject sound insight— "The fear of the LORD is the beginning of knowledge, but fools despise wisdom and instruction" (Proverbs 1: 7, NIV). To be clearer, "Discretion will protect you, and understanding will guard you. Wisdom will save you from the ways of wicked men, from men whose words are perverse, who have left the straight paths to walk in dark ways…" (Proverbs 2: 11 – 13, NIV).

A vital part of the game is the boy getting next to the girl in a private way, and this varies based on the two parties. "Boys talk to girls on the phone over a period of days or weeks," Harding (2010) stated the purpose is "to establish some level of familiarity, and then they meet to have sex. …A boy will often tell the girl that he loves her in order to move the relationship along, even if he does not" (p. 163). Keep in mind, these aspects are all a part of the game. Harding was able to glean three frames (names) and two statuses to which the boys categorized girls within their surroundings: Stunts, Gold Diggers, Good Girls, wifey and shorty.

In this first frame, "the stunt," according to the boys within this study, "is a girl who is primarily interested in sex rather than a relationship," Harding (2010) noted. It gets a little more interesting as he continued on to share these boys' view of the girls in this category when he wrote:

> Boys think of these girls as the ones who enjoy sex for its own sake and so not connect sexual behavior with emotional intimacy. Nor is a stunt after money or the status that comes from associating with particularly popular or high-status boys. Since she is mostly interested in sex, a stunt is easy to get into bed, and accordingly she is most likely to respond to the guy who "hollering" at her… She is also extremely likely to cheat on a boyfriend or husband because relationships are not a priority for her… ..She is also extremely likely to cheat on a boyfriend or husband relationships are not a priority for her…" (p. 164).

As I reviewed this information, I thought about my own experiences during early adolescence as I "discovered" girls and my curiosities about them. Yes, I imagined touching them, feeling them, and enjoying their scent, but there was a limit to my curiosity because of my upbringing. My mom and dad repeatedly, almost obsessively, said to my older brothers and I, "Don't be out there treating somebody's daughter like a piece of meat." They made it clear that there was no double standard in the way they were raising us up to be young men. But Harding's (2010) insight reflected upon this sentiment, when he asserted:

Traditional gender roles inflect the way that young men think about stunts. Boys are revered for being "players," reveling in sexual relationships with multiple girls without the entanglements of emotional commitment. Stunts, the female equivalents, are stigmatized. They are "hos" (whores). A girl who is (or once was) a stunt is not a good candidate for a romantic relationship, and boys who get too involved with stunts are made fun of (p. 165).

"Stunts" are most likely to advise the boy *not* to "catch feelings" because they are not looking for a relationship, but are only interested in having a good time and that's it. The next group of girls are the "gold diggers." These are the girls who have agendas to use their sexual acts and/or favors to obtain what she wants. Harding (2010) wrote the following narrative:

"Gold diggers" are girls who are, according to the boys, interested in a man's money or other resources. She looks for a man with a car and a job (legitimate or not) and seeks to extract gifts, rides, and money from him, using the relationship with him to that end. She wants a boyfriend who will take her shopping, out to eat, and to the movies. She will have sex with a young man in order to create and preserve a relation, but unlike a stunt, a gold digger is not interested in sex for its own sake. Rather, she uses it to extract resources from her boyfriend and to control him. Since the gold digger is interested only in a man's resources, she is very likely to cheat on her boyfriend with another boy who has a thicker wallet. She will also end a relationship when a partner loses his job or runs out of cash, or when another partner comes along with a nicer car or more expensive gifts. …To be a gold digger she must consider material resources a primary factor in the relationship (p. 165).

Next, we have the most under-rated group, especially amongst boys who are "sowing their wild oats," the "good girl." The good girl is goal oriented, "who is focused on her future, not on boyfriends or parties. She goes to school regularly, studies, and has plans to go to college or at least some sort of job training after high school" (Harding, 2010; p. 166). Unfortunately, the good girl is oftentimes overlooked for those who "give it up," or those who "got that action." Harding continued on to say:

> She probably has a job of her own, so she does not need a man's money. The good girl is watched over by her family, close to her mother or father [or both], attends church regularly, and is usually uninterested in a boyfriend. She does not have time for a boyfriend, at least not until she graduates from high school. This make the good girl inexperienced, as she usually has never had a boyfriend and has at most one prior sexual partner. There is no chance the good girl is going to let herself get pregnant. She is the one a boy could bring home to meet his mother. She will be a positive influence because she has her own priorities "straight." The good girl is the type of girl you could have a long-term relationship with…" (p. 166).

Then we have the two status types: the wifey and the shorty. The wifey is "the primary girlfriend. She take priority over the others, the shorties," Harding (2010, p. 150) said. He also clarified the wifey's position in the following:

> … [She is the one the boy] spends the most time with time with… and she is the girlfriend with whom he is having a

long-term relationship, based on emotional as well as sexual intimacy. She is the protowife, the girlfriend he might someday have children with and someday marry, and, as the names suggests, this is the type of relationship that comes closest to an idealized "middle-class" romantic relationship" (pp. 166 – 67).

The "shorty" type "is casual, intermittent, and nonexclusive, but it is not a 'one-night' stand and it is not only a sexual relationship. A young man can have multiple shorties, girls he 'talks to' (spend time with) and has sex with from time to time, without the level of commitment or the long-term orientation of a wifey" (Harding, 2010; p. 167).

African American young men oftentimes fall victim to circumstances of their own devices, choices, and sometimes, their surroundings by choice. These components lead to many African American males being incarcerated, under-educated and/or untrained, unemployable, etc. As these things occur, they affect Black men's counterpart as well, the Black woman. But the same fate befalls African American females but, too often, their children are added into the mix. However, if opportunities are taken, "Black women, armed with the means to adequately support themselves," Washington (1996) wrote, "set their sights on partners with similar assets and credentials. Many refuse to accept a mate who has any less and as are hesitating to marry at all" (p. 47). This also adds to the rift between African American men and women. Yet both African American males and females follow the aforementioned codes and behaviors. However, it is the hope that the young Black females would grow into mature young African American women; and those young Black males would mature into young African American men.

The reality is far too many young African Americans girls choose to relinquish their gifts, talents, and strengths in order to have a *man* or to be that "ride or die chick." There are some women/girls who will support their man at any cost, even if it costs her freedom. These are the young African American girls/women will entertain the "bad boys," "the thugs," and the "knuckle heads," but will not give the "decent guys" a chance. Leaving the "good guys" to suffer from the deeds (or should I say misdeeds) of their contemporaries. African American women and girls will sacrifice herself by becoming mother figures or workhorses for their *man*. Some of these girls/women, faced with "slim pickings," will downplay their ambitions to equate themselves to their boyfriends or husbands, for the sake of having a man. But what she fails to realize is that the "bad boy scheme" becomes inadequate in terms of support and the responsibilities that accompanies life as an adult. Once again, this is where the presence of the elders could be valuable.

Yet, for African American men and boys, some never grow out of the gaming mindset because they are not required to grow up (mature) and be held accountable for their actions. They look for women, and not just Black women and girls, who are willing to take care of them like their momma may have. Having limited marketable skills, many will resort to criminal activities to make ends meet, and with this scheme comes law enforcement and the penal system. What's more disparaging is that these entities are not in people of color's favor to begin with. In some cases, the women end up tangled in his dirt because she *loves him*. Yet a large number of African American men and boys immerse themselves in self-sabotaging behaviors based on distrust and rancor due to his unpremeditated engagement within an assortment of relationships. This is when and how they continue to enter into negative relationships that do not work out. Whether it is known or not, this is an old scheme which prolongs oppositional positions amongst African American males and females. In fact, Harding (2010) offered this explanation:

> ...The high likelihood of a mismatch between what a boy is looking for in a relationship and what he perceives the typical girl is looking for means that in most nascent relationships the partners' goals well appear to be different. In this situation, distrust follows directly from the assumption that the partner will try to take advantage of the relationship. Boys use the expectation to justify their own attempts to take advantage of the relationship for personal ends, material or sexual.
>
> Having multiple models of girls and girlfriends cause trust problems in the boys' relationships, another example of the model shifting engendered by cultural heterogeneity. Even when a boy believes he has found a girl of a certain type, when other frames are also available, events or observations can trigger these alternative frames... (p 176).

So, what happens to the Black female following the unsteady behavior of her counterpart? I revert to Persaud's (2004) stance on what becomes of the Black woman: "She eventually becomes part of a half-ass relationship that caters only to the whims of her 'man.' In the end, many black women 'tolerate poor treatment hoping that if they hold out long enough, the negative behavior will stop..." (p. 26). This treatment is related to the *prince charming* wishes discussed earlier. However, Persaud went on to expose something far more damaging to African American woman:

> ...the black man finds it easy to stray because she [the Black

woman] will always be there. She is so often taken for granted and unwanted that she hopelessly seeks the love and attention from those (including her own children) who are taught to despise her. She is easily exploited, but most important, she will always be available… (p. 26).

Unfortunately, too many African Americans end up in situations where they use up their natural resources without ever pursuing or achieving the experience of engaging in a healthy relationship. Regrets and other mental anguish ensue because many African Americans may eventually see a lapse in judgment in terms of their choice in mates. Black women might think back on some of the decent suitors they overlooked or turned down through the years. "I had to have bad boy," she might think, "and he ain't shit." "I wasted my time with this…" he might say. Yet Anderson (1999) offered a description of this good man and how he is oftentimes viewed by his Black female counterpart:

> … [In this social climate] the good man, who would aspire to play the role of the decent daddy of old, is considerate of his mate and provides for her and her children, but at the same time he runs the risk of being seen as a pu**y by the women as by his peer group. This inversion in the idea of the good man underscores the ambivalent position of girls squeezed between their middle-class dreams and the ghetto reality (pp. 167 – 68, once again, I altered the slang for the female anatomy).

For those men, they remain true to themselves and are "decent, good men," they run the risk of being mistreated in their effort to relate to Black women. Please be mindful that my intent is not to talk negatively of Black women or men nor to paint them in a negative light. Many of the comments/statements expressed here are based solely on my "jaded" views based on my experiences.

Someone cautioned me years ago, "I'm afraid for boys like you. Y'all have to go through a lot of shit to find your treasure." I really didn't understand what that meant, so I asked questions. After a while, I was told: "You're a good boy and will be a decent young man someday. Some women will take your kindness for a weakness and take advantage of you." In hindsight, I see what they meant and felt the pangs of repeated sorrow and discontent as I sought to find and enjoy a healthy, loving, nurturing relationship with a Black woman. I've heard too many times, "your edges weren't rough enough for her" and "you weren't hard enough." Not all Black men are "rough necks" or "thugs." That's stereotypical BS! It's something we need to work on because it reflects how we see and feel about ourselves. I'm not interested in changing into someone I am not just to relate to or be in a relationship with a Black woman. Yet I still believe in Black love.

Can You Stop?

Realizing that wisdom and knowledge are two invaluable elements I can possess, knowing myself became all the more important because without it I remained last. A substantial portion of my alone time was not only about getting to know myself but to also get more comfortable in my own skin. I believe, now more than ever, self-knowledge and self-awareness are not just clichés to be taken lightly. They contain keys on this journey called life and all that's entailed. As one of my mentors repeatedly said, "The answers to the questions about one's self are always found in one's self." That can be no further from the truth. Knowing thy self is a source of power. In fact, Akbar (2005) defined and discussed this power in the following fashion:

> ***Power is the ability to influence the environment consistent with one's self-interest.*** …Power is intended to put people into the unique position that they can obtain and achieve within the context of their environment those things that maximize their survival and the continuation of themselves to the best of their ability. Power in this sense does not require the conquest of other people but only the acquisition of those things which have been realistically assigned for the advancement of one's own people as participants in the human community (p. 35, emphasis mine).

How does one obtain this type of power? one might ask. Akbar wrote, "We must use our inner resources in order to take from the environment those resources that insure our advancement as human beings" (p. 35).

This was an appropriate place on my journey towards self-exploration to dig deeper. I reached back to the wisdom and information I'd attained in past interactions with others. Starting with Wimberly's (2003) discussion on "externalization," which "refers to the process of reflection that helps persons look at ways their recruitment takes place and the impact that recruitment has on growth and development" (p. 18). How is this important to me as an individual? "A point of externalization is to lessen the impact of negative conversations and to promote more positive conversations through exploring one's recruitment," Wimberly explained (p. 28). Recruitment is, from my understanding, one's involvement in discussions, negative or positive, that supports our place in life. That is why Wimberly also wrote: "Human striving for meaning is never fully satisfied with negative conversations.

Negative stories always impoverish the person; positive stories enhance and enrich" (p. 27). This is an important feature of learning myself because the stories and conversations I've heard and engaged in gives me clues as to how I was seen by others and, therefore, I held of myself.

When I was in seminary, I learned the significance of knowing the story my conception and birth (my birth narrative). My mom told me of my birth story a long time ago. It was powerful in that she risked her life for me, even before the birthing process. You see, my mom was diagnosed with stomach cancer and her doctors wanted to begin treatment right away, but then, she discovered she was pregnant. I'm not sure of the timeframe, but my mother and father had a difficult decision to make—whether they should abort the child to save her life or risk losing both she and the unborn child. This went on for some time until my eldest brother, Willie, at the ripe age of 10 or 11, stepped in. "Don't get rid of the baby, momma," he implored. "If you do, I'll never speak to you again." Yikes! For a child to express such strong feelings for an unborn baby says a lot about my brother—I later discovered we share a number of characteristics and personality traits.

Needless to say, I was born October 11, 1971 at 1:18 a. m. Through the years, especially when I was struggling to find purpose in life, I questioned why my mother listened to a child on such a critical issue such as life and death. As it turned out that child *knew* I was supposed to be here and also *knew* our mother would be fine. Recently, my mom shared how she presented this decision to her doctors: "I have this baby now, so I'm going to keep my baby." Awesome! (Thanks, mommy!)

My brother and I did not get the chance to get to know one another until we were adults. Willie joined the U. S. Army when I was a child and I only got to see him when he came home on leave. My brother invited me into his home when I lost my job, my home, my car, etc. years later. He did this because I was family, but then, something amazing happened: We connected. My brother and I discovered we had so many things in common. It was like looking at a coin. He is much more reserved, while I am more animated. We both speak our minds, but we sounded differently—I have the cussing gene. However, whenever Willie does become animated and boisterous, move out the way! Overall, we both found that the strongest thread of our bond was not only our mother but we also have similar personalities.

I shared this because it lends to and supports what Wimberly (2005) explained about externalization—a person deciding "to face the pain caused by privileging negative stories and conversations" (p. 28). Such discussions that caused me pain were those that did not show me in a positive light. There were a few people who did not wish the best for me, and that was hurtful, especially as a child. Instead of encouraging or inspiring greatness, some of the sentiments were the opposite. I stopped believing those stories and did something different. I now know this process was a form of self-evaluating and getting rid of those stories that meant me no good—"...this process is the ego looking directly at the conversation basis of one's personality" (pp. 27 – 28). Before I could stop believing what others said about me, I had to examine what was said and weigh them against who I was. The pain came I saw what people thought of me in a certain way. But, in the end, their words did not count. It was what God thought of and made me to be that counted.

Learning who you are carries a lot of weight because it mitigates uncertainties and promotes resolute aspirations, purpose, and most of all, your place in this world. The gateway to relating to others in such a way that exerts confidence is knowing the direction I am traveling. This is why the axiom: "Learning where you came from helps you to get where you're going is so beneficial." Akbar (2005) astutely wrote, "People can only belong to themselves if their identity is an outgrowth of their history, their culture, their reality and their survival needs" (p. 4). When I started focusing on myself, setting limits and boundaries were not so hard. Not knowing myself created space and opportunities for others to take advantage of me, and that's not who I was designed to be in this world. "Self-knowledge requires us to inspect these components of ourselves," Akbar said, "and appreciate the role they have played in structuring the path that we are travelling" (p. 26).

Making changes in my life required a process of transforming the way I saw myself and what I believed myself to be. In order for change to occur, rewriting the *fairytales* about me was called for. Wimberly (1997) called this procedure, "Reauthoring the Myths that Bind Us," in that he taught: "We can transform the beliefs and convictions we have long held about our sense of self, ourselves in relation to others, and how we engage in the activity of caring" (p. 73). Going back to the trait I shared in Chapter Seven, "the giving spirit." I examined the stories and examples I'd seen throughout my life to see how and why I engaged in this behavior. Something had to be done about it because of the pain and dissonance it caused in my life and psyche. Wimberly continued on to expound on this reauthoring concept:

> Reauthoring recognized that change in convictions and beliefs is possible; we are not totally at the mercy of our

early childhood experiences, unconscious processes, and cultural conventions. While altering our myths is a slow process with much struggle and resistance, reauthoring moves forward as our resolve grows that we are neither totally passive in creating and formulating myths nor acquiescent in living out the stories that myths entail.

Myths are not just handed down. We play an active part in developing the myths that inform our lives. We have the capacity to interpret events and give them meaning and significance. …Myth making, then, assumes that we ae not powerless, not without agency in shaping the myths that inform our lives. Within realistic limits, it is possible to take responsibility for how we interpret reality and give meaning to it (1997, p. 73).

I disclosed how my giving and helping others affected many areas of my life, to the point where they negatively impacted the way I related to others. In a previous work, *Perpetual Victim* (2018), I discussed a character named "Alonzo, 'Mr. Savoir Faire'." Alonzo reached a point in his life where his altruism caused problems in his life, and his loved ones brought it to his attention to which it was not well received. This is how others saw him: "Alonzo was known by many as a 'guy who would give you the shirt off his back,' literally. He had a heart for people and did not like seeing others suffer. By no stretch of the imagination did Alonzo try to portray himself as perfect or that he had it all together, but he tried to show compassion at all costs—sometimes at the expense of his own peace of mind" (p. 22). For Alonzo, this was a way of life and he felt it was necessary to help others no matter what. He never imagined he would be faced with the challenge of examining such an important aspect of his life.

Alonzo's dilemma was:

> He worked hard and oftentimes more than those he tried to help. Alonzo attributed his overcompensation to his "love of people" and "sharing the load with others." Therefore, his "helping" others led him to feeling abandoned, betrayed, and disappointed once the people he assisted needs or wants were met. However, there was another aspect to Alonzo's lending a hand. Alonzo had a tendency of meeting and dating women whom were struggling in their lives. He took the position of the "knight in shining armor," bringing temporary relief to whatever situation they were in—whether it was emotionally or financially, he stepped in and tried to save the day (p. 72).

Don't get me wrong, helping others isn't a terrible thing because we all need assistance of some kind at some point in our lives. However, in Alonzo's case, there were a couple of things working against him: he sometimes put in too much work and his rationale was not clear in his heart and mind. When faced with consternation in this regard, Alfonzo struggled to reconcile the lessons he learned because this "was something he observed his parents do his entire life, but he never really gained a clear understanding as to why they behaved the way they did or why they chose to do so... He failed to put in the work of developing his own spin on 'giving'" (pp. 71 – 72).

Here's a little secret: I wrote those words to describe myself over two years prior to writing of this book. It is amazing how God's timing reins sovereign over everything we do. I picked up on this a while ago and am now coming to grips with it as I began reinterpreting how I see myself in this regard. Yet this is not surprising because I had to continue to live and function in my *dysfunction* so I would be able to observe myself as I continued to relate to others. Yet Wimberly (1997) offered a sense of relief when he wrote:

> Attribution assigns meaning to experience; attribution or assigning meaning, which gives significance to our experience. …Attribution, or assigning meaning to life experiences, is the result of our encounters with life transitions and traumatic events. Myths are formed from attributions that help us make sense of things… Existing attributions are often *inadequate* in helping us respond to new challenges… …As we face challenges to our existing mythic formulations and interpretations of reality, not all of us will do the necessary editing and updating. Some of us resist changing them, feeling secure with what we already have done regarding our beliefs. Others of us, however, readily welcome the challenges and grow as a result. We see the new challenges as opportunities rather than dangers (pp. 74, 75; emphasis mine).

How accurate those words were in describing where I was in this process. I did not recognize my giving as a of the sign, or shall I say a catalyst, for examining and rewriting those stories that explained why I functioned that way I did. I knew I needed to be clear on why I did things for others (intentions), but somehow I never considered how or why helping others became a burden until it disrupted my peace of mind. Being a giver for so long, I struggled with letting it go, stepping out of the way, and making the proper adjustments in the roles I played. Accepting this was a process; a long, arduous process. However, it was necessary because I was able to see what I needed to work on as I moved onto the next phase of my life.

Getting to know myself is not an absolute process where I do it once and it's done for good. It is a repetitive undertaking that should be done ever-so-often, especially in the wake of noteworthy life-changing events. In fact, "...Self-knowledge, in part, has to do with understanding the impact of these influences," Akbar (2005, p. 26) explained. "...This process of self-exploration not only permits you to discover those hidden gems in yourself, which are special to you, but it helps you to identify those things which you do not do very well" (p. 27). To be clear, this process is an opportunity for growth and direction; it is not intended to beat yourself up but to rewrite the stories of your life. Taking time for myself has offered opportunities for restoration of relationships that were important to me.

Before I move on, I want to share the stages of reauthoring your beliefs and myths:

1. Identify the themes that make up our personal myth.
2. Assess the influence of these themes on our lives over a period of time. This assessment determines if the themes are growth-facilitating or growth-inhibiting, and whether they contribute to our being wounded healers rather than remaining walking wounded.
3. Attempt to discern God's presence or a spiritual force at work in transforming these themes into themes of a wounded healer.
4. Make plans to alter the themes of the personal myth in order to increase our growth possibilities (Wimberly, 1997; p. 77).

Allow me to expound on the difference between a "wounded healer" and "walking wounded." First, both are states of being, but differs in that one merely exists, and the other lives a full life in spite of one's woundedness. A person can have a cut on their finger that is bleeding. The cut does not cause the person to stop living as infection sets in because the proper attention was not given. To prevent the spread of contamination, the person has to take care of the wound by cleaning and bandaging it. Therefore, the person might be wounded, but they are still able to live on (walking wounded).

Is It True?

One of the ways I was able to begin reauthoring my story was continuously reminding myself that "I cannot keep taking on assignments that were not given to me." In other words, I had to allow others to figure out their own situations without jumping in to save them and doing the work for them. I had to get out of the way so people could solve their own problems and grow. If I did not do this, seeds of resentment would have been planted, and I would have deprived myself of the opportunity to live my life to the fullest. I am mindful that my actions may have been interfering with a person's reaping what they may have sown. Like Alonzo (wink, wink), I did not like seeing people suffer, but my actions impeded the lessons and experiences they needed for *their* journey. Arriving at this place helped me to forgive of myself for a lot of reasons, and on a lot of levels.

I started my reauthoring process by looking at an area I struggled with over the years—grappling with what others thought of me and trying to please them. Don't get me wrong, I did not dwell on others' opinions or observations of me, or at least tried not to; yet there were times when some of their words cut deeply. I learned to limit how much time I invested in certain people's thoughts and/or opinions of me because most times I did not know what their agendas were. I didn't trust them enough to accept their words to begin with. I found that the views of others were a disruption from what I needed to do on my journey.

* * * * *

In DeGruy's (2017) discussion of "vacant esteem," which is "the state of believing oneself to have little or no worth, exacerbated by similar pronouncements of inferiority from the personal sphere and larger society" (p, 108). Is imperative to our understanding of this context. Vacant esteem is more intense than low self-esteem in that it renders a person as worthless or useless in the world. This does not necessarily mean a person doesn't want to live. They fail to live up to his or her full potential based on the conversations, view and myths others may have created for them.

I thought about this concept long and hard to ensure that I did not fit into this category, which I did not because "When these influences (my family, community and society) all promote a disparaging and limiting identity to which we believe we are confined…," (p. 108). Had this been the case, it would have been extremely difficult for me to have set and pursue goals in my life. I consider myself blessed because I was born into a familial environment that pushed me and others to pursue higher heights in life. However, DeGruy spoke of this type of family setting, which is contrary to my origins:

> When parents believe themselves to have little or no value, it reflects itself in behaviors that can instill a similar belief in their children. This belief is passed down through generations in the form of unexamined, and often long established, child-rearing practices. Some of the extreme ways we have worked to make our children submissive and

docile provide examples of established parenting that can contribute to vacant esteem (p. 109).

I became aware of these types of occurrences as I began taking my wellbeing seriously in order to submit to this change process, which included looking at various aspects of my life's story. It required me to look for clues that were similar to the above-mentioned quote. I identified many positive qualities that were instilled in me, such as a strong work ethic, standards, values, and morals. To my knowledge, there was no tearing down or belittling, beyond jokes and teasing, which could have caused me to possess vacant esteem.

DeGruy (2017) also spoke on features of vacant esteem and African Americans when she wrote: "Another indication of vacant esteem is the effort to undermine the achievements of other African Americans. We all know this by the euphemistic phrase, 'crabs in the barrel.' Whether we are talking about youth in school or adults in the workplace, there are those who seek to bring down those who look like them" (p. 110). Unfortunately, this phenomenon occurs frequently; and it is the source of great trepidation within the African American community. It happens several ways: folk tearing others down or individuals cutting off those who believe in their potential and abilities. The crab in a barrel mentality affects those who are satisfied in their mediocre, complacent with their station in life, while convincing others to be satisfied with them. In some cases, people will sabotage another person's progress in order to keep him or her with them.

Another sad but true example of vacant esteem, is when one person believes, supports, and pushes another person to pursue the goals that *that* person may have shared. The ally may observe the people around the other person and find that they might be comfortable with their life's station. Little to no encouragement occurs and the person that attempted to motivate him or her becomes "an outsider," and cast out of that person's inner-circle.

Boundaries are useful in this area because "You can lead a horse to water," the old adage says, "but you can't make them drink." Although I've heard similar messages about boundaries, I did not get it until it was my time to do so. I was reminded of the lesson Dr. Al taught not only through his books but also face-to-face contact—"You cannot be affective in another person's life if they are not ready." Again, one of the most important takeaways during my time of transition was not to interfere in other people's lives because they have to experience life for themselves. I had gotten so accustomed with giving/helping that it became requisite for some. I've learned to mind my own business and leave people alone. I arrived at a point in my life where I do not have to be available to everyone, all the time; and I certainly do not have to present.

Can This Last?

I listened to a song by an old school R&B group by the name of Skyy (1989) throughout this process; their song called "Real Love." The lyrics, performed by the female lead singer, implores her lover to give love another chance. These are some of the words: "Don't be afraid of the way you feel (don't be afraid) Open your heart and you'll see it's real, it's real love." This soulful song speaks volumes in that the singer expresses an understanding of her lover's past hurts and disappointments. She goes on to assure him that she does not intend to hurt him, but there was no guarantee that neither one of them will not feel pain. This song is inspirational because it helped me to see I needed to first love myself before I could love anyone. Don't get me wrong, I've always *liked* myself but not so sure if I fully loved, embraced, and accepted myself for who I was (am). By engaging in the reauthoring process, I began an incredible walk where I carefully considered how things/people affected my peace and wellbeing. Now, you would be hard-pressed to get a rise out of me. I've learned to remove myself from situations and let folk go on their way before I allowed them to upset me in any way. So, let's discuss how I got there.

    One of the reoccurring themes that came to mind during this process was my ability to set and maintain healthy **boundaries**, because I had loose to none with most of the people I was affiliated with. As one of the therapists I worked with used to say to me: "Your boundaries are for you. They can and will prevent others from going too far with you because your boundaries will not allow them to." My challenge was not knowing how to set boundaries because I did so for others, which was what I was used to doing. I needed to do so for myself and that caused a number of challenges for me. But here's another piece to this puzzle: I had to get to the point where I was not only ready to ascertain healthy boundaries, but to reinforce and maintain them. There are some folks, for example, I will not communicate with them unless it is absolutely necessary. Even then, I am very careful to stick to the purpose as to why I am communicating and not allowing violations or abuse to occur. Yup, those sentiments people held about me being cold and distant became the way I presented myself to some because it tells them the contact is about *that business* only.

    Can you imagine how many people either blocked me or changed their numbers without letting me know or passing on the new one? I can tell you I truly did not give a damn. In fact, it was funny because they put in the effort and the dollars to make this happen when I was not interested in communicating with them any longer. I decided to get out of the "crab in a barrel" environment because of who I was created to be, which did not include a self-loathing, coveting lifestyle. I made the conscious decision to put certain things, behaviors, and people aside and live my life. This started when I began seeing myself in a new light, which did not include being anyone's emotional doormat.

I evaluated my relationship with God. One of the things my mother and other family members repeatedly pounded in my siblings and I heads was "You gotta know God for yourself." So, I reconnect with God. I quit being mad at church folks. I stopped blaming others for the way they treated me, and then, getting mad at God because "God allowed these things to happen to me." I had to see how I played into this situation because I allowed people to treat me the way they did.

I stopped going to church long before COVID-19 and all of its restrictions. In fact, it was almost two years beforehand. Religion, in the traditional sense, was killing me—body, mind and soul. I needed to understand *my* relationship with GOD!!!! As I encouraged a friend and sister in Christ, "When we set out to know ourselves, we can't help but to encounter God along the way." It was at that very moment that I realized the magnitude of such this statement that I understood the necessity of letting go of the need to feel needed by others—namely those who only wanted to use me for whatever reason that benefitted them—because I need me more. I am valued in God's sight. There was much more I had to do in this world and for myself. Was this an easy feat? It was not at first, but then, it became less painful once I counted up the cost.

There were several aspects of my relationship with God that were uncovered during this time of learning and reauthoring my story. First thing's first, who I am is not tied into others. This is a two-fold revelation: No one, but God and myself, defines who I am and am not because of what I can do or be for anyone else. Back in the day, we had a saying: "Never let a (explicative) make you." What this means is you cannot allow yourself to get so wrapped up in another person, a position, or a title, to the point that they define who you are.

The biggest misstep I made was letting people determine what I should and should not do because of my position, credentials, or title. For years, I tried to conform to many expectations. My life became discombobulated in a number of ways. I lost sight of who I was called to be. The people who supported and loved me enough to let me know when something was out of sync. I got caught up in false purposes. I became so wrapped up in helping others because I thought I was obligated to do so. Before I knew it, years had gone by and I did not have the chance to live for myself. Sure, I accomplished a number of goals along the way, but I wasn't living in a way that was enjoyable. I got caught up in what Galatians 6: 2 – 6 (*NIV*) says, while missing the instructions:

> Carry each other's burdens, and in this way you will fulfill the law of Christ. If anyone thinks they are something when they are not, they deceive themselves. Each one should test their own actions. Then they can take pride in themselves alone, without comparing themselves to someone else, for each one should carry their own load. Nevertheless, the one who receives instruction in the word should share all good things with their instructor.

I took time to study myself in various situations and they no longer worked for me. I didn't like what I saw in hindsight, of course. Again, "I cannot take on assignments that were not given to me," helped me to see how/why I did so. I cannot be who/what people want or need if it's not what I am/was supposed to do. Many times, people are in search of something and they may not be in a position to receive it. I cannot find out what it is, and then, conform to whatever that might be. I am in the way, out of order, and in the wrong position when I do so because I am not GOD!!! If God did not put me in that position, then it is not mine to step into. God is the giver of all things and meets every need. I had to respect that!

If you believe in the power of prayer, you know God (or your Higher Power) hears you when you cry out. I prayed that God would show me the way I needed go. Slowly but surely, it began to come to pass. I started seeing this request come to fruition. It was painful but I knew if I did not take heed, I would down the wrong path.

I looked at it this way: There are four seasons, and those seasons are different. Each season serves a different purpose and they have certain durations. So does many things and people in our lives. Holding on too long can and will cause irreparable damage. I accepted the fact that a number of people had served their purpose and the time had come for us to move on along like the changing of the seasons. I had to give up my sentimental holds of them and move on with my life. When these things began to happen, there is nothing I could do about it. Otherwise, I'd probably be doing too much in that relationship.

What's Next?

It was time to move forward while not forgetting from whence I came. I know there are many things I must continue to examine and process. But as I said before: It was my time to redefine myself, to reinvent myself and to reauthor what I believed myself to be. You see, when this is done in a healthy way, the chances of something knocking me off my square becomes less likely. Thus, I must further explore meaning in my life. In other words, I consorted with God to give meaning in my life.

Viktor Emil Frankl, who is recognized as the "Father of Logotherapy," discussed our existence to which he noted: "…existence is a way of being, characteristic to human beings, which is not a factual being, but a facultative way of being. It is a not a unique and never-changing way of being, as neurotic people tend to misinterpret it, but the possibility to always change oneself" (1994, p. 61). In other words, we are able to participate in the way we live and we can always change how we live. Yet, Marshall and Marshall (2012) said this about us:

> Human beings are the only creatures who can reach beyond themselves in the search for purposeful goals and values. They have a body, and a mind. But beyond, their bodies and minds, they are equipped with *Freedom of Will* to explore, and to decide, the direction of their actions, even if this means acting in the belief of something that is greater than them (p. 13).

What makes this so awesome is that Frankl called this the "Freedom of Will" in that we, human beings, have the ability to decide on what and/or how we will live. For many, this choosing can be in concert with a Higher Power/Being. Marshall and Marshall (2012) also stated: "While in body and mind we are determined, and/or influenced by physical, and psychological mechanisms, there is a dimension—a uniquely human dimension—which allows us to reach beyond ourselves in the search for meaning" (p. 13). This dimension, the third dimension, is called the spirit, Frankl (1975) refers to as "specifically human dimension" (p. 90).

There's great power in the human spirit. We are able to transcend many obstacles and overcome barriers because we can reach beyond what seems impossible. What makes the human spirit so special is it "is a not a substance. It is a dynamic" (Frankl, 1975). To further explain the characteristics of the human spirit, I'll share a few of several:

> The spirit cannot be divided, reduced, or duplicated. The spirit as a whole is greater than the sum of its parts. Spirit is the essence of a person. It is, with each person, an entirely new creation, not inherited from one's parents, or encoded in the genes. The spirit is not constrained to here-and-now. Spirit is essentially "trans-spacial," and "trans-temporal" dynamism, spanning the past, and the present in the search of meaning. It is essentially open to the future. It cannot be damaged, or destroyed, and it does not become ill… Spirit is that dimension through which human beings can rise above their psychological and physical dimensions, and take a stand towards it. In other words, to exist means "…to come back to oneself by rising above, and beyond oneself, and one's circumstances" (Frankl, 1994, p. 61; in Marshall and Marshall, 2012, p. 15, 16).

I shared all of this to say that the human spirit has the ability to endure, rise above tough times, and is not be confined to our physical bodies. The spirit is the core of who we are and is our being. However, we function within the limits of our physical being because we are imperfect mortals. Yet we still have the ability to change our situations by altering our wills. Marshall and Marshall (2012) elucidated on the confines and the freedom of the human will in the following terms:

> Within the limitations of being vulnerable, fallible, and finite human beings, we are essentially free to distance ourselves, and to rise above, and beyond our instincts, genetic inheritance, and environment. We can choose our response to our genes, upbringing, to events of fate, and even to our own selves.
>
> Our freedom and responsibility extend to the point that our conscience allows us to discern meaning possibilities, with the provision, that it is the conscience of a fallible and mortal human being… we need not fight against our instincts drives, genetic inheritance, and environment all the time, and at all costs. For, as much as we express ourselves "despite," or act "in-response-to" our physical and psychological realities, so we become ourselves exactly with "help of" and "through" our physical, social, and psychological realities (p. 17, containing Frankl 1984 and 1994).

With an understanding of the Freedom of Will, human beings are at liberty to be whom they were called to be by being aware of all aspects of their being. Wimberly (2000) added this dimension when he wrote: "Humans beings also develop a positive self-understanding by adopting and identifying with positive narratives and roles through which they can orient their lives" (p. 24). When a person is in touch with themselves, which comes with what they believe about themselves, then he or she can "will" themselves to new heights. This includes their relationships— "Instead, they are fleeing former relationships in the pursuit of what they consider higher. Perhaps the relationships in which they were involved did not produce the kinds of rewards that they have come to expect" (p. 24). I concur. Again, one must know thy self in order to recognize their worth and their purpose.

Returning to Logotherapy, which means "healing through meaning" (Frankl, 1978, p. 19), and how it can be beneficial in the process of reauthoring myths and beliefs about oneself. I concentrated on various aspects of my life in order to reconstruct what I believed about myself. I had to discern who or what was holding me from who and what I am supposed to be. I was not what Wimberly (2000) called a "Relational Refugee," "...persons not grounded in nurturing and liberating relationships. They [relational refugees] are detached and without significant connections with others who promote self-development" (p. 20). Fortunately, I did have people in my life who supported and encouraged me to care for and love on myself more. This is contrary to "They [relational refugees] lack a warm relational environment in which to define and nurture their self-identity. As a consequence, they withdraw into destructive relationships that exacerbate rather than alleviate their predicament" (p. 20).

I'll have to admit that I can be a bit complicated given that one moment I enjoy being by myself because of the absence of "drama," and then, I might want to be in a relationship. Having made the decision to take a break after my last relationship to focus on who I am and what I need has been very productive. The urge to be with someone were overshadowed by the benefit of my purpose for this period in my life. I need(ed) to achieve happiness within myself, and what I have been destined to fulfil. "Humans beings need to be surrounded by people who have positive attitudes towards them," Wimberly (2000) said, "because such attitudes become the basis for one's own positive self-image. People become selves by internalizing the attitudes of others" (p. 23). Because the processes of knowing oneself and reauthoring myths in our lives is mostly done by oneself, having people who genuinely love me certainly made a difference. Wimberly asserted the following:

> Human beings learn to live in a healthy, whole manner by seeing such practices demonstrated by others they trust, imitating these patterns and rehearsing their own ways of living. Such experiences form internalized scenarios that govern how people interpret subsequent experiences. If people internalize only negative experiences, they will develop negative scenarios, which then become patterns of response to later experience, whether positive or negative (p. 23).

Here's where Wimberly's teachings came in handy. Several people warned and encouraged me to be careful of who I associated with over the years, but it really did not click (or denied) until I started feeling the coldness from some individuals. I retreated to sort things out and threw out a few tests to see if they would bite. Those individuals took the bait each time. Though it did not shock me, it stung because I knew these individuals had to be let go. Their willingness to breach my trust with such ease that made it easier for me to let go. In doing so, demonstrated my willingness to respect myself and show them how to treat me. Discerning who genuinely loved me for me made all the difference. However, Wimberly (1997) called this behavior a result of "The myth of self-sacrifice or unlovability." He captured its essence as the following:

> This myth relates to the belief that we will only be loved if we hide our true selves. The love we received as children was often conditional, based on performing up to others' expectations, to the detriment of self. A major theme in this myth is unrequited or unreturned love. We hide our real selves, burying deeply our anger about having to sacrifice selfhood (pp. 25 – 26).

I said all of that to say, the roles I willingly took on and the parts I played were at my discretion. I cannot complain about how I am treated if I was not willing to acknowledge *my* behaviors. After all, I was in control of my choices and my actions. Once I knew my actions were causing me problems and cost more than I was willing to pay, changes were made with no regrets. One writer said it this way: "The ability to contemplate and to be aware of life's ending makes life precious. In the knowledge of the finiteness of life it makes sense to act. To find what is meaningful becomes urgent" (Marshall and Marshall, 2012; p. 21). This statement took on a new meaning when I discovered there was far more to life than trying to assist others on their "come ups," when in actuality, they were only trying to sustain for the moment.

*****

At some point, I became "jaded." This state of jadedness prevented me from embracing a number of things with hope and usefulness. Knowing that I wanted to live more productively, this was a good place to start. I had to first accept my woundedness, which contributed to my weariness, before I could look at myself clearly. I knew if I did not address some of the hurt in my life, I would continue hurting myself as well as others. I had to do my part so I could move forward and hope to find someone who is working on themselves. I contemplated my desire to find a suitable mate and assigned value to an enriching experience in that regard. Having a loving relationship based on mutual respect is where I am in my life, and I am confident that it is achievable. I'm ready to receive the skills and knowledge that would serve me best in this regard.

This process has helped me to recognize that there are a lot of hurting people in the world; and, unfortunately, many are stuck in either their pain or their dysfunction, or both. I was one of them and did not know the depth of my pain until I saw my ex-girlfriend face-to-face. It was an acrimonious situation and I realized it was contrary to who I am. Once I processed that meeting, I found myself empathizing for us. I saw so much pain between us but in diverse ways. I made the choice not to live that way any longer because, although love is a complicated entity, there is no room for animosity towards anyone. That's not who I am.

I often wonder how we can allow ourselves to get so stuck in seeking revenge that we don't see how hurt we truly are. In this "interesting" climate the world is currently in, I pray for humanity's inhumanities, and that includes our interpersonal connections. Therefore, if there ever comes a time when I see any of my exes, I pray that we are able to be civil towards one another because this is what's needed. We need to help one another heal in order to restore our communities.

Needless to say, I've found that my level of skepticism have decreased from the time I started working on this book. I'm open to the possibilities that lie ahead as well as the new opportunities that are waiting for me to step into. I listened LaBelle's (1974) *What Can You Do for Me?* "People want to live not merely exist...," these words struck a chord in my soul because these lyrics speaks to helping people to move past complacent spaces in their lives. "…In some respects, it is easier today [1946]: we can now speak freely again so many things," Frankl said, "things that are inherently connected with the problem of the meaningfulness of human existence and its value, and with human dignity" (2019). It's interesting to see that the more things change, the more they remain the same. I really believe many of my difficulties, as they relate to my romantic aspirations and relationships in general, are linked to how I see myself.

If I could assemble a soundtrack of my life, it would have a variety of genres as well as songs. I listened to the late Jermaine Steward's, "We Don't Have to Take our Clothes Off," released in the spring of 1986. I was in the eighth grade and my girlfriend and I experienced the purest form of puppy love. As I told you earlier on, it thrilled me to the bone to have been able to simply hold her hand. Since then, my approach to love and romance grew significantly. I went from innocence, to the "nitty-gritty," to now, pure longing for something more concrete in the sense that the games I played before are long gone. As India.Arie (2001) melodically expressed, "I am ready for love. Why are you hiding from me…? I am ready for love. Will you take me in your hands? I will learn what you teach and do the best that I can…." With that being said, there is no better way to end this book. *Is It Just Me* or am I truly ready for love?

Afterthoughts:

Isn't Life Interesting?

Now that we have come to the end of this book, I thought about some of the changes I've made in my life. My perceptions are not the same because I've matured tremendously. I have acquired levels of awareness beyond what I'd expected. I am more open, compassionate, and understanding, while at the same time, not very intolerant of unnecessary drama and commotion. I just won't stand for it because maintaining my peace became more important than ruckus. I finally learned how to get out of the way and let things go how they go. Continuous confrontations, contentions and strife is no way to live. So, I leave folks alone, while *not* allowing others to mistreat, use or handle me. Doing so was (and is) optimal because I appreciate my worth, which is far more than some might think or see. Working on this book has shown me a number of wonderful aspects of myself and ways to pursue my dreams without depriving myself when helping others. I will live a blessed life in such a way that I will no longer limit myself in order to *be* myself. I've found my peace and will protect it at all costs.

Speaking of living, one of the best gems of wisdom I've gleaned during this process was becoming comfortable in my own skin. This means I am learning to be and "do me" without pausing to see if I'm what others *want* me to be. I was reminded of this during two discussions I had—one with my mom and the other with a good friend. My mom, who imparted great wisdom all of my life, repeatedly emphasized a critical lesson: "You cannot be everything to everybody. All you can do is be yourself." It's time for me to live for me, unapologetically!

Not very long after my talk with my mom, my friend and I made the same observation because we had to be who and what others wanted for so long that we had to unlearn that behavior in order to discover better ways to live. I must have said this a thousand times: "I cannot be who you want me to be and still be sane." Therefore, I remind myself to relax and enjoy being my authentic self.

One of the most liberating aspects of this entire project was affirming that I can be myself without selling myself short. It became crystal clear that conceding who I am in order to appease others creates misery, unnecessary suffering, and regret. Having genuine friendships will happen naturally as I show who I am. This progression does not mean I should reveal myself to just anyone because there are sharks out there waiting to devour and/or distract me. I started trusting myself more, while utilizing the skills I possess as it pertains to me associating with others. I have taken small steps in allowing others to get to know me, did so while taking great care of observing what people say and what they show me.

Is It Just Me has inspired me to continue writing in such a way that's beyond the mundane and trendy. There is a great deal of work to be done, especially during these turbulent times. People are disparately looking for relief as we face a multitude of political and social issues. We must be cognizant, however, of who we are while remaining safe. In times like these, I'm reminded of what the late Dr. June Dobbs Butts emphasized during a classroom lecture: "When people are in pain they search for ways to feel good at any cost, even if it's on someone else's dime." The context to which Dr. Dobbs Butts made this statement referred to inappropriate and nonconsenting sexual contact. Essentially, she helped us to make the connection between forcible and nonconsensual encounters, which are crimes, with hurt people perpetrating egregious acts on others who do/did not give permission to them. Dr. Dobbs Butts' overall point was "People just wanna feel good."

At juncture of this process, I've had the chance to ponder one of the questions posed therein: Does my sexual assault still affect my life? Honestly, it does but not as intensely as it once had. I am grateful to have supportive people in my life as well as others who have endured horrific experiences of their own. To be clear, I do have people with whom I consistently communicate with and consider my friends, who are also survivors. Rarely do we speak on our experiences but will support one another when needed. We authentically push and prod each other to be better than our past circumstances. Carefully yet essentially, we checked in during those times of restriction and isolation.

Nevertheless, those who survived COVID-19 were affected in some way akin to a type of Post-Traumatic Stress Disorder. I chose to use some of the restriction time to work on me, to find ways to develop and become a better me. *Is It Just Me* or am I not the only hopeful soul who believes in the power of unity and healing? Although many things have taken place, both good and bad, negative, and positive, I feel things will change for the betterment of humanity. I say this because this is where my faith is grounded. Finally, *Is It Just Me* or I am the only one who believes in the power of love, and where there's love, there's hope.

K. A. S. J.

December 1, 2020

Acknowledgements

I give honor and glory to the Creator of the universe, God, and thanks to God's son, my Lord and Savior, Jesus the Christ. I am nothing without Your presence. I thank You for Your power, Your protection, and most importantly, Your love. Amen!

To my awesome parents: Shirley Ann Jones-Bryant (Anderson), the late Curtis Mutammadine Bey Calloway (my earthly father), and the late Charles Levi Anderson (my earthly dad). Thank you all for your tremendous sacrifices, lessons and love you've shed upon me. You've helped me become the man I am and will be. I give you the earthly credit for all that I am, and I thank you for being the conduit for me. I can go on-and-on but for the sake of time and space: Words cannot express my gratitude. So, I say, thank you. I love you. And I miss you much (father and dad).

To my brothers, sisters, and in-laws: Willie, III, Roy J., Sr., Duane C. B. Jones, Roy W. J. Anderson, Tihira S. Jones-Anderson and Connie C. H. Anderson, Shannon (Roy, Sr.), Keisha (Duane), Thomasena, and LaShondria (my birthday twin). To my nieces and nephews: Pamela, LaShay, Anamarie, Nicole, Ivory, Roy, Jr., Kai-El, Ra-El, Jacoby, MacKenzie, David Walker, David McCray, Naomi and Denise Petterson, Miracle Jefferson, and the late Niakia Desre. To my grand nieces and nephews, aunts, uncles, and cousins: Too many for me to name and/or remember (I'm just being honest). To my "second heartbeat": Timothy J. Troupe, Roy J. "Doughboy" Jones, Jr., Elijah J. "E-Dub" Walker, Kionna M. R. "B. B. Butterfly" Richards and Brianna N. "Sunshine" Jefferson. And to my mentees, past and present. Much love.

To my god sisters, god brothers, and friends, who supported, encouraged and pushed me during this process (and there are many): Minnettia and Nicole Durant, Keesha and Terry Walker, Angelita (Angel) Young, Anjamilah Gregory, Tiyan and Timothy Petterson, Olayinka Olubumni-Williams (Dr. O.) and Gary Williams, Antionette (Toni B.) Betton, Glennisha S. White, Charlene Sims, Jeneice Richards, Memi Elliot, Phillip and La Quanda Barber, Dr. Dana Taylor (PBS), and Robin Johnson. My VA crew: Felicia McGrue, Cherreca Scandrett, Sharrion Beard, Jennifer Young, Deborah Mayo, Dawn Turner, Rhonda Meeks, Brenda Whitfield, Chardenay Jones, Michelle Washington, LaTonya Butler-Palmer, Trecialeen "Tricia" Young, and Aisha Bryant.

And to my fur baby: Libra Beauty Jones, Daddy's heart.

To my gifted, creative, collaborative team:

Kionna M. R. "BBB" Richards: Thank you for writing the "Special Note" for this book. My heart was full of joy as I read your words and I must say they were on point. Being a part of your life, even as an adult, is both an honor and a great joy. It's been an interesting journey thus far, and there are many miles to go. I am privileged to be considered an important part of your life.

Many times, young adults tend to push people away as they seek to find and identify their places in the world. You understand and appreciate God's purpose for my presence in your life, as do I respect your place in mine. I prayerfully do my best to *stay in order* (as you know) as I *obediently* interact with you. I pray that our journeys continue to be filled with lessons to be learned and applied to our lives as well as the lives of others. Never forget that you were created for *GREATNESS* and not distractions! Continued blessings. I love you much, my precious B. B. B.

Lisa Brown, Kelly Gorham, Annie T. Shaw-Spellman, and Erica Harry: I am truly grateful to have met you. All of you have been a source of inspiration, motivation, and support throughout this process. You've provided great constructive criticism and feedback, and gave me parse for the course as I grappled with the information presented in this book. You've (Lisa and Kelly) read and reassured me that what is presented was needed and necessary. You've (Annie and Erica) shared your perspective, when you could have simply brushed me off, but encouraged me to keep digging around for truths that were not readily accessible. Thank you all for your time and enthusiasm. I truly appreciate you.

Please charge it to my mind if your name is not listed. This is why I don't like "***name dropping***."

ABOUT THE AUTHOR

Kasim Ali Sidney Jones earned a Bachelor of Social Work from Kean University (Union, New Jersey), a Master of Divinity from the Interdenominational Theological Center (Atlanta, GA); and a Doctor of Education from Argosy University (Sarasota, FL). Dr. Jones is the author of *No Shame in the Game*, *Tamar's Healing*, and *Perpetual Victim*. He is also an ordained minister, Board Certified Christian Therapist/Counselor, the sole proprietor of Tamar's Healing, LLC, and employed by the Veteran Health Administration. Dr. Jones is the middle child of seven and resides in Georgia.

References

Akbar, N. (1996). *Breaking the chains of psychological slavery.* Tallahassee, FL: Mind Productions.

Anderson, E. (1999). *Code of the street: Decency, violence, and the moral life of the inner city.* New York: W. W. Norton & Company.

Baack, G. A. (2016). *The Inheritors: Moving forward from generational trauma.* She Writes Press.

Berry, M. F. and Blassingame, J. W. (1982). *Long memory: The Black experience in America.* New York: Oxford University Press.

Birch, A. (2014). *Boundaries: After a pathological relationship.*

Blassingame, J. W. (1979). *The slave community: Plantation life in the Antebellum South* (Revised & Enlarged ed.). New York: Oxford University Press.

Bradshaw, J. (2005). *Healing the shame that binds you* (Expanded and Updated Ed.). Deerfield, FL: Health Communications, Inc.

_____. (1995). *Family secrets: The path from shame to healing.* New York: Bantam Books.

Brown, C. R. (2009). *Brain damage: The slave mentality of African Americans.* Elmont, NY: Enaz Publications.

Brown, D. L., White-Johnson, R. L., and Griffin-Fennell, F. D. (2013). Breaking the chains: Examining the endorsement of modern Jezebel images and racial-ethnic esteem among African American women, *Culture, Health & Sexuality*, vol. 15, no. 5, 525 – 539. Retrieved from http://dx.doi.org/10.1080/13691058.772240.

Charak, R., Eshelman, L. R., and Messman-Moore, T. L. (2019). "Latent Classes of Childhood Maltreatment, Adult Sexual Assault, and Revictimization in Men: Differences in Masculinity, Anger, and Substance Use," *Psychology of Men & Masculinities*, vol. 20, no. 4, 503 – 514.

Cress Welsing, F. (1991). *The Isis Papers: The keys to the colors.* Chicago, IL: Third World Press.

Cross, D. (2006). *Soul ties: Unseen bond in relationships.* Lancaster, LA: Sovereign World.

DeGruy, J. (2017). *Post Traumatic Slave Syndrome: America's legacy of enduring injury & healing.* Dr. Joy DeGruy Be the Healing.

Easton, S. D., Saltzman, L. Y., and Willis, D. G. (2014). "'Would You Tell Under Circumstances Like That?': Barriers to Disclosure of Child Sexual Abuse for Men," *Psychology of Men & Masculinity*, vol. 15, no. 4, 460 – 469.

Eddy, B. (2018). *5 Types of people who can ruin your life: Identifying and dealing with narcissists, sociopaths, and other High-Conflict Personalities.* New York: TarcherPerigee.

Eyerman, R. (2001). *Cultural Trauma: Slavery and the formation of African American identity.* Cambridge, N. Y.: Cambridge University Press.

Foster, T. A. (2019). *Rethinking Rufus: Sexual violations of enslaved men.* Athens, GA: The University of Georgia Press.

Frankl, V. E. (2019). *Yes to life: In spite of everything.* Boston: Beacon Press.

Genovese, E. D. (1974). *Roll, Jordan, Roll: The world the slaves made.* New York: Vintage Books.

Gutman, H. G. (1976). *The Black family in slavery and freedom, 1750 – 1925.* New York: Vintage Books.

Harding, D. J. (2010). *Living the drama: Community, conflict, and culture among inner-city boys.* Chicago, IL: The University of Chicago Press.

Harris-Perry, M. V. (2011). *Sister citizen: Shame, stereotypes, and Black women in America.* New Haven: Yale University Press.

Head, J. (2004). *Black men and depression: Saving our lives, healing our families and friends*. New York: Harlem Moon.

Huggins, N. I. (1977). *Black odyssey: The African-American ordeal in slavery.* New York: Vintage Books.

Jimerson, R. O. (2016). *Greatness is in our DNA: From being worshipped like gods and goddesses to victims of Post-Traumatic Slave Syndrome* (Vol. 1).

Jones-Rogers, S. E. (2019). *They were her property: White women as slave owners in the American South.* New Haven: Yale University Press.

Jordan, W. D. (1974). *The white man's burden: Historical origins of racism in the United States.* New York: Oxford University Press.

Kaufman, G. and Raphael, L. (1996). *Coming out of shame: Transforming gay and lesbian lives.* New York, NY: DoubleDay.

Kendi, I. X. (2016). *Stamped from the beginning: The definitive history of racist ideas in America.* New York, NY: Nation Books.

Lewis, M. (1995). *Shame: The exposed self.* New York: The Free Press.

Litwack, L. F. (1979). *Been in the storm so long: The aftermath of slavery.* New York, NY: Vintage Books.

Marshall, M. and Marshall, E. (2012). *Logotherapy revisited: Review of the tenets of Viktor. E. Frankl's logotherapy.* Ottawa, Ontario: Ottawa Institute of Logotherapy.

MacKenzie, J. (2019). *Whole again: Healing your heart and rediscovering your true self after toxic relationships and emotional abuse.* New York: TarcherPerigee.

Menakem, R. (2017). *My grandmother's hands: Racialized trauma and the pathway to mending our hearts and bodies.* Las Vegas, NV: Central Recovery Press.

Menter, J. E. (2015). *You're not crazy—you're codependent* (2nd Ed.). J2 Publications.

New International Version Holy Bible (2011). Grand Rapids, MI: Zondervan.

Persaud, R. (2004). *Why Black men love white women: Going beyond sexual politics to the heart of the matter.* New York, NY: Pockets Books.

Ramos, L. (2015). *Sexual assault [rape]: Moving from victim to survivor.* Denver, CO: Outskirts Press.

Reya, E. (2007). *The death of Black America.* Bloomington, IL: AuthorHouse.

Skeen, M. (2014). *Love me don't leave me: Overcoming fear of abandonment & building lasting, loving relationships.* New Harbinger Publications, Inc.

Snyder, A. (2020). *Black mental health matters: The ultimate guide for mental health awareness in the Black community.* Toledo, OH: Majestic Publishing.

Stampp, K. M. (1989). *The peculiar institution: Slavery in the Ante-Bellum South.* New York: Vantage Books.

Stephens, D. P. and Phillips, L. D. (2003). Freaks, Gold Diggers, Divas, and Dykes: The Sociohistorical Development of Adolescent African American Women's Sexual Scripts, *Sexuality & Culture,* 3 - 49.

Stewart, D. M. (2020). *Black women, Black love: America's war on African American marriage.* New York, N. Y.: Seal Press.

Street. R. (2016). *You can help: A guide for family & friends of survivors of sexual abuse and assault.*

Ture, K. (formerly Stokely Carmichael) & Hamilton, C. V. (1967/1992). *Black power: The politics of liberation.* New York, N. Y.: Vintage Books.

Ullman, S. F. (2011). "Is Disclosure of Sexual Traumas Helpful? Comparing Experimental Laboratory Versus Field Study

Results," *Journal of Aggression, Maltreatment & Trauma*, vol. 20, 148 – 162.

Van Der Kolk, B. (2014). *The body keeps score: Brain, mind, and body in the healing of trauma.* New York, NY: Penguin Books.

Walker, R. (2020). *The unapologetic guide to Black mental health: Navigate and unequal system, learn tools for emotional wellness, and get the help you deserve.* Oakland, CA: New Harbinger, Inc.

Washington, E. B. (1996). *Uncivil war: The struggle between Black men and women.* Chicago, IL: The Nobel Press, Inc.

Willis, J. T. (2020). *Got my own song to sing: Post-Traumatic Slave Syndrome in my family.* Bloomington, IN: iUniverse.

Wimberly, E. P. (1997). *Recalling our own stories: Spiritual renewal for religious caregivers.* San Francisco: Jossey-Bass Publishers.

_____. (1999). *Moving from shame to self-worth: Preaching & pastoral care.* Nashville, TN: Abingdon Press.

_____. (2000). *Relational refugees: Alienation and reincorporation in African American churches and communities.* Nashville, TN: Abingdon Press.

_____. (2003). *Claiming God reclaiming dignity: African American pastoral care.* Nashville, TN: Abingdon Press.

Winters, M. (2020). *Black fatigue: How racism erodes the mind, body, and spirit.* Oakland, CA: Berrett-Koeler Publishers, Inc.

Wolhandler, S. J. (2018). *Protecting yourself from emotional predators: Neutralize the users, abusers and manipulators hidden among us.* Boulder, CO: Amare Press.

Wolynn, M. (2016). *It didn't start with you: How inherited family trauma shapes who we are and how to end the cycle.* New York, NY: Penguin Books.

Wright, H. N. (2011). *The complete guide to crisis & trauma counseling: What to do and say when it matters most!* Updated and expanded. Ventura, CA: Regal.

Dr. Kasim Ali Sidney Jones

www.ingramcontent.com/pod-product-compliance
Lightning Source LLC
Chambersburg PA
CBHW072045110526
44590CB00018B/3042